100 MAIN COURSE RECIPES

HALIBUT WITH PEPPER SAUCE

Serves 4

800 g/1¾ lb halibut fillets
1 tsp salt
freshly ground black pepper
2 tbsp plain flour
2-3 tbsp butter

Sauce:
2 red peppers
2 shallots
200 ml 7 fl oz double cream
50 ml 2 fl oz white wine
salt
cayenne pepper

Garnish:
finely chopped strips of red, yellow and green peppers sautéed in a little oil

Serve with:
boiled potatoes or rice

1 First make the sauce. Cut the peppers lengthwise and remove the seeds. Cut into thin slices. Slice the shallots finely.

2 Bring the cream to the boil in a saucepan, add the peppers and shallots and continue boiling for 15-20 minutes until the peppers are soft. Blend the sauce in a mixer or food processor. Pour it back into the saucepan, add the wine and season with salt and cayenne pepper to taste. Keep the sauce warm.

3 Cut the fish into even-sized portions if the fillets are very big. Remove the skin and any bones, season with salt and pepper and coat in the flour.

4 Melt the butter in a frying-pan and fry the fish on both sides over medium heat. Do not overcook.

5 Put the fish on a warm serving dish and garnish with the strips of pepper. Serve the sauce in a separate bowl or put the sauce on four plates and place the fish slices on top.

Variations:
This sauce is also good with other types of fish, such as fried pike, perch or cod fillet.

HALIBUT WITH PEPPER SAUCE 200

TO DRINK
dry white wine or lightly chilled red wine

LEVEL OF DIFFICULTY
easy

PREPARATION TIME
1 hr

PREPARE IN ADVANCE
partly

HERRING 'SANDWICHES'

Serves 4

6 tbsp grated celeriac
200 ml /7fl oz crème fraîche
16 cleaned, filleted herrings
8 anchovies
85 g/3 oz breadcrumbs or rye flour
85 g/3 oz butter

Sauce:
100 ml/3½ fl oz water
80 ml/3 fl oz white wine vinegar
large bunch chives, finely chopped
1 bay leaf
15 white peppercorns
100 ml/3½ fl oz double cream
250 g/8¾ oz unsalted butter
salt
white pepper
pinch cayenne

Serve with:
boiled potatoes

1 Mix the celeriac with the crème fraîche. Put 8 herring fillets, flesh side up, on a work surface. Place one anchovy fillet on each and place equal quantities of the celeriac cream mixture on top of each one. Cover with the rest of the fillets making 8 'sandwiches'. Salt sparingly and carefully coat the 'sandwiches' in breadcrumbs or rye flour.

2 Melt the butter in a frying-pan and fry the 'sandwiches' until golden brown on both sides.

3 Make the sauce. Mix the water, vinegar, chives, bay leaf and white peppercorns in a saucepan and boil until reduced by half. Strain the sauce and discard the flavourings. Pour it back into the saucepan. Add the cream and boil for a further 3-4 minutes. Stir in the butter, approximately one-third at a time. Season to taste with salt, white pepper and cayenne.

TO DRINK
dry white wine

LEVEL OF DIFFICULTY medium difficult
PREPARATION TIME 30 mins
PREPARE IN ADVANCE no

FILLET OF FISH DUGLÉRÉ

Serves 4

4 tomatoes
4 tbsp butter
1 onion, finely chopped
6 tbsp chopped parsley
600 g/1¼ lb fish fillets - plaice or other similar fish
½-1 tsp salt
freshly ground black pepper
1 fish stock cube
200 ml/7 fl oz dry white wine
100 ml/3½ fl oz water
juice of ½ lemon
150 ml/5 fl oz double cream

Garnish:
finely chopped parsley

Serve with:
rice or boiled potatoes

1 Scald the tomatoes with boiling water and peel. Cut in half, remove the seeds and dice the flesh.

2 Grease a skillet with 1 tbsp of the butter. Add the onion, chopped tomatoes and 5 tbsp of the parsley. Carefully place the fish fillets in the pan, flesh side uppermost. Add salt and pepper and crumble over the fish stock cube. Pour in the wine, water and lemon juice.

3 Bring to the boil and simmer, covered, over low heat for 7-8 minutes. Remove the fish with a slotted spoon and put on to a warm serving plate. Cover with foil.

4 Heat the pan and bring the sauce to the boil. Add half the cream and simmer for a few minutes. Beat the egg yolks with the rest of the cream. Gradually add to the hot sauce mixture, stirring constantly. Heat gently without allowing the mixture to boil, otherwise it will curdle. Remove from the heat and beat in the remaining butter. Season with a little salt and pepper.

5 Pour the sauce over the fish. Sprinkle over the remaining parsley and serve immediately.

FILLET OF FISH DUGLERÉRÉ 202

TO DRINK
Spanish or Portuguese white wine

LEVEL OF DIFFICULTY
easy
PREPARATION TIME
30 mins
PREPARE IN ADVANCE
yes

FISH MOULD

Serves 4-6

2 tbsp butter
2 tbsp breadcrumbs
500 g/18 oz white fish, such as cod
1½ tsp salt
freshly ground white pepper
1½ tbsp cornflour
30 g/1 oz soft butter
300 ml/10 fl oz double cream
2 eggs

Garnish:
peeled prawns

Serve with:
prawn sauce, mushroom sauce, (recipe 420) or white wine sauce (recipe 432)
Boiled, mashed potatoes or rice

1 Preheat the oven to 200° C/ 400° F, gas mark 6. Grease a 1½ litre/2¾ pint oblong dish or ring mould with half the butter and coat with breadcrumbs.

2 Clean the fish and remove any bones. Cut the fish into small pieces and put in a blender or food processor. Sprinkle with a little salt. Blend until the fish is finely minced. Stop the processor and add white pepper, butter, cornflour and egg.

3 Re-start the processor. Gradually add cream until the mixture is smooth. Do not overwork the mixture or it will separate.

4 Pour the mixture into the prepared dish or mould; do not fill more than two-thirds of the dish as the mixture will rise during cooking. Cover with buttered greaseproof paper or foil. Put the mould in a roasting tin with enough water to reach halfway up the side of the mould.

5 Bake in the oven for 50-60 minutes. The mould should be firm when tested with a skewer.

6 Allow the mould to cool slightly and then loosen around the edges with a knife or spatula. Turn out on to a plate. Garnish with peeled prawns and serve with one of the sauces as suggested above.

Variation:
The mould can be flavoured with 6 tbsp finely chopped dill.

TO DRINK
dry or medium white wine

LEVEL OF DIFFICULTY easy
PREPARATION TIME 1½ hrs
PREPARE IN ADVANCE yes

TROUT PARCELS

Serves 4

4 x 250 g/9 oz whole rainbow trout, cleaned
salt
freshly ground black pepper
2 tbsp chopped parsley
2 tbsp chopped fresh dill
2 tbsp chopped chives
juice of 2 lemons
4 tbsp dry white wine
8 tbsp butter

Serve with:
boiled potatoes, hollandaise sauce (see recipe 422)

1 Rinse the trout and pat dry with kitchen paper. Remove the gills and cut off fins. Preheat the oven to 200° C/400° F, gas mark 6.

2 Take 4 sheets of foil, each big enough to take one fish, and put 1 tbsp of butter in the middle of each. Place one trout on each sheet, with the spine of the fish just above the middle.

3 Season the inside of the fish with salt and pepper. Sprinkle ½ tbsp each of parsley, dill and chives over each fish. Pour the juice of ½ lemon and 1 tbsp white wine over each fish. Top with 1 tbsp butter each.

4 Fold the foil over the fish to make parcels, ensuring that the edges meet. Fold the edges over at least twice to secure and to make airtight parcels.

5 Put the parcels in an ovenproof dish and bake in the oven. After 20 minutes the trout should be ready and the parcels will be swollen like balloons.

6 Serve the fish directly from the parcels which should be opened carefully as they will be very hot.

TROUT PARCELS 204

TO DRINK
dry or medium dry white wine

LEVEL OF DIFFICULTY
easy

PREPARATION TIME
30 mins

PREPARE IN ADVANCE
yes

GERDA'S FISH RAGOUT

Serves 4

1 small courgette
1 red pepper, seeded
1 yellow pepper, seeded
3 tbsp butter
salt
600 g/1¼ lb firm white fish fillets
200 ml/7 fl oz fish stock
100 ml/ 3½ fl oz dry white wine

Sauce:
2 tbsp butter
2 tbsp flour
200 ml/7 fl oz fish stock
100 ml/3½ fl oz double cream
25 ml/1 fl oz dry white vermouth
1 egg yolk
salt
freshly ground black pepper
½ tsp lemon juice

Garnish:
12 radishes and boiled potatoes

1 Cut the courgette and peppers into strips. Fry separately in two-thirds of the butter until soft; do not brown.

2 Grease a shallow pan with the remaining butter. Lightly salt the fillets and put them in it. Add the fish stock and wine. Cover and simmer for 6-8 minutes. Transfer the fish to a plate and keep warm under foil.

3 Strain the stock and reserve 200 ml/7 fl oz.

4 To make the sauce, melt the butter and stir in the flour. Cook, stirring for 1 minute. Gradually stir in the fish stock and half the cream. Add the vermouth. Simmer over low heat for 5 minutes. Beat together the egg yolk and the rest of the cream. Add to the sauce, beating constantly. Add salt and black pepper to taste and ½ tsp lemon juice. Keep the sauce warm.

5 Trim the radishes and boil them for a few minutes in lightly salted water.

6 Put the fish fillets in a deep sided serving dish. Pour the sauce over the top. Add the fried vegetables in neat piles on the top. Garnish with the radishes and potatoes.

TO DRINK
dry white wine

LEVEL OF DIFFICULTY
medium difficult

PREPARATION TIME
1 hr

PREPARE IN ADVANCE
partly

GRAVAD LAX

Serves 6

1 kg/2¼ lb middle-cut fresh salmon
3 tbsp castor sugar
3 tbsp salt
1 tbsp coarsely ground white pepper
1 bunch roughly chopped fresh dill

Sauce:
3 tbsp mild mustard
1 tbsp French mustard
2 tsp salt
1½ tbsp vinegar
200-250 ml/7-8¾ fl oz vegetable oil
3 tbsp finely chopped dill

Serve with:
boiled or creamed potatoes

1 Fillet the salmon but leave the skin on. Slice along the backbone of the fish with a sharp, straight-bladed knife. Remove the fillet. Repeat on the other side. Pluck out any smaller bones away with tweezers.

2 Mix together the sugar, salt, pepper and dill and lightly rub on the flesh side of the fillets. Put the two fillets together, flesh sides facing and place in a dish. Sprinkle over the remaining sugar mixture. Cover with clingfilm or put in a sealed plastic bag. Keep in the refrigerator for 1½-2 days, turning over halfway through this time.

3 Make the sauce. Mix the mustards together. Add the sugar, salt, ground black pepper and vinegar. Add the oil, a little at a time, beating constantly. Finally mix in the dill.

4 Thinly slice the salmon on a slant or cut into 1 cm/½ inch thick slices crossways. Serve with boiled dill potatoes and the sauce, or with creamed potatoes and salad.

Variation:
A good variation is to pan-fry thickly sliced gravad lax (with the skin left on) in a dry frying-pan, or grill over a hot barbecue, allowing about 1 minute per side.

GRAVAD LAX 206

TO DRINK
dry white wine, lager or beer

LEVEL OF DIFFICULTY
easy

PREPARATION TIME
$1\frac{1}{2}$ - 2 days

PREPARE IN ADVANCE
yes

GRAVAD LAX AND CUCUMBER SAUCE

Serves 4

300 ml/10 fl oz double cream
1 large cucumber
50 ml/2 fl oz dry white wine
100 ml/ 3$^1/_2$ fl oz fish stock
juice of 1 lemon
salt
freshly ground black pepper
50 g/$^3/_4$ oz butter, diced
1 tbsp finely chopped chives
4 slices gravad lax, 2 cm/$^3/_4$ inch thick (see recipe 206)
2 tbsp vegetable oil

Serve with:
boiled potatoes or mashed potatoes

1 Bring the cream to the boil, reduce the heat and simmer for a short while.

2 Peel the cucumber. Cut lengthwise and scrape out the seeds. Cut into 5 mm/$^1/_{10}$ inch thick slices. Add the cucumber slices to the simmering cream. Stir in the wine and a little of the fish stock. Simmer until the cucumber is soft. Add the remaining fish stock, lemon juice, salt and pepper to taste. Add the chives.

3 Brush the salmon slices with a little oil. Grill for a few minutes on each side.

4 Serve immediately with the cucumber sauce and boiled or mashed potatoes.

TO DRINK
white wine

LEVEL OF DIFFICULTY
easy

PREPARATION TIME
30 mins

PREPARE IN ADVANCE
partly

STUFFED CABBAGE ROLLS

Serves 4-6

500 g/1 lb perch fillets
½ tbsp salt
1 tsp freshly ground black pepper
3 egg whites
400 ml/14 fl oz double cream
1 savoy cabbage or iceberg lettuce
2 tbsp butter
500 ml/17 fl oz fish stock
200 ml/7 fl oz dry white wine

Sauce:
200 ml/7 fl oz double cream
2 egg yolks
salt
freshly ground black pepper

Serve with:
boiled potatoes or rice

1 Cut the fish into small pieces and remove any bones. Process in a food processor using the finest blade. Mix in salt, pepper and the egg whites. Add the cream, a little at a time, and stir until the mixture is smooth.

2 Separate the cabbage leaves, wash and blanch in lightly salted boiling water for 10-12 minutes. Blanch lettuce leaves for 2-3 minutes. Drain on kitchen paper.

3 Spread out the leaves and place 1 tbsp of the fish mixture on each. Fold into small parcels, tucking in the sides.

4 Grease a large saucepan. Arrange the rolls, seam sides downwards. If the rolls do not fit in one layer, arrange the second layer in the hollows of the first. Pour over the stock and wine and simmer for 10 minutes. Remove from the pan and keep warm.

5 Strain the cooking liquid and return to the pan. Add the cream and simmer gently until smooth and slightly thickened. Remove the pan from the heat. Beat the egg yolks with a little of the warm sauce and pour the mixture into the remaining sauce, beating vigorously.

6 Warm the sauce but do not allow to boil. Add salt and pepper to taste.

7 Place the rolls on warm serving plates and pour the sauce over them.

STUFFED CABBAGE ROLLS 208

TO DRINK
dry white wine

LEVEL OF DIFFICULTY
medium difficult

PREPARATION TIME
2 hrs

PREPARE IN ADVANCE
partly

QUENELLES

Serves 6-8

500 g/1 lb perch fillets, skinned
salt
freshly ground white pepper
400 ml/4 fl oz double cream
2 egg whites

Mushrooms:
3 tbsp butter
1 shallot, finely chopped
250 g/8 oz button mushrooms, finely chopped
50 ml/2 fl oz dry white wine

Sauce:
4 tbsp butter
4 tbsp plain flour
700 ml/1¼ pints milk
120 g/4 oz cheese grated
2 tbsp melted butter

Serve with:
mashed potatoes or rice

1 Cut the fish into small pieces and remove any bones. Chop finely.

2 Season and add the cream, a little at a time. Beat the egg whites until they form stiff peaks and fold into the mixture. Add more cream if the mixture is too firm; stir in a little cornflour if it is too thin.

3 Bring a large saucepan of lightly salted water to the boil. Shape the fish mixture into balls. Cook, a few at a time, in the simmering water for 10 minutes, until they float to the top. Remove and keep warm while you cook the rest.

4 Melt the butter and sweat the shallot for 5 minutes. Add the mushrooms and cook for 2-3 minutes. Pour over the wine and simmer for 3-4 minutes.

5 Make the sauce. Melt the butter and stir in the flour. Cook, stirring for 1 minute. Gradually stir in the milk, season and bring to the boil. Simmer for 5 minutes, stirring constantly.

6 Preheat the oven to 250° C/ 500° F, gas mark 10. Grease an ovenproof dish. Spread the mushroom mixture over the base and arrange the quenelles on top. Pour over the sauce, sprinkle with grated cheese and melted butter. Bake until golden.

TO DRINK
dry white wine or chilled Beaujolais

LEVEL OF DIFFICULTY medium difficult
PREPARATION TIME 2 hrs
PREPARE IN ADVANCE yes

PERCH OR PIKE WITH CHIVE SAUCE

Serves 4

2 tbsp butter
2 shallots, finely chopped
4 perch or pike fillets
salt
freshly ground black pepper
200 ml/7 fl oz dry white wine
300 ml/10 fl oz double cream
1 egg yolk
1 bunch parsley, finely chopped
1 bunch chives, snipped

Fish stock:
Fish bones and trimmings
1 small carrot, chopped
1 small onion, sliced
3 sprigs parsley
1 small bay leaf
5 white peppercorns
500-600 ml/17 fl oz-1 pint water

Garnish:
8 tbsp trout roe (optional)

Serve with:
boiled potatoes or rice

1 First make the stock. Put the fish bones and trimmings, carrot, onion, parsley, bay leaf and peppercorns in a saucepan. Pour over water to cover. Bring to the boil and simmer for 20 minutes. Strain the fish stock.

2 Melt 1 tbsp of the butter in a flameproof casserole and add the shallots, fish, salt and pepper. Pour over the fish stock so that it almost covers the fish. Add the wine and simmer the fillets for approximately 5 minutes. Remove the fillets with a slotted spoon and keep them warm under foil.

3 Pour the cream into the pan, stir and simmer. When the sauce is starting to thicken after 5-6 minutes, remove the pan from the heat.

4 Beat the egg yolk and mix with 2-3 tbsp of the warm sauce. Beat the mixture into the sauce. Warm the sauce but do not allow to boil. Stir in the remaining butter.

5 Add the parsley and chives. Adjust the seasoning and pour the sauce over the warm fish. Garnish with a little trout roe, if desired.

PERCH OR PIKE WITH CHIVE SAUCE 210

TO DRINK
dry white wine

LEVEL OF DIFFICULTY
medium difficult

PREPARATION TIME
1 hr

PREPARE IN ADVANCE
partly

JAMBALAYA

Serves 6

3 tbsp vegetable oil or butter
1 large onion, finely chopped
255 g/9 oz rice
600 ml/1 pint chicken stock
1 x 400 g/14 oz can tomatoes
¼ tsp chili powder
¼ tsp thyme
¼ tsp oregano
½ tsp basil
2 garlic cloves, crushed
salt
½ tsp black peppercorns
60 g/2 oz butter
1 chicken, roasted
300 g/10 oz smoked ham, cut into strips
1 green pepper, cut into strips
300g /10 oz cooked prawns, peeled

1 Heat 2 tbsp of the oil or melt 2 tbsp of the butter in a large saucepan or flameproof casserole and sauté the onion. Add the rice, stir and fry for a couple of minutes. Add the stock, and the tomatoes with the can juice. Add the garlic, chili, herbs, salt and black peppercorns. Bring to the boil, cover and simmer for 18-20 minutes, or until the rice has absorbed the liquid.

2 Bone the chicken and dice the meat. Heat the remaining oil or melt the remaining butter. Fry the ham and pepper strips.

3 Stir the diced chicken, ham and peppers into the cooked rice. This dish can be prepared in advance as far as this stage.

4 Warm the dish before serving and make sure it is hot all the way through. Finally add the prawns leaving on the heat just long enough to warm them through.

TO DRINK
white wine or lager

LEVEL OF DIFFICULTY fairly easy
PREPARATION TIME 1 hr
PREPARE IN ADVANCE yes

SALMON MOULD

Serves 8

1-1.25 kg/2¼-2¾ lb fresh salmon
750 g/½ lb cooked prawns
5 hard boiled eggs, sliced
dill sprigs

Stock:
1 litre/1¾ pints water
100 ml/3½ fl oz white wine vinegar
1 tbsp salt
1 tbsp sugar
dill sprigs
10 white peppercorns
1 onion, sliced
1 small carrot

Jelly:
200 ml/7 fl oz dry white wine
10-12 gelatine leaves

Garnish:
cucumber slices
lemon wedges
dill sprigs

Serve with:
boiled potatoes and green sauce (see recipe 429)

1 Mix all the stock ingredients in a pan, cover and boil for 15 minutes. Add the fish; the stock should not completely cover it. Simmer for 15-20 minutes.

2 Allow the salmon to cool slightly in the stock. Remove and discard the bones and skin. Cut the fish into bite-sized pieces. Reserve the stock.

3 Strain the stock. Soak the gelatine in cold water for 20 minutes. Drain and dissolve the gelatine over a low heat in 100 ml/3½ fl oz fish stock. Stir into the remaining fish stock and wine. Rinse a loaf tin with cold water and pour in a little fish stock, 5 mm/¼ inch deep. Put the tin in the refrigerator and leave the jelly to set.

4 Peel the prawns. Arrange a layer of prawns, egg slices, salmon pieces, and dill sprigs on top of the set jelly. Pour over a little more jelly and allow to set. Continue adding layers in this way. Cover with foil and leave to set in the refrigerator.

5 Loosen the edges with a knife, dip the mould in warm water and invert on to a serving dish. Garnish with cucumber, lemon wedges and dill.

SALMON MOULD 212

To drink
medium white wine

LEVEL OF DIFFICULTY
medium difficult

PREPARATION TIME
1 hr + setting time

PREPARE IN ADVANCE
yes

BUTTERFLY SALMON WITH HERB SAUCE

Serves 4

600 g/1¼ lb salmon fillet
1½ tsp salt
butter or oil

Sauce:
100 ml/3½ fl oz white wine
100 ml/3½ fl oz water
1 fish stock cube
200 ml/7 fl oz crème fraîche
3 tbsp finely chopped parsley
3 tbsp finely chopped chives
3 tbsp finely chopped dill
1 tsp dried tarragon
freshly ground black pepper
1 tbsp butter

Serve with:
boiled potatoes

1 Ask the fishmonger to cut butterfly steaks, or alternatively make them yourself by the following method. Clean the salmon fillet and remove an bones.

2 Cut a slice, approximately 1½ cm/½ inch thick straight into the fish without cutting through the skin. Cut another equally thick slice, but this time cut through the skin. Fold out both slices; they are held together in the middle by the skin to form the butterfly. Cut the rest of the salmon this way, making 4 butterflies.

3 Make the sauce. Mix the wine and water in a pan and crumble in the fish stock cube . Bring to the boil. Stir in the crème fraîche and bring back to the boil. Boil for approximately 10 minutes over high heat, stirring occasionally. Add salt and pepper to taste. Add the herbs and the butter. Keep the sauce warm without further boiling.

4 Preheat the grill. Sprinkle the salmon slices with salt and brush then with a little oil. Grill for 2-3 minutes on each side. Alternatively, fry the salmon slices on both sides in melted butter in a frying-pan.

5 Spoon the sauce on to warm plates and top with the butterfly salmon. Alternatively, place the salmon on a serving plate and serve the sauce separately.

TO DRINK
dry white wine

LEVEL OF DIFFICULTY
easy

PREPARATION TIME
30 mins

PREPARE IN ADVANCE
partly

WHITE FISH WITH SMOKED SALMON

Serves 4

8 dab or plaice fillets
salt
freshly ground pepper
100 g/3½ oz smoked salmon, thinly sliced
3 tbsp butter
2 shallots, finely chopped
2 tbsp white wine vinegar
200-300 ml/7-10 fl oz dry white wine
200 ml/7 fl oz fish stock
15 fresh basil leaves or 1 tsp dried basil
200 g/7 fl oz crème fraîche

Serve with:
boiled or mashed potatoes, mange tout and baby carrots

1 Place the fish fillets, flesh side down on a work surface. Season with a little salt and pepper. Cover with thinly sliced smoked salmon and fold the fillets.

2 Melt 1 tbsp of the butter in a saucepan or flameproof casserole. Add the shallots and sauté without colouring. Add the vinegar and white wine. Allow to boil until reduced to 50 ml/2 fl oz. Pour in the stock.

3 Add the folded fish fillets and simmer over very low heat for 7-8 minutes.

4 Melt 1 tbsp of the remaining butter. Fry the basil very quickly. Set aside.

5 Remove the fish fillets with a slotted spoon and keep warm. Stir the crème fraîche into the stock and bring to the boil. Remove the pan from the heat and beat in the remaining butter. Do not let the sauce boil. Finally mix in the basil and add salt and pepper to taste.

6 Spoon the sauce on to warm plates and put the fish fillets on top. Alternatively, place the fish on a large serving dish, pour a little sauce over the top and serve the remaining sauce in a separate bowl.

WHITE FISH WITH SMOKED SALMON 214

TO DRINK
dry white wine

LEVEL OF DIFFICULTY
easy

PREPARATION TIME
1 hr

PREPARE IN ADVANCE
no

SALMON AND POTATO BAKE

Serves 4

2 tbsp + 1 tsp butter
2 onions, chopped
8-10 cold boiled potatoes
300-400 g/10-14 oz salmon
 or river trout
1 bunch dill, finely chopped
freshly ground white pepper
3 eggs
400 ml/14 fl oz milk

Serve with:
green beans

1 Preheat the oven to 220° C/425° F, gas mark 7. Melt 1 tbsp of the butter and add the onions. Fry them without colouring. Peel and slice the potatoes. Cut the salmon into slices.

2 Grease an ovenproof dish with 1 tsp butter. Layer the potatoes, onion, salmon, and dill in the dish. Add a little pepper between layers. The final layer should be potatoes.

3 Beat together the eggs and milk and pour the mixture over the dish. Dice the remaining butter and dot it over the top.

4 Place the dish in the oven and bake for approximately 45 minutes.

Variations:
Instead of boiled, sliced potatoes use raw sliced potatoes. Bake on a slightly lower oven heat, 200° C/400° F, gas mark 6, for approximately 1 hour.

SALMON AND POTATO BAKE 215

TO DRINK
lager

LEVEL OF DIFFICULTY
easy
PREPARATION TIME
1 hr
PREPARE IN ADVANCE
yes

MADEMOISELLE'S FISH

Serves 4

1 tbsp butter
4 pike or perch fillets
about 300 g/10½ oz vermicelli

Fish stock:
fish bones and trimmings
about 1 litre/1¾ pints water
½ carrot, chopped
1 piece celeriac, chopped
1 small onion, chopped
parsley sprigs
6 white peppercorns
1½ tsp salt
pepper
50 ml/2 fl oz dry white vermouth

Sauce:
4 tbsp butter
4 tbsp flour
200 ml/7 fl oz double cream
2-3 tbsp tomato purée
2-3 tsp tarragon vinegar
salt
freshly ground black pepper

1 Make the stock. Put the fish trimmings, water, vegetables, parsley and peppercorns in a saucepan. Boil for 20 minutes. Strain and add salt and pepper and vermouth to taste.

2 Grease a saucepan or fish kettle with 1 tsp of the butter. Place the fillets on the base, pour over the stock just to cover and bring to the boil. Lower the heat and simmer for 5 minutes. Remove and set aside.

3 Preheat the oven to 220° C /425° F, gas mark 7. Boil the vermicelli as instructed on the packet. Drain and rinse with cold water. Drain well.

4 Make the sauce. Melt the butter, add the flour and cook for 1 minute, stirring. Gradually stir in the stock. Add the cream, stir and simmer for 5 minutes. Add the tomato purée, a little at a time, to taste. Add the tarragon vinegar and season with salt and pepper to taste.

5 Grease an ovenproof dish with the remaining butter and arrange the vermicelli. Place the fish on top. Pour over the sauce.

6 Place the dish in the oven and leave until it is fully heated and the sauce is bubbling.

MADEMOISELLE'S FISH 216

To drink
dry white wine

LEVEL OF DIFFICULTY easy
PREPARATION TIME 1 hr
PREPARE IN ADVANCE yes

QUICK CURRIED PRAWNS

Serves 4

255 g/9 oz long grain rice
600 g/1¼ lb cooked prawns
100-150 g/3½-5 oz butter
1 tbsp curry powder
bunch parsley, chopped
1 garlic clove, crushed (optional)
salt
freshly ground black pepper

1 Boil the rice in lightly salted water for 15 minutes. Drain and rinse in boiling water. Peel the prawns.

2 Put the butter in a serving dish. Add the prawns, curry powder, chopped parsley and garlic, if using.

3 When the rice is cooked and the water has been fully absorbed, put the hot rice into the serving dish. Leave for approximately 5 minutes so that the butter will melt and the prawns become warm. Mix well just before serving. Add seasoning to taste.

TO DRINK
lager, medium white wine

LEVEL OF DIFFICULTY
easy
PREPARATION TIME
30 mins
PREPARE IN ADVANCE
no

SOLE WITH PRAWNS

Serves 4

300 g/10 oz cooked large prawns
500-600 g/1-1¼ lb sole fillets
salt
30 g/1 oz flour
30 g/1 oz butter
1 can green asparagus tips

Potato purée (Pommes duchesse)
(see recipe 406)

Mushroom sauce:
400 g/14 oz mushrooms
1 tbsp butter
½ tbsp cornflour
300 ml/10 fl oz double cream
salt
freshly ground white pepper

Béarnaise sauce (see recipe 419)

1 Make the potato purée, following recipe 406. Pipe the potato mixture around the edge of a large, circular, ovenproof dish. Pipe a second circle near the centre. Pipe strips of potato, like wheel spokes, to form one section for each fish fillet.

2 Make the mushroom sauce. Wipe and slice the mushrooms. Melt the butter and sauté the mushrooms until any liquid has been absorbed. Remove the pan from the heat and sprinkle over the flour. Add the cream, return to the heat and bring to the boil, stirring constantly. Simmer the sauce until it has the consistency of thick cream. Add salt and pepper to taste.

3 Make the Béarnaise sauce.

4 Peel the prawns. Preheat the oven to 250° C/500° F, gas mark 10. Season the fillets with salt, fold in half, flesh side upwards and coat them lightly with flour.

5 Heat the butter in a large frying-pan and fry the fillets slowly over low heat for approximately 5 minutes each side.

6 Place the potato-decorated dish in the oven and bake until golden yellow.

7 Warm the asparagus and the mushroom sauce. Arrange the asparagus and sole on the dish. Spoon the mushroom sauce into the inner circle. Garnish the fish with prawns. Serve immediately with the Béarnaise sauce in a separate bowl.

SOLE WITH PRAWNS 218

TO DRINK
dry white wine

LEVEL OF DIFFICULTY
medium difficult

PREPARATION TIME
2 hrs

PREPARE IN ADVANCE
partly

PLAICE ROLLS WITH PRAWNS

Serves 6

2 tsp butter
1 kg/2¼ lb plaice fillets
500 g/1 lb cooked, peeled prawns
150 g/5 oz fish roe
1 lemon
salt

Sauce:
3 tbsp butter, softened
1 small onion, finely chopped
300 ml/10 fl oz dry white wine
2 fish stock cubes
1½ tbsp flour
700 ml/1¼ pints double cream
salt
cayenne pepper

Serve with:
mashed potato or rice and puff pastry crescents (see recipe 437)

1 Make the sauce. Melt 1 tbsp of the butter and sauté the onion. Add the wine and fish stock cubes. Boil until reduced to about 100 ml/3½ fl oz.

2 Strain the liquid and discard the onion. Mix the flour with the remaining butter to form a *beurre manié*. Add to the liquid, together with 200 ml/7 fl oz of the cream. Bring the sauce to the boil, at the same time slowly adding the remaining cream, stirring constantly. Continue to cook until it is the consistency of thick cream. Stir the sauce thoroughly. Add salt and cayenne pepper to taste.

3 Grease a fish kettle or large pan with the butter. Roll up each fillet and arrange in the pan. Cover and keep in the refrigerator until ready to use.

4 Make the pastry decorations as described in recipe 437.

5 Cook the fish just before serving. Sprinkle over 1 tsp of salt and pour over the juice of ½ lemon. Add enough water almost to cover the fish, bring to the boil, cover and simmer for 5-8 minutes.

6 Transfer the fish to a warm serving dish, draining it well. Add some of the prawns and cover with the hot sauce. Garnish with remaining prawns, fish roe and puff pastry decorations.

PLAICE ROLLS WITH PRAWNS 219

TO DRINK
dry white wine

LEVEL OF DIFFICULTY easy
PREPARATION TIME 1 hr
PREPARE IN ADVANCE yes

BAKED TURBOT

Serves 6

1 x 2 kg/4½ lb turbot

Serve with:
boiled potatoes, grated horseradish and thin lemon wedges

1 Preheat the oven to 110° C/225° F, gas mark ¼. Clean the fish and remove the gills. Dry with kitchen paper. Put the fish into a fish kettle, turbot kettle or a large ovenproof dish. The dark side of the fish should face upwards. Note that the container should not be greased and no liquid should be added.

2 Put the container into the oven. Bake for approximately 1 hour. To test whether the turbot is ready, check carefully with a fork that the fish flesh can be parted easily from the backbone. The fish meat should be white and opaque.

3 Serve the turbot directly from the fish kettle or ovenproof dish. Slit the skin along the backbone, lift away the skin and serve the fish on individual plates.

Suggestion:
The body of the turbot is lozenge shaped and broader than it is long. Because it difficult to fit into conventional utensils, the turbot kettle or *turbotière* was invented. This is a square or diamond-shaped fish kettle, usually made of copper, aluminium or stainless steel. It is also useful for cooking other flatfish, such as brill and skate.

BAKED TURBOT 220

To drink
dry white wine

LEVEL OF DIFFICULTY
easy

PREPARATION TIME
just over 1 hr

PREPARE IN ADVANCE
partly

BAKED SALMON

Serves 6

1 kg/2¼ lb salmon fillet
1 egg, lightly beaten
2-3 tbsp fine breadcrumbs
1 tbsp melted butter
salt
freshly ground black pepper

Garnish:
cucumber slices
lemon slices
smooth leaf parsley

Serve with:
butter-fried spinach, boiled new potatoes and
Hollandaise sauce (see recipe 422)

1 Clean the salmon and remove any bones with tweezers. Leave the skin on.

2 Place the fish, skin side down, in a small ovenproof dish or fish kettle covered with greaseproof paper. Brush the flesh with beaten egg. Sprinkle over the breadcrumbs and set aside in the refrigerator for 1 hour.

3 Preheat the oven to 200° C/ 400° F, gas mark 6. Brush the top of the fish with the melted butter and season with salt and pepper. Place the fish in the middle of the oven and cook for 10-15 minutes.

4 Place the salmon on a serving dish and garnish with cucumber, lemon and parsley.

Variations:
Instead of using butter-fried spinach and Hollandaise sauce, spinach sauce made with frozen leaf spinach may be served. Thaw the spinach over low heat. Strain the liquid and add 300-400 ml/10-14 fl oz crème fraîche. Season with salt, pepper and grated nutmeg to taste. Serve the sauce warm.

TO DRINK
dry white wine

LEVEL OF DIFFICULTY
easy

PREPARATION TIME
30 mins

PREPARE IN ADVANCE
partly

STUFFED SEA BASS

Serves 4

1-1¼ kg/2¼-2¾ lb smoked sea bass
juice of ½ lemon

Spinach timbales
200 g/7 fl oz chopped frozen spinach, thawed
2 eggs
100 ml/3½ fl oz crème fraîche
salt
freshly ground white pepper
pinch grated nutmeg
1½ tbsp butter

Stuffing:
100 g/3½ oz butter
50 g/1¾ oz chives, chopped
freshly ground black pepper
rind of 1 lemon

Sauce:
200 ml/7 fl oz mayonnaise
100 ml/3½ fl oz sour cream
1-2 tbsp grated horseradish

Serve with:
boiled new potatoes and lemon wedges

1 Preheat the oven to200° C/ 400° F, gas mark 6. Make the spinach timbales. Drain any excess liquid from the spinach. Beat the eggs together with the cream. Stir in the spinach. Add salt, pepper and nutmeg to taste.

2 Grease 4 small metal moulds, 2-3 cm/¾-1 inch wide, with the butter and fill them with the spinach mixture. Put them in a roasting tin and half filled with hot water. Bake in the oven for 20 minutes, or until cooked. Test with a skewer. Cover with foil and keep them warm in the hot water.

3 Sprinkle the lemon juice over the fish. Mix together all the stuffing ingredients. Fill the fish and press the sides together.

4 Place the fish on a large foil square and fold over the edges to form a parcel. Put the parcel in an ovenproof dish. Bake for 20-30 minutes.

5 Meanwhile, make the sauce. Mix together the mayonnaise, sour cream and horseradish.

6 Serve the fish straight from the foil parcel and serve the horseradish sauce separately.

STUFFED SEA BASS 222

To drink
dry white wine, lager or beer

LEVEL OF DIFFICULTY
easy

PREPARATION TIME
1 hr

PREPARE IN ADVANCE
yes

EASTER FISH STEW

Serves 4

400 g/14 oz firm white fish
1 celery stalk
2 carrots
½ small leek
50 g/1¾ oz + 1 tsp butter
1 x 400 g/14 oz can plum tomatoes
1 tsp salt
freshly ground black pepper
250 ml/8¾ fl oz white wine
150 g/5 oz cooked peeled prawns
150-200 g/5-7 oz cooked or canned mussels or clams
8 cooked peeled crayfish tails
8 cooked Pacific mussels in their shells (optional)
1 bunch dill, finely chopped

Serve with:
boiled potatoes

1 Roughly grate the celery and carrots and slice the leek. Place them in a pan with 100 ml/3½ fl oz water and 1 tsp of the butter. Bring to the boil and simmer for 2 minutes. Drain and reserve.

2 Pour the tomatoes, together with their can juice into a large saucepan. Cut the fish fillets into 2-cm/¾-inch thick slices and add them to the tomatoes. Season with salt and pepper to taste. Add the reserved cooked vegetables, the wine and the remaining butter and simmer over very low heat for approximately 5 minutes. Do not stir very frequently.

3 Add the prawns, mussels, crayfish tails and the Pacific mussels, if using. Warm thoroughly without boiling. (Boiling will make shellfish very chewy). Sprinkle over the dill and add seasoning to taste. Serve immediately.

TO DRINK
dry white wine

LEVEL OF DIFFICULTY
easy

PREPARATION TIME
30 mins

PREPARE IN ADVANCE
partly

BEEF RYDBERG

Serves 4

500 g/17 oz fillet of beef
6-8 medium-sized potatoes
salt
2-3 onions
85 g/3 oz butter
freshly ground white pepper

Garnish:
1 tbsp chopped parsley
4 eggs

1 Peel the potatoes and cut into 5 mm/¼ inch cubes. Melt 30 g/1 oz of the butter and fry the potato cubes until they are soft inside and slightly browned. Sprinkle with a little salt. Keep warm.

2 Chop the onions and fry in 15 g/½ oz of the remaining butter over low heat, until soft and golden.

3 Cut the meat into 1 cm/½ inch cubes. Melt the remaining butter in a frying-pan and fry the meat until it is brown all over but still pink inside. Season with salt and pepper.

4 Mix the onions and meat and warm thoroughly. Arrange the meat on one side of a serving dish and the potatoes on the other. Sprinkle with chopped parsley and serve with raw egg yolks in eggshell halves.

BEEF RYDBERG 224

TO DRINK
a robust red wine

LEVEL OF DIFFICULTY
easy

PREPARATION TIME
30 mins

PREPARE IN ADVANCE
no

BEEF STROGANOV

Serves 4

500 g/1 lb boneless beef, fillet or rump steak
200 g/7 oz mushrooms
2-3 tbsp butter
1 onion, finely chopped
1 tsp salt
freshly ground black pepper
3 tbsp tomato purée
1-2 tbsp French mustard
200 ml/7 fl oz crème fraîche
100 ml/3½ fl oz sour cream

Serve with:
rice or boiled potatoes

1 Cut the meat into long, thin strips, 3-4 cm/1-1½ inches long. Wipe the mushrooms and, if large, slice them.

2 Melt 1 tbsp of the butter in a heavy frying-pan and sauté the onions for a 3-5 minutes without colouring. Add the mushrooms, increase the heat and cook until the liquid has been absorbed.

3 Melt the remaining butter in a large frying-pan. Add the meat and brown quickly on high heat, turning as often as necessary. Season with salt and pepper.

4 Transfer the meat to the pan with the onions and mushrooms. Stir in tomato purée and mustard. Add the crème fraîche and sour cream, stir well and simmer for 2-3 minutes. Warm thoroughly, without boiling, before serving.

TO DRINK
red wine or beer

LEVEL OF DIFFICULTY
easy

PREPARATION TIME
30 mins

PREPARE IN ADVANCE
yes

BOEUF BOURGUIGNONNE

Serves 8

1.2 kg/2½ lb top rump beef
3 tbsp butter
150 g/5 oz bacon, cut into strips
2 onions, chopped
1 carrot, diced
salt
freshly ground white pepper
½ tsp dried thyme
2 tbsp flour
4 tsp tomato purée
1 bay leaf
½ bottle red wine
200 ml/7 fl oz beef stock
20 small shallots
300 g/10½ oz button mushrooms
2 cloves garlic, crushed
2 tbsp chopped chives

Serve with:
boiled potatoes, pickled onions and pickled gherkins

1 Cut the beef into 2-cm/¾-inch cubes. Melt 2 tbsp of the butter in a frying-pan. Add half the meat and brown well all over. Remove from the pan and brown the remainder.

2 Set a heavy pan over medium heat and lightly fry the bacon strips. Add the onion and carrot and fry for 4-5 minutes. Add the browned meat cubes, salt, white pepper and thyme. Sprinkle over the flour and stir. Add the tomato purée, bay leaf and wine. Bring to the boil and simmer over low heat for 1½ hours. Add a little stock and more wine if necessary.

3 Peel the shallots. Melt the remaining butter and brown the shallots. Wipe the mushrooms and fry them.

4 Add the shallots, mushrooms and garlic to the meat 30 minutes before the end of the cooking time.

5 Add salt and pepper to taste, sprinkle over the chives and serve.

BOEUF BOURGUIGNONNE 226

TO DRINK
red wine

LEVEL OF DIFFICULTY
fairly easy

PREPARATION TIME
2 hrs

PREPARE IN ADVANCE
yes

ENTRECÔTE WITH TARRAGON

Serves 4

4 x 150 g/5 oz entrecôte steaks
freshly ground black pepper
3 tbsp butter
1 tsp salt

Sauce:
200 ml/7 fl oz crème fraîche
2 tsp French mustard
2 tsp dried tarragon
1 tbsp chopped parsley
salt
freshly ground black pepper
50 ml/2 fl oz whisky
water

Serve with:
fried, sliced courgettes, French beans and sauté potatoes

1 Set the meat aside at room temperature for 1 hour. This helps it to become more tender. Season with freshly ground black pepper.

2 Melt the butter in a large frying-pan and fry the meat for 2 minutes on each side, or a little longer if you like it well done. Add salt after you have finished frying.

3 Remove the pan from the heat. Gently heat the whisky and pour over the meat. Set alight and shake the pan until the flames die down.

4 Place the meat on warm dinner plates or a warm serving dish. Keep warm.

5 Put the crème fraîche, mustard, tarragon and parsley into the frying-pan. Bring to the boil, stirring. Add pepper and salt to taste and a few drops of whisky, if liked. Dilute with a little water if the sauce is too thick.

TO DRINK
red Bordeaux or Italian red wine

LEVEL OF DIFFICULTY
easy

PREPARATION TIME
30 mins

PREPARE IN ADVANCE
no

FLAMBÉED FILLET OF BEEF

Serves 4

4 x 150 g/5 oz slices fillet of beef
6 tbsp creamy Gorgonzola
3 tbsp butter
salt
freshly ground black pepper
2 tbsp finely chopped shallots
50 ml/2 fl oz brandy
150 ml/5 fl oz red wine
1 tbsp soya sauce
200 ml/7 fl oz double cream
1 tbsp butter

Serve with:
duchesse potatoes or baked potatoes
chopped parsley
sliced butter-fried courgettes

1 Cut a small pocket on the side of each fillet and fill each with approximately 1 tbsp of cheese. Secure with a cocktail stick.

2 Melt 2 tbsp of the butter in a frying-pan. Fry the fillets for 4-6 minutes on each side, depending on whether they are to be rare or well done. Season with salt and pepper. Add the chopped shallots just before the fillets are cooked and fry for a few minutes without allowing them to colour.

3 Gently heat the brandy. Pour the brandy over the beef and set alight. Shake the pan until the flames die down and remove the fillets. Keep them warm in foil.

4 Set the frying-pan over high heat. Pour in the red wine and soya sauce and boil until reduced by two-thirds.

5 Add the cream and the remaining Gorgonzola. Boil the sauce, stirring constantly until it is the consistency of thick cream. If necessary, add a little extra salt, pepper and soya sauce. Strain the sauce and stir in the remaining butter.

6 Place the fillets on warm plates and pour over the sauce. Serve with lightly fried courgette slices sprinkled with chopped parsley and duchesse potatoes or baked potatoes.

FLAMBÉED FILLET OF BEEF 228

TO DRINK
full bodied red wine

LEVEL OF DIFFICULTY
fairly easy

PREPARATION TIME
30 mins

PREPARE IN ADVANCE
no

CARBONADE OF BEEF

Serves 4

8 small beef steaks
3-4 tbsp butter
salt
freshly ground white pepper
1 stock cube (optional)
4-5 large onions
1 tbsp water
2 bottles beer
85 g/3 oz breadcrumbs made from day old white bread

Serve with:
boiled potatoes

1 Tenderize the beef by hitting it with your hand or a steak hammer. Melt 2 tbsp of the butter in a frying-pan and brown the beef quickly on both sides. Season with salt and pepper. Rinse the pan with a little water, and add the crumbled stock cube, if desired. Reserve the gravy.

2 Cut the onions into thin slices. Melt 1 tbsp of the remaining butter and fry the onions slowly in butter over low heat until soft and golden. Stir in the water; the onions will absorb it.

3 Layer the fried beef and onions in a pan, finishing with a layer of onions. Pour the beer and reserved gravy over the beef and bring to the boil. Cover and simmer until tender.

4 Preheat oven to 220° C/425° F, gas mark 7.

5 Remove the steaks and place them overlapping each other on an ovenproof dish, greased with 1 tsp of the remaining butter. Boil the onion sauce. Check the seasoning, adjust if necessary, and pour over the beef.

6 Sprinkle over the breadcrumbs. Dice the remaining butter and dot over the top. Bake in the oven until heated through and crunchy on top.

TO DRINK
beer or red wine

LEVEL OF DIFFICULTY
fairly easy

PREPARATION
1 hr

PREPARE IN ADVANCE
yes

STUFFED BEEF

Serves 4

4 large thin rump steaks beaten flat
1 tsp salt
freshly ground black pepper
2 tbsp butter

Stuffing:
1 small onion, finely chopped
2 egg yolks
1½ tbsp French mustard
½ tbsp Swedish or German mustard
2 tbsp chopped capers
2 tbsp finely chopped beetroot
2 tsp grated horseradish

Serve with:
sauté potatoes

1 Mix all the ingredients for the stuffing together. Place the beef on a work surface. Season with salt and pepper.

2 Divide the stuffing equally between the beef slices. Place the stuffing on one half of each beef slice and fold the other side over the top. Pinch the edges so that the stuffing does not seep out.

3 Melt the butter in a frying-pan. Fry the beef quickly over fairly high heat, for 1-2 minutes on each side.

4 Place the beef on warm plates and serve immediately.

STUFFED BEEF 230

TO DRINK
beer or red wine

LEVEL OF DIFFICULTY easy
PREPARATION TIME 30 mins
PREPARE IN ADVANCE no

BRAISED BEEF ROLL

Serves 4-6

1 x 800 g/1¾ lb boned topside
1 tbsp salt
freshly ground white pepper
1 small soft cheese with garlic
1 tbsp paprika
1 tsp dried rosemary
1 x 200 g/7 oz can small button mushrooms
2 tbsp butter
1 carrot, sliced
1 large onion, sliced
300 ml/10 fl oz stock

Sauce:
1½ tbsp flour
150-200 ml/5-7 fl oz double cream
400 ml stock
soya sauce
salt
freshly ground black pepper

Serve with:
boiled potatoes, seasonal vegetables and pickled gherkins

1 Season the meat with salt and pepper. Spread with the cheese and sprinkle with paprika and rosemary. Drain the mushrooms and reserve the can juice. Add the mushrooms, pressing them into the cheese. Roll up the meat. Swiss roll style, and tie with cotton string.

2 Melt the butter in a flameproof casserole and brown the beef all over. Add the carrot and onion. Add half the stock and simmer, covered, for 45 minutes, until tender. Add more stock if required.

3 Remove the meat and keep warm. Add any remaining stock and the reserved mushroom can juice to the pan. Bring to the boil and stir to deglaze.

4 Make the sauce. Strain the gravy into a clean saucepan. Rub the vegetables through a wire strainer. Add the stock and bring to the boil. Stir the flour into a little cold water and pour the mixture into the sauce, stirring constantly until it thickens. Add the cream and simmer for 5 minutes, stirring occasionally. Add salt, pepper and soya sauce to taste.

5 Cut the roll into slices and place on a warm serving dish. Garnish with lightly boiled vegetables.

TO DRINK
red wine

LEVEL OF DIFFICULTY
fairly easy

PREPARATION TIME
1 hr

PREPARE IN ADVANCE
yes

FESTIVE MIXED GRILL

Serves 4

8 thin slices lean beef
salt
freshly ground pepper

Red filling:
4 tbsp chili sauce
12-16 pickled onions

Yellow filling:
4 tbsp French mustard
1 bunch chives, finely chopped

Green filling:
4 tbsp crushed green peppercorns
1 tbsp vegetable oil

Marinade (optional):
150 ml/5 fl oz soya sauce
1 tbsp paprika
freshly ground black pepper
spices and herbs to taste

Serve with:
baked potatoes or potato salad, green salad, tomato salad (see recipe 199), cucumber salad with hazelnuts (see recipe 403)

1 Prepare the marinade, if using, by beating all the marinade ingredients together.

2 Preheat the grill or barbecue. Prepare the pinwheels. Choose and prepare one of the fillings. Lay the meat on a work surface and season. Turn the meat over, spread the filling over and roll up. Cut the roll into 15-20 mm/½-¾ inch thick slices and spear them with skewers. Brush with cooking oil or with marinade, if using.

3 Grill the meat for 3 minutes on each side.

Variations:
Chops, steaks and frankfurters can be brushed with the marinade, grilled and served with vegetable kebabs.

To make vegetable kebabs, spear 3-4 different vegetables on to the skewers. Choose from cherry tomatoes, cucumber slices, small onions, whole mushrooms, whole radishes, courgette slices and slices of corn on the cob. Brush with cooking oil and season with salt and pepper or brush with the marinade. Grill for a few minutes, turning frequently.

FESTIVE MIXED GRILL 232

TO DRINK
red wine, white wine or beer

LEVEL OF DIFFICULTY
easy

PREPARATION TIME
varied

PREPARE IN ADVANCE
partly

FILLET OF BEEF PROVENÇAL

Serves 4

500-600 g/1-1¼ lb fillet of beef
salt
freshly ground white pepper

Fried potatoes:
10-12 potatoes
2-3 tbsp butter
1 tsp salt

Garlic butter:
100 g/3½ oz butter
2 cloves garlic, crushed
1 tsp lemon juice (optional)

Garnish:
chopped parsley

1 Preheat the oven to 130° C/250° F, gas mark ½. Trim the beef and rub with salt and pepper. Place in an ovenproof dish, insert a meat thermometer and roast in the oven for about 1 hour. When the thermometer registers 55° C/131° F the meat will be rare, 60° C/140° F the meat will become pink and at 65° C/149° F light pink. Turn the meat halfway through the cooking time. Do not baste.

2 Remove the meat from the oven and set aside to rest for 15 minutes. Increase the oven temperature to 250° C/500° F, gas mark 10. Return the meat to the oven.

3 Meanwhile, make the garlic butter. Mix all the ingredients together, shape into a roll, cover with foil and refrigerate.

4 Peel and thinly slice the potatoes. Melt the butter in a large frying-pan and fry the potatoes until completely soft and golden. Add salt. Place the potatoes in an ovenproof dish.

5 Cut the meat into 5-mm/¼-inch thick slices. Arrange overlapping slices of the meat on top of the potatoes.

6 Slice the garlic butter and place on top of the meat. Heat in the oven for approximately 2 minutes or until the butter has started to melt.

7 Sprinkle with chopped parsley and serve immediately.

FILLET OF BEEF PROVENÇAL

TO DRINK
full-bodied red wine

LEVEL OF DIFFICULTY
easy

PREPARATION TIME
$1\frac{1}{2}$ hrs

PREPARE IN ADVANCE
yes

PEPPER STEAK

Serves 4

2-3 black or green peppercorns
4 x 150 g/5¼ oz steaks
2 tbsp butter
½ tsp salt
3 tbsp brandy
300 ml/10 fl oz double cream

Serve with:
sauté potatoes or baked potatoes

1 Roughly crush the peppercorns. Do not use a pepper grinder as the pepper would become too fine. Coat the steaks with the pepper; press one side into the crushed peppercorns, turn over and do the same to the other side. Set aside for approximately 1 hour.

2 Melt the butter in a frying-pan. Add the steaks and fry for 2-3 minutes on each side. Add salt to taste. Pour over the brandy and heat gently. Set alight and gently shake the pan until the flames die down. Remove the steaks from the pan and keep warm.

3 Pour the cream into the frying-pan. Increase the heat and simmer, stirring, until it has become a fairly thick sauce. Adjust the seasoning if required. Pour the sauce over the steaks.

Variations:
100 ml/3½ fl oz white wine or Marsala can be used instead of brandy, but you will not be able to flambé the steaks.

PEPPER STEAK 234

TO DRINK
red wine

LEVEL OF DIFFICULTY
easy

PREPARATION TIME
30 mins + resting time

PREPARE IN ADVANCE
partly

BEEF IN RED WINE SAUCE

Serves 4

600 g/1¼ lb fillet of beef
1 litre/1¾ pints beef stock
3-4 different vegetables e.g. fried beans, baby carrots, small whole onions, leeks

Sauce:
1 tbsp finely chopped onion
1 clove garlic, crushed
1 tsp paprika
100 ml/3½ fl oz red wine
1 tbsp tomato purée
300 ml/10 fl oz stock
4 tsp butter
4 tsp flour

1 Tie the fillet with cotton string to hold it together while it is cooking. Prepare the vegetables.

2 Bring the stock to the boil, add the fillet and simmer for 10 minutes. It should be very rare and red inside; if you prefer it pink, simmer for 15 minutes. Remove from the heat. Leave the fillet in the stock for 10 minutes to absorb the flavours.

3 Meanwhile, boil the vegetables in some of the stock until tender.

4 To make the sauce, mix the onion, garlic, paprika and wine in a saucepan. Simmer until reduced by half. Add the tomato purée and stock and cook for a few minutes.

5 Mix together the butter and flour to make a *beurre manié*. Add a little at a time, stirring each piece in thoroughly before adding the next.

6 Cut the fillet into attractive slices and place on warm dinner plates together with the sauce and vegetables.

BEEF IN RED WINE SAUCE 235

TO DRINK
light red wine

LEVEL OF DIFFICULTY
easy
PREPARATION TIME
1 hr
PREPARE IN ADVANCE
no

SHOEMAKER'S DISH

Serves 4

400-500 g/14 oz-1 lb fillet of beef
8 slices bacon or 100 g/3½ oz smoked ham, diced
1 tsp salt
freshly ground white pepper
2 tbsp butter
150 ml/5 fl oz water or stock
4 lightly browned cocktail frankfurters (optional)

Mashed potatoes:
1 kg/2¼ lb potatoes
1 tbsp salt
freshly ground white pepper
2 tbsp butter
250-300 ml/9-10 fl oz hot milk or single cream
finely chopped chives

Garnish:
parsley butter
tomato quarters

1 Make the mashed potatoes. Peel the potatoes, cut into small pieces and boil in unsalted water until soft. Drain. Mash in the saucepan. Add salt, pepper, butter and hot milk or single cream. Beat the purée with an electric mixer until light and airy. Keep covered and warm.

2 Prepare the meat. Cut into slices and pound the meat gently by hand or with a steak hammer. Heat a saucepan and fry the bacon slices or smoked ham.

3 Melt the butter in a frying-pan and fry the beef slices for 2-3 minutes on each side. Season with salt and pepper. Deglaze the frying-pan with a little water or stock to make the gravy.

4 Place the beef slices, bacon or ham, cocktail frankfurters and mashed potatoes on warm dinner plates. Pour a little gravy on top of the fillets. Sprinkle finely chopped chives over the mashed potatoes, and garnish with parsley butter and small quarters of tomato.

SHOEMAKER'S DISH 236

TO DRINK
red wine or beer

LEVEL OF DIFFICULTY
easy

PREPARATION TIME
30 mins

PREPARE IN ADVANCE
partly

SLOTTS STEAK

Serves 6-8

1-1.5 kg/2¼-3¼ lb boneless beef, e.g. topside or brisket
2-3 tbsp butter
2 onions, quartered
1 carrot, sliced
1 tsp salt
1 bay leaf
6 white peppercorns
4 anchovies
400 ml/14 fl oz beef stock
1 tbsp vinegar

Sauce:
600 ml/1 pint water
3 tbsp flour
100 ml/3½ fl oz double cream
salt
freshly ground white pepper
soya sauce

Serve with:
boiled potatoes, seasonal vegetables, redcurrant jelly, and pickled gherkins

1 Prepare the meat and tie with cotton string if unevenly shaped.

2 Cut the onion into quarters. Peel and slice the carrot. Melt the butter in a flameproof casserole. Brown the meat on all sides. Insert a meat thermometer. Add the onions and brown them with the meat. Add the carrot, salt, bay leaf, peppercorns, anchovies, stock and vinegar.

3 Cover and simmer over low heat until the thermometer registers 70-75° C/158-167° F, about 1¼-1½ hours. Add more water or more stock, if required.

4 Transfer the meat to a carving dish and cover with foil.

5 Strain the cooking juices and make up to 600 ml/1 pint with water. Bring to the boil. Mix the flour with a little water and add to the boiling gravy, stirring all the time. Add the cream and cook for approximately 5 minutes. Add salt and pepper and a little soya sauce to taste.

6 Carve the meat into thin slices and place on a warm serving dish. Pour over a little of the sauce and serve the rest separately.

TO DRINK
red wine

LEVEL OF DIFFICULTY
easy

PREPARATION TIME
2 hrs

PREPARE IN ADVANCE
yes

TAFELSPITZ

Serves 4-6

1-1.5 kg/2¼-3¼ lb topside
1 tbsp salt
freshly ground black pepper
300 ml/10 fl oz water
300 ml/10 fl oz dry white wine
1 large onion, chopped
1 thick slice lemon
3 carrots
4 leeks
1 small stick celery

Apple Sauce with Horseradish:
6-7 tart eating apples or small cooking apples
150 ml/5 fl oz water
2 tbsp sugar
2-3 tbsp fresh horseradish
1 tsp vinegar

Serve with:
boiled or sauté potatoes

1 Rub the meat with salt and . Place it in a small saucepan so that it fits tightly. Pour over equal quantities of water and white wine, so that the meat is fully covered. Add the onion and lemon slice. Bring to the boil and skim. Simmer the meat for approximately 30 minutes.

2 Prepare the carrots, leeks and celery and add to the saucepan. Simmer for further 30-45 minutes or until the meat is tender. If you are using a meat thermometer, it should register 75° C/167° F.

3 Meanwhile, make the apple and horseradish sauce. Peel and core the apples. Using as little water as possible, boil until soft. Add sugar to taste. Purée the apples in a food processor or mash to a purée. Leave to cool. Grate 2 or more tbsp horseradish into the purée and add the vinegar.

4 Remove the meat from the saucepan and cut into slices. Place on a warm serving dish. Remove the vegetables from the saucepan and use to garnish the meat. Pour a little of the cooking liquid over the meat. Serve the apple and horseradish sauce separately.

TAFELSPITZ 238

TO DRINK
white wine

LEVEL OF DIFFICULTY
easy

PREPARATION TIME
2 hrs

PREPARE IN ADVANCE
yes

HUNGARIAN GOULASH

Serves 4

600 g/1¼ lb boneless beef
2 tbsp butter
2 large onions, finely chopped
salt
freshly ground white pepper
500 ml/17 fl oz stock
2-3 tbsp tomato purée
1-1½ tsp paprika
½ tsp ground cumin
1 x 800 g/1¾ lb can sauerkraut
200 ml/7 fl oz crème fraîche

Serve with:
rice or mashed potatoes

1 Cut the meat into cubes. Melt the butter in a large pan and brown the meat. Add the onion and cook until golden. Season with salt and pepper. Pour over the stock so that it almost covers the meat. Add the tomato purée, paprika and cumin and simmer, covered, for approximately 25 minutes or until the meat is tender.

2 Add the sauerkraut and boil for approximately 10 minutes.

3 Stir in the crème fraîche and serve.

Variation:
Goulash can also be made with veal.

TO DRINK
red wine

LEVEL OF DIFFICULTY
easy
PREPARATION TIME
1 hr
PREPARE IN ADVANCE
yes

HERBY SALT BEEF

Serves 4

1.5 kg/3¼ lb topside

Herb marinade:
1 litre/1¾ pints water
3 tbsp salt
1 tbsp black and white peppercorns, crushed
1 large onion, sliced
2 cloves garlic, sliced
fresh herbs e.g. basil, tarragon, rosemary, parsley

Serve with:
boiled new potatoes or potato gratinée (see recipe 411)
fried small onions
green salad
pickles

1 Preheat the oven to 30°C / 250° F, gas mark ½. Prepare the meat and place on a close-fitting ovenproof dish or tray. Insert a meat thermometer.

2 Roast the meat in the lower part of the oven until the thermometer reads 55-60° C/ 131-140° F, depending on how rare you like the meat. It will take approximately 1½-2 hours.

3 Bring the water for the marinade to the boil. Add the salt, peppercorns, onion, garlic and herbs. Continue to boil for 3-4 minutes. Cool the marinade by placing the saucepan in cold water.

4 Remove the meat from the oven and extract the thermometer. Place the warm meat in a small, tight-fitting container and pour over the marinade. Set aside in the refrigerator for 4-5 hours.

5 Remove the meat from the marinade, wrap tightly in foil and leave in the refrigerator until serving.

6 Cut the meat into thin slices and serve with the recommended accompaniments.

HERBY SALT BEEF 240

TO DRINK
red wine or lager

LEVEL OF DIFFICULTY
easy
PREPARATION TIME
2 hrs + marinating time
PREPARE IN ADVANCE
yes

HOLSTEIN SCHNITZEL

Serves 4

4 x 150 g/5 oz fillet of veal or veal escalopes
1 tsp salt
freshly ground white pepper
3 tbsp flour
1 egg, beaten
85 g/3 oz breadcrumbs
2-3 tbsp butter

Garnish:
4 fried eggs
8 anchovy fillets
capers

Serve with:
French fries or boiled potatoes
petit pois
baby carrots
asparagus

1 Pound the veal until thin. Season with salt and pepper. Coat the veal in flour, then in the beaten egg and lastly in breadcrumbs. Set aside until the breadcrumb mixture has set.

2 Melt the butter in a frying-pan. Fry the veal for approximately 3-4 minutes each side over medium heat. Do not allow to burn. Remove from the pan and keep warm

3 Fry the eggs. Place the schnitzels on a warm serving dish, top each with 1 fried egg and garnish with anchovies and capers.

Variations:
Holstein Schnitzel is traditionally served with fried egg, different varieties of boiled vegetables warmed in butter, and French fries, together with fried bread croûtons and dressed with Russian black caviar or smoked salmon. This is a complete meal, with both starter and main course served at the same time.

TO DRINK
dry white wine, light red wine or lager

LEVEL OF DIFFICULTY
easy

PREPARATION TIME
30 mins

PREPARE IN ADVANCE
partly

VEAL FILLET OSCAR

Serves 4

2 tbsp butter
4 slices veal fillet
1 tsp salt
freshly ground white pepper

Sauce:
Béarnaise sauce (see recipe 419)
1-1½ tbsp tomato purée

Garnish:
1 boiled lobster tail
8 canned or cooked asparagus spears
4 slices truffle or preserved truffle parings

Serve with:
sauté potatoes or French fries

1 Make the sauce and stir in the tomato purée. Peel the lobster tail and cut into slices.

2 Melt the butter in a frying-pan. Fry the veal fillets for 2-3 minutes on each side. Season with salt and pepper. Place on a warm serving dish.

3 Carefully pour the warm sauce around the edges of the fillets to form a ring around the meat. Place 2 asparagus spears side by side on top of each fillet. Place a truffle garnished lobster slice on top of the asparagus. (The garnish symbolizes the Swedish King Oscar II's crest and his initials.) Serve the rest of the sauce in a separate bowl.

Variations:
The lobster can be replaced with a few fresh, cooked peeled prawns.

VEAL FILLET OSCAR 242

To drink
red wine

LEVEL OF DIFFICULTY
easy

PREPARATION TIME
30 mins

PREPARE IN ADVANCE
partly

VEAL FRICASSÉE

Serves 6

1 kg/2$^{1}/_{4}$ lb boneless veal, shoulder or breast
1 litre/1$^{3}/_{4}$ pints chicken stock
2 leeks
2 carrots
1 bay leaf
1 tsp sage
1 tsp salt
10 white peppercorns
2 tbsp flour
2 tbsp butter
3 egg yolks
juice of $^{1}/_{2}$ lemon
100 ml/3$^{1}/_{2}$ fl oz single cream
salt
freshly ground pepper

Serve with:
boiled potatoes or rice

1 Cut off and reserve the green part of the leeks. Rinse and tie together. Reserve the whites of the leeks. Cut the carrots into 3-cm/1-inch cubes.

2 Place the meat in a large pan in plenty of water. Bring to the boil. Cook for 5 minutes. Drain and rinse the meat under cold running water.

3 Place the meat in a clean pan. Pour over the stock to cover. Add the carrots, leek greens, bay leaf, sage, salt and peppercorns. Bring to the boil and simmer for 1 hour.

4 Meanwhile, cut the white of the leeks into 2-cm/$^{3}/_{4}$-inch lengths. Add to pan when the meat has been simmering for 30 minutes.

5 When the meat is cooked, discard the bay leaf and leek greens. Place the meat, carrots and leek white in a deep serving dish and keep warm.

6 Strain the stock into a saucepan. Simmer, uncovered, until reduced to 500 ml/17 fl oz.

7 Work the flour and butter together to make a *beurre manié*. Beat the egg yolks with the cream.

8 Bring the stock to the boil. Stir in the *beurre manié*, a little at a time. Remove from the heat and beat in the egg mixture. Simmer for 2-3 minutes. Add the lemon juice and season with salt and pepper to taste.

9 Pour the sauce over the meat and vegetables and serve.

To drink
white wine

LEVEL OF DIFFICULTY medium difficult
PREPARATION TIME 2 hrs
PREPARE IN ADVANCE yes

OSSO BUCO

Serves 4

1.5 kg/3¼ lb knuckle of veal chopped into 8 pieces
30 g/1 oz flour
3 tbsp butter or vegetable oil
3 onions, chopped
1 small carrot, chopped
1 stick celery, chopped
1 bay leaf
1 x 400 g/14 oz can plum tomatoes
200 ml/7 fl oz white wine or Marsala
salt
freshly ground black pepper
200 ml/7 fl oz stock
2 cloves garlic, crushed
grated rind of ½ lemon
6 tbsp finely chopped parsley

Serve with:
boiled rice or pasta

1 Coat the meat with the flour. Melt the butter or heat the oil in a large heavy based pan and brown the meat on both sides. Transfer to a dish.

2 Add the onion, carrot, celery and bay leaf to the pan. Lower the heat and fry slowly for approximately 5 minutes, stirring constantly. Return the meat to the pan, making sure the pieces lie flat so that the meat does not fall off the bone.

3 Add the tomatoes, wine, salt, pepper, and a little of the stock. Bring to the boil, cover and simmer for approximately 1½ hours until the meat is tender. Add more wine and stock if the dish becomes too dry.

4 Mix in the garlic and lemon rind just before serving and sprinkle with chopped parsley.

OSSO BUCO 244

To drink
Italian red wine

LEVEL OF DIFFICULTY easy
PREPARATION TIME 2 hrs
PREPARE IN ADVANCE yes

SWISS SCHNITZEL

Serves 4

4 thin slices veal fillet or veal escalopes
8 slices Emmental cheese
4 thin slices cooked ham
salt
freshly ground white pepper
3 tbsp flour
1 egg, beaten with a little water
85 g/3 oz breadcrumbs
2-3 tbsp butter

Serve with:
sauté or baked potatoes
petit pois
tomato salad

1 Pound the veal until it is thin. Place 2 slices of cheese on top of 2 pieces of veal. Place 2 slices of ham on each and add a further two slices of cheese. Finally cover with the remaining slices of veal. Season with salt and pepper.

2 Coat the schnitzels with flour, then with the beaten egg and lastly with breadcrumbs. Set aside until the breadcrumb mixture has hardened.

3 Melt the butter in a frying-pan and fry the schnitzels for 6-8 minutes on each side over low heat, making sure that they do not burn.

4 Cut the schnitzels into thick slices and place on a warm serving dish. Pour a little melted brown butter over the top.

TO DRINK
dry white wine or light red wine

LEVEL OF DIFFICULTY
easy

PREPARATION TIME
30 mins

PREPARE IN ADVANCE
partly

VITELLO TONNATO

Serves 8

1.25 kg/2¾ lb boneless leg or loin of veal
salt
freshly ground white pepper

Sauce:
1 x 185 g/6½ oz can tuna in oil
4 anchovy fillets
2 tbsp capers
4 tbsp lemon juice
2 egg yolks
200 ml/7 fl oz vegetable oil
salt
freshly ground black pepper

Garnish:
anchovy fillets
capers or sliced green olives
lemon wedges

Serve with:
boiled potatoes

1 Preheat the oven to 170° C/325° F, gas mark 3. Rub the meat with salt and pepper. Place on a wire rack over a baking tray. Insert a meat thermometer into the thickest part. Bake in the oven until the thermometer registers 70° C/158° F (rare) or 75° C/167° F (well done), approximately 1½ hours. Set aside to cool.

2 Make the sauce. Drain the tuna. Beat the tuna, anchovies, capers and lemon juice together or work in a food processor until smooth. Add the egg yolks, one at a time, and mix. Slowly add the oil in a thin stream, beating constantly or while the machine is going. The consistency of the sauce should be that of mayonnaise. Add salt and pepper to taste.

3 Cut the cold meat into thin slices and place on a serving dish. Pour over the sauce and garnish with anchovies, capers or sliced olives and lemon wedges.

Variations:
This meal can be made from leftover roast veal. Cold boiled or roast sliced turkey may also be used.

VITELLO TONNATO 246

To drink
white or red wine

LEVEL OF DIFFICULTY
fairly easy

PREPARATION TIME
2 hrs

PREPARE IN ADVANCE
yes

HAZELNUT PORK SCHNITZEL

Serves 4

4 slices pork fillet or lean shoulder of pork
salt
freshly ground black pepper
3 tbsp flour
1 egg, beaten
85 g/3 oz ground hazelnuts
2 tbsp butter

Serve with:
mashed potatoes and steamed broccoli

1 Prepare the meat. Season with salt and pepper. Coat first with flour, then with beaten egg and lastly with the ground nuts.

2 Melt the butter in a frying-pan, add the meat, lower the heat and fry the meat slowly making sure that it is golden brown on each side.

3 Place the schnitzels on a warm serving dish. Serve with mashed potatoes and boiled broccoli.

HAZELNUT PORK SCHNITZEL

TO DRINK
white wine

LEVEL OF DIFFICULTY
easy

PREPARATION
30 mins

PREPARE IN ADVANCE
partly

OVEN BAKED FILLET OF PORK

Serves 6-8

1-1.2 kg/2¼-2½ lb pork fillet
85 g/3 oz butter
salt
freshly ground pepper
16 canned artichoke hearts
600 ml/1 pint Béarnaise sauce
2 tbsp whole green peppercorns

Tomatoes à la provençal:
4 tomatoes, halved
85 g/3 oz butter
5 tbsp coarse breadcrumbs
2 cloves garlic, crushed
6 tbsp chopped parsley

Serve with:
sauté potatoes
green salad

1 Preheat the oven to 250° C/ 500° F, gas mark 10. Start with the Tomatoes à la provençal. Grease an ovenproof dish with a little of the butter. Place the tomatoes, cut side up, in the dish. Mix together the remaining butter, breadcrumbs, garlic and parsley. Spread the mixture evenly over the tomato halves. Set aside

2 Grease a gratin dish with a little of the butter and set aside. Cut the pork into 16 slices. Melt the remaining butter in a frying-pan and fry the pork for 1 minute on each side. Season with salt and pepper.

3 Drain the artichoke hearts and place them in the gratin dish. Place 1 slice of pork fillet on each artichoke heart.

4 Mix the Béarnaise sauce with the peppercorns and spoon the mixture evenly over the fillets.

5 Place the two dishes in the oven and bake for approximately 8 minutes. Serve with sauté potatoes and green salad.

Variations:
Instead of green peppercorns and Béarnaise sauce, use creamed mushrooms.

OVEN BAKED FILLET OF PORK 248

TO DRINK
red wine

LEVEL OF DIFFICULTY
easy

PREPARATION TIME
1 hr

PREPARE IN ADVANCE
yes

PORK WITH PEPPERCORN SAUCE

Serves 4

500-600 g/1-1¼ lb fillet of pork
2 tbsp butter
salt
freshly ground white pepper

Green pepper sauce:
1 tbsp butter
1 onion, finely chopped
1-2 tbsp green peppercorns, lightly crushed
1 tbsp French mustard
100 ml/3½ fl oz stock
300 ml/10 fl oz double cream
salt
freshly ground white pepper

Serve with:
sauté potatoes or Hasselback potatoes (see recipe 408), mangetout or French beans

1 Start with the sauce. Melt the butter and sauté the onion over low heat without colouring. Add the peppercorns and fry for a couple of minutes. Stir in the mustard, stock and cream. Simmer, stirring constantly, until thick and smooth. Season with salt and pepper.

2 Trim the meat. Melt the butter in a frying-pan. Place the whole fillet in the frying-pan and fry for 10-15 minutes, turning once. Season with salt and pepper.

3 Cut the fillet into fairly thick, diagonal slices and place on a warm serving dish. Spoon over a little of the warm sauce and serve the rest of the sauce separately.

PORK WITH PEPPERCORN SAUCE 249

TO DRINK
red wine

LEVEL OF DIFFICULTY
easy

PREPARATION TIME
30 mins

PREPARE IN ADVANCE
partly

HIRAM'S ROLLED PORK FILLET WITH DILL

Serves 4

8 slices lean pork fillet
salt
freshly ground black pepper
3 tbsp chopped dill
3 tbsp chili sauce or tomato purée
2 tbsp butter
400 ml/4 fl oz stock
½ tsp cornflour or plain flour

Serve with:
sauté or mashed potatoes

1 Place the meat slices on a work surface. Season with salt and pepper. Put 1 large tsp dill and 1 tsp chili sauce or tomato purée on top of each slice. Roll up the slices and secure with a cocktail stick, or tie with string.

2 Melt the butter in a frying-pan. Brown the rolls all over. Add a little stock and let the rolls absorb it. Shake the pan so that the rolls do not stick to the base. Add a little more stock twice and allow it to be absorbed. Pour over the remaining stock and simmer, covered, for 20 minutes or until the fillets are tender.

3 Add the cornflour or plain flour to thicken the sauce, if necessary. It should be thin, brown and shiny.

4 Remove the string or cocktail sticks and serve the rolls in the sauce. with sauté or mashed potatoes.

HIRAM'S ROLLED PORK FILLET WITH DILL 250

TO DRINK
dry white wine or lager

LEVEL OF DIFFICULTY easy
PREPARATION TIME 1 hr
PREPARE IN ADVANCE yes

GAMMON IN FOIL PACKETS

Serves 4

1 tbsp butter
4 x 125 g/3½ oz lightly smoked gammon steaks
8 medium-sized potatoes
2 large onions
4 tomatoes
4 tsp chopped parsley

Garlic butter:
4-5 tbsp butter
2 garlic cloves, crushed

1 Cut 4 pieces of foil about 30 cm/12 inches square. Make the garlic butter. Mash the butter until soft and mix in the crushed garlic.

2 Preheat the oven to 170° C/ 325° F, gas mark 3. Grease the middle of each foil square with the butter. Slice the onions and push out into rings. Slice the tomatoes. Peel the potatoes and cut into very thin slices, using a food processor with a slicing blade or a cheese slicer.

3 Divide the potatoes equally between the 4 pieces of foil, add plenty of raw onion rings on top and finally add a gammon steak. Top each with the tomato slices. Fold the foil packets together so that they are airtight.

4 Bake the parcels for approximately 50-60 minutes. Open the packets and sprinkle with chopped parsley.

TO DRINK
dry white wine

LEVEL OF DIFFICULTY
easy

PREPARATION TIME
1½ hrs

PREPARE IN ADVANCE
partly

SUNDAY CREOLE STEW

Serves 4-6

600 g/1¼ lb pork fillet
30 g/1 oz butter
2 bratwurst or spiced frankfurter
1 red pepper, sliced
salt
freshly ground black pepper
1 tsp dried marjoram
1 tbsp flour
300 ml/10 fl oz double cream
100 g/3½ oz pickled onions
150 g/5 oz black olives
50 g/1¾ oz pickled gherkins, chopped

Serve with:
rice, pasta or boiled potatoes

1 Prepare the fillets and cut into chunky slices. Cut the sausages into 1 cm/½ inch cubes.

2 Melt the butter in a heavy-based saucepan. Brown the pork and sausages. Add the red pepper. Season with salt, pepper and marjoram. Sprinkle over the flour and stir. Add the cream and bring to the boil. Add the pickled onions, olives and gherkins.

3 Simmer for 10-15 minutes. Add a little stock or more cream, if necessary, and season to taste.

4 Warm through thoroughly before serving.

SUNDAY CREOLE STEW 252

To drink
red wine

LEVEL OF DIFFICULTY easy
PREPARATION TIME 30 mins
PREPARE IN ADVANCE yes

SPICY SPARE RIBS

Serves 6

1.5 kg/3¼ lb pork spare rib,
thickly cut

Marinade:
250 ml/9 fl oz mild or medium
chili sauce
25 g/¾ oz onion, finely chopped
2 cloves garlic, crushed
1 tsp vinegar
1 tsp mild mustard
salt
freshly ground black pepper
1 tsp ground ginger
2 tsp Worcestershire sauce
2 tsp soya sauce
2 tsp vegetable oil or melted
butter

Serve with:
baked, sauté or boiled potatoes
Brussels sprouts or broccoli
apple sauce

1 Preheat the oven to 170° C/225° F, gas mark 3. Place the spare ribs, bone upwards, in an oblong dish or pan.

2 Mix together all the marinade ingredients and brush over the spare ribs. Bake in the oven for approximately 45 minutes.

3 Turn the spare ribs over, and brush with the marinade. Bake for a further 45 minutes. Brush once or twice with the marinade during cooking. When the bones are almost separating from the meat, the dish is ready.

4 Cut the spare ribs into portions and arrange on a serving dish.

TO DRINK
lager or robust red wine

LEVEL OF DIFFICULTY
easy
PREPARATION TIME
$1^1/_2$ hrs
PREPARE IN ADVANCE
partly

HOSTESS HAM RING

Serves 4

3 sheets frozen puff pastry sheets, thawed
1 tbsp butter
1tbsp flour

Filling:
2 tbsp butter
2 onions, finely chopped
200 g/7 oz smoked ham
100 g/3½ oz leaf spinach
3 eggs
300 ml/10 fl oz single cream
75 g/2½ oz strongly flavoured cheese, grated
salt
freshly ground black pepper
grated nutmeg or paprika

Garnish:
lettuce
rings of red and green peppers

1 Preheat the oven to 250° C/500° F, gas mark 10. Grease a 1.5 litre/2½ pint ring mould with the butter and coat with the flour. Brush the edges of the pastry sheets with water and place them so that they overlap slightly. Roll out the dough and place in the mould. Chill in the refrigerator for approximately 30 minutes.

2 Meanwhile, make the filling. Melt the butter in a pan and sauté the onions over low heat until soft and transparent. Cut the ham into thin strips and roughly chop the spinach.

3 Put the onions, ham and spinach into the base of the pastry-lined mould. Beat together the remaining ingredients. Pour the mixture into the mould and bake in the bottom of the oven for approximately 15 minutes until golden. Cover with foil and bake for further 15 minutes. Lower the heat to 200° C/400° F, gas mark 6, and bake for a further 10 minutes. Test with a skewer.

4 Leave for 10 minutes before turning out. It is best served warm but may be served cold.

HOSTESS HAM RING 254

TO DRINK
lager or light red wine

LEVEL OF DIFFICULTY
easy

PREPARATION TIME
1½ hrs + resting time

PREPARE IN ADVANCE
yes

NASI GORENG

Serves 4

5 tbsp oil
Nasi Goreng or Indonesian spices (available from specialist delicatessens and oriental grocers)
2-3 tbsp grated onion
4 tbsp finely chopped onion
1 red chili, cut into strips
1 leek, cut into strips
340 g/12 oz long grain rice, boiled, drained and cooled
2 chicken breasts, cooked and cut into strips
250 g/8 oz lean pork, fried and cut in strips
1-2 tbsp ketjap benteng (Indonesian soya sauce)
salt
freshly ground black pepper
1 omelette, made from 2 eggs, cut into long, narrow strips
100 g/3½ oz cooked, peeled prawns

Serve with:
prawn crackers (traditionally these are much larger than Chinese prawn crackers), sliced tomatoes, cucumber, chutney

1 Heat 1 tbsp of the oil and fry the grated onion until golden. Add the spices to taste.

2 Heat 3 tbsp of the remaining oil and fry the chopped onion, chili and leeks. Stir in the boiled rice and fry over low heat, stirring constantly. Stir in the fried grated onions.

3 Fry the chicken and pork lightly in the remaining oil. Stir in the soya sauce, salt and pepper.

4 Mix the rice and meat together and, if necessary, add more spices or soya sauce. Keep warm.

5 Deep-fry the prawn crackers. Drain on kitchen paper.

6 Place the rice mixture in a bowl. Garnish with prawns, prawn crackers and strips of omelette.

TO DRINK
tea or lager

LEVEL OF DIFFICULTY
medium difficult

PREPARATION TIME
1 hr

PREPARE IN ADVANCE
partly

PORK AND SAFFRON RICE

Serves 4

500 g/1 lb pork fillet
3 g/1 oz flour
2-3 tsp butter

Tomato sauce:
1 tbsp butter
3 tbsp finely chopped onion
1 x 400 g/14 oz can chopped tomatoes
1 tsp dried basil
1 clove garlic, crushed
salt
freshly ground white pepper

Batter:
2 eggs
2½ tbsp water
75 g/2½ oz Parmesan cheese, grated
½ tsp paprika
salt
freshly ground white pepper

Saffron rice:
½ onion, finely chopped
250 g/9 oz rice
2 tbsp butter or vegetable oil
pinch crushed saffron
600 ml/1 pint chicken stock

1 Make the tomato sauce. Melt the butter and fry the onion until soft. Add the tomatoes, basil, garlic, salt and pepper. Simmer for 5-10 minutes.

2 Make the batter. Break the eggs into a bowl, add the water, cheese, paprika, salt and pepper. Stir well. Let the mixture stand until it has thickened.

3 Cook the saffron rice. Heat the butter or oil and fry the onion and rice. Stir in the saffron, add the stock and simmer, covered, over low heat for 18-20 minutes. (The cooking time will vary depending upon the type of rice used).

4 Prepare the meat. Cut into 8 equal-sized pieces and beat flat to form escalopes.

5 Coat the meat in the flour and then in the batter.

6 Melt the butter in a large frying-pan and add the meat. The butter should not be too hot. Fry for approximately 3 minutes on each side.

PORK AND SAFFRON RICE 256

To drink
Italian red wine

LEVEL OF DIFFICULTY
fairly easy

PREPARATION
1 hr

PREPARE IN ADVANCE
partly

REGATTA PORK CHOPS

Serves 4

4 pork chops
freshly ground white pepper
1/2 tsp paprika
2 tbsp butter
1 tsp salt
1/2 tsp four-spice (quatre-épices)
8 tomatoes
1 onion, finely chopped
1/4 tsp dried thyme
1 clove garlic, crushed (optional)
1 bay leaf

Garnish:
finely chopped dill
finely chopped parsley

Serve with:
spaghetti or boiled potatoes

1 Season the pork chops with pepper and paprika.

2 Melt the butter in a frying-pan and brown the chops on both sides. Transfer them to a flameproof casserole and add salt and four-spice.

3 Blanch, peel and chop the tomatoes. Fry the onion in the same pan in which the chops were browned. Add the tomatoes, thyme, garlic, if using, and a crumbled bay leaf. Boil the mixture for 2-3 minutes. Season with salt to taste and pour over the chops. Cover and simmer for approximately 10 minutes or until the pork chops are cooked and tender.

4 Sprinkle with chopped dill and parsley and serve.

TO DRINK
lager or red wine

LEVEL OF DIFFICULTY
easy

PREPARATION TIME
30 mins

PREPARE IN ADVANCE
yes

ROAST PORK WITH ROSEMARY

Serves 8-10

2.5 kg/5½ lb joint of pork
freshly ground black pepper
salt
3-4 cloves garlic
1 tbsp rosemary
500 ml/17 fl oz stock
1 tbsp soya sauce

Sauce:
300-400 ml/10-14 fl oz stock
4 tbsp flour
100 ml/3½ fl oz white or red wine
200-300 ml/7-10 fl oz double cream
salt
freshly ground black pepper
2 tbsp blackcurrant jelly

Serve with:
gratinée mashed potatoes layered with assorted vegetables (see recipe 413) or sauté potatoes
fried whole small onions,
Brussels sprouts

1 Preheat the oven to 170° C/ 325° F, gas mark 3. Prepare the meat and rub with salt and pepper. Slice the garlic cloves into 2 or 3 pieces lengthwise. Cut several slits in the meat close to the bone and insert the slivers of garlic. Sprinkle over the rosemary. Place the meat on a wire rack over a roasting tin. Insert a meat thermometer. Place the roasting tin in the bottom of the oven and leave until the thermometer reads 80-85° C/ 176-185° F, approximately 2-2½ hours. Baste the meat several times during the last 30 minutes of cooking with the stock mixed with soya sauce.

2 Place the meat on a carving board and cover with foil. Allow to stand

3 Make the sauce. Drain the cooking juices from the meat and dilute with stock. Mix the flour with a little of the wine and stir into the mixture. Add the remaining wine and cream and allow the sauce to boil for approximately 5 minutes. Add salt, pepper, and blackcurrant jelly to taste.

4 Carve the meat into slices. Place on a warm serving dish. Serve the sauce separately.

ROAST PORK WITH ROSEMARY 258

TO DRINK
red wine

LEVEL OF DIFFICULTY
easy

PREPARATION TIME
3 hrs

PREPARE IN ADVANCE
partly

SUPPER TIME KEBABS

Serves 4

250 g/8 oz pork fillet
250 g/8 oz calves' kidneys
6 slices bacon
2 bratwurst or frankfurters
1 large onion
salt
freshly ground black pepper
2 tbsp vegetable oil

Sauce:
1 onion
3 small peppers
200 g/7 oz mushrooms
2 tbsp butter
200 ml/7 fl oz double cream
salt
freshly ground black pepper
1-2 tbsp brandy (optional)
soya sauce

Serve with:
crème fraîche
croquette potatoes (see recipe 412), or boiled potatoes or rice

1 Cut the pork into 8-12 chunky slices. Skin and core the kidneys and soak in cold water. Cut into 12 slices. Cut the bacon slices in half and roll around the kidney slices. Cut the bratwurst or frankfurters into 2-3 cm/¾-1 inch lengths. Peel and cut the onion into 4 pieces and separate into layers.

2 Brush 4 skewers with the oil. Thread the pork, kidneys and bratwurst alternately on to the skewers with one piece of onion between each. Season with salt and pepper and brush with a little oil.

3 Preheat the grill. Make the sauce. Thinly slice the onion and slice. Seed the peppers and cut into very thin rings. Slice the mushrooms.

4 Melt the butter in a frying-pan. Fry the onions, peppers and mushrooms over low heat without colouring. Add the cream and simmer gently to allow the flavours to merge. Season with salt and pepper and add brandy and soya sauce to taste. Keep the sauce warm.

5 Grill the kebabs, turning once during cooking. Do not overcook the meat as it will become dry and tough.

6 Place the sauce on 4 dinner plates. Place the kebabs on top. Garnish with crème fraîche.

TO DRINK
red wine

LEVEL OF DIFFICULTY easy
PREPARATION TIME 1 hr
PREPARE IN ADVANCE partly

GAMMON PASTIES

Serves 4

2 sheets frozen puff pastry
2 tsp butter
150 g/5 oz Emmental or Gruyère cheese
approximately 500 g/1 lb smoked gammon
1 tbsp French mustard
1 egg, lightly beaten

Sauce:
2 tbsp butter
2 shallots or small onions, finely chopped
300 ml/10 fl oz meat or vegetable stock
2-3 tbsp tomato purée
50 ml/2 fl oz Madeira

Serve with:
cauliflower, broccoli or butter-fried leaf spinach

1 Thaw the puff pastry for approximately 10 minutes. Preheat the oven to 220° C/ 425° F, gas mark 7. Grease a baking sheet with the butter. Thinly slice the cheese. Cut the gammon into 8 slices. Sandwich in pairs with the mustard and cheese.

2 Cut the puff pastry sheets in half. Roll out each half until approximately 15 cm/6 inches square. Cover the double gammon slices with puff pastry. Fold the edges under the meat to form a parcel. Cut away excess dough and press the edges together to seal. Cut decorations out of the leftover puff pastry and place on top of the pasties. Place the pasties on the greased baking tray and brush with beaten egg.

3 Bake in the bottom of the oven for approximately 20 minutes.

4 Meanwhile, prepare the sauce. Melt the butter in a saucepan and sauté the shallots or small onions over low heat. Stir in the stock, tomato purée and Madeira and bring to the boil. Simmer for 3-4 minutes. Add seasoning and, possibly, more wine, to taste.

5 Serve with cauliflower, broccoli or leaf spinach.

GAMMON PASTIES 260

To drink
red wine

LEVEL OF DIFFICULTY
easy

PREPARATION TIME
1 hr

PREPARE IN ADVANCE
partly

HAM WITH BLACKCURRANT SAUCE

Serves 8-10

1.5 kg/3¼ lb boneless slightly salted ham
300 ml/10 fl oz water
300 ml/10 fl oz diluted blackcurrant juice
2 cloves garlic, sliced
1 piece root ginger
1 stick cinnamon
parsley sprigs

Sauce:
4 tsp cornflour
100 ml/3½ fl oz water
salt
freshly ground black pepper

Serve with:
boiled baby carrots, mangetout, boiled potatoes and pickled fresh cucumber (see recipe 402)

1 Place the ham in a tightly fitting pan. Check that the meat thermometer will fit when covered with a lid. Remove the ham from the pan.

2 Bring the water and blackcurrant juice to the boil in the pan. Add the garlic, ginger, cinnamon and parsley.

3 Insert the thermometer into the thickest part of the ham.

4 Place the ham in the boiling liquid and simmer, covered. Turn the ham over once during the cooking time. Remove the pan from the heat when the thermometer registers 70° C/ 158° F, approximately 1 hour.

5 Leave the ham in the liquid for 20 minutes if serving at room temperature. Otherwise, allow cool completely in the cooking juices.

6 Make the sauce. Strain the cooking liquid into a saucepan. Mix together the cornflour and 100 ml/3½ fl oz cold water and beat into the cooking liquid. Bring to the boil, season with salt and pepper to taste.

7 Serve with fresh, tender young vegetables, such as baby carrots or mangetout, boiled potatoes or pickled fresh cucumber.

To drink
white wine or lager

LEVEL OF DIFFICULTY
easy
PREPARATION TIME
2 hrs
PREPARE IN ADVANCE
yes

LAMB CUTLET GRATINÉE

Serves 4

12 double lamb cutlets
garlic salt
2 tbsp butter
salt
freshly ground white pepper
250 ml/8 fl oz stock or water
1 onion, finely chopped
Gorgonzola or other blue cheese

Serve with:
sauté potatoes, French beans and fried tomatoes

1 Preheat the oven to 220° C/425° F, gas mark 7. Rub the meat with garlic salt. Melt the butter in a frying-pan and fry the lamb chops for 2-3 minutes on each side. Season with salt and pepper.

2 Place the lamb chops on an ovenproof dish. Rinse the frying-pan with a little water or stock and pour over the meat. Place a large teaspoon of finely chopped onion on each cutlet and top with one slice of Gorgonzola.

3 Place the dish in the oven and bake for approximately 10 minutes until the cheese has melted and the onions have softened.

LAMB CUTLET GRATINÉE 262

TO DRINK
white wine or retsina

LEVEL OF DIFFICULTY
easy

PREPARATION TIME
30 mins

PREPARE IN ADVANCE
partly

LAMB STEW WITH HARICOT BEANS

Serves 6

1 kg/2¼ lb boned breast or shoulder of lamb
2-3 tbsp butter
1 large onion, chopped
2-3 cloves garlic, crushed
1 x 400 g/4 oz can plum tomatoes
1 tsp dried rosemary
salt
freshly ground black pepper
250 g/8 oz haricot beans, soaked overnight and drained
400 g/14 oz carrots
20 black olives

Serve with:
rice or boiled potatoes

1 Cut the meat into 2 cm/¾ inch cubes. Melt 2 tbsp of the butter in a frying-pan and brown the meat in batches. It should be well browned on all sides.

2 Melt the remaining butter in a heavy-based pan and fry the onion. Stir in the garlic. Add the tomatoes with the can juice, rosemary, salt and pepper. Simmer for 3-4 minutes, stirring.

3 Add the meat cubes and the haricot beans to the pan and enough water to cover. Cover with a lid and simmer for approximately 2 hours.

4 Meanwhile, cut the carrots into 5 mm/¼ inch thick slices. Add the carrots and olives to the pan and boil for approximately 30 minutes. Add a little water if the mixture is becoming dry. Adjust the seasoning.

5 Serve the stew with rice or boiled potatoes.

LAMB STEW WITH HARICOT BEANS 263

To drink
red wine

LEVEL OF DIFFICULTY
easy

PREPARATION TIME
3 hrs

PREPARE IN ADVANCE
yes

ROAST LEG OF LAMB PROVENÇAL

Serves 6-8

1 x 2 kg/4½ lb leg of lamb
6 cloves garlic
parsley sprigs
2 tsp salt
freshly ground black pepper
1 tsp dried rosemary
1 tsp dried oregano
1 tbsp butter
1 tsp soya sauce
200 ml/7 fl oz white wine

Serve with:
baked vegetables, potato gratin (see recipe 414 and 411) or sauté potatoes and French beans

1 Preheat the oven to 170° C/ 325° F, gas mark 3. Prepare the meat. Peel the garlic cloves and cut each lengthwise into three slices. Cut several pockets in the lamb and insert slivers of garlic and parsley sprigs.

2 Mix together the salt, pepper, rosemary and oregano and rub into the lamb. Place the lamb in a roasting tin and insert a meat thermometer. Roast the lamb in the oven for 1½-1¾ hours. Baste the lamb with melted butter and soya sauce during the roasting time until it is well coloured.

3 When the thermometer registers 70° C/158° F, the meat will be pink inside. At 75° C/ 167° F, the lamb will be well done. If required, deglaze the roasting tin with a little white wine or stock to make gravy.

ROAST LEG OF LAMB PROVENÇAL 264

To drink
red wine

LEVEL OF DIFFICULTY
easy
PREPARATION TIME
2 hrs
PREPARE IN ADVANCE
yes

LAMB CUTLETS WITH RATATOUILLE

Serves 4

8 double lamb cutlets
85 g/3 oz butter

Ratatouille:
1 small courgette
1 small aubergine
½ leek
2 sticks celery
1 red pepper
1 green pepper
2 tbsp olive oil
1 x 400 g/14 oz can chopped tomatoes
2 tbsp tomato purée
1-2 cloves garlic, crushed
1 vegetable stock cube, crumbled
50-100 ml/2-3½ fl oz white wine (optional)
salt
freshly ground black pepper

Marinade:
juice of ½ lemon
1 tbsp soya sauce
1 tbsp vegetable oil
2 tbsp finely chopped fresh herbs or 2 tsp dried mixed herbs

Serve with:
French beans, boiled potatoes or rice

1 Make the ratatouille. Cut the courgette and aubergine in half lengthwise and chop. Slice the leek. Cut the celery into 1 cm/¼ inch long pieces. Cut the peppers in half, remove the seeds and cut into pieces. Heat the oil and fry the vegetables. Add the tomatoes with the can juice, the tomato purée, garlic, stock cube and wine. Simmer until the vegetables are soft and the sauce is thick. If necessary, add more wine or water. Season to taste.

2 Meanwhile, mix together all the ingredients for the marinade. Add the lamb cutlets and set aside for approximately 20 minutes. Turn them once during this time.

3 Grill or fry the cutlets in the butter for 2-3 minutes on each side.

4 Serve with ratatouille, boiled French beans and potatoes or rice.

TO DRINK
rosé wine

LEVEL OF DIFFICULTY
easy

PREPARATION TIME
1 hr

PREPARE IN ADVANCE
partly

SCANDINAVIAN SUPPER

Serves 4-5

2 x 240 g/8½ oz packets frozen minced reindeer meat or minced beef
2-3 tbsp butter
salt
freshly ground black pepper
2 large onions, finely chopped
½-1 stock cube
200-300 ml/7-10 fl oz double cream or crème fraîche
2 tbsp grated horseradish
2 tbsp finely chopped parsley

Serve with:
boiled or sauté potatoes
salted or pickled gherkins

1 Melt the butter in a large frying-pan and add the frozen meat. Separate the meat with a fork gradually while it thaws so that it is evenly browned. The heat should not be too high. Season with salt and pepper. Transfer the meat to a large saucepan.

2 Fry the onion in the same butter, until soft and golden. Stir it into the meat and crumble over the stock cube. Stir in the cream. Simmer over low heat for approximately 15 minutes. Add a little stock, water or cream if the sauce is too thick.

3 Stir in the horseradish when the dish is cooked. Taste and adjust the seasoning if necessary.

4 Sprinkle over the chopped parsley and serve with boiled or sauté potatoes, and salted or pickled gherkins.

Note:
Reindeer is a popular and economic meat in Sweden, where this recipe comes from. The form of reindeer traditionally used is off-cuts and awkwardly shaped pieces. Minced beef may be substituted, although the texture and flavour will be somewhat different.

SCANDINAVIAN SUPPER 266

TO DRINK
red wine or lager

LEVEL OF DIFFICULTY
easy

PREPARATION TIME
30 mins

PREPARE IN ADVANCE
yes

JUNIPER CHOPS

Serves 6

12 single or 6 double venison chops
salt
freshly ground pepper
1 tsp four-spice (quatre-épices)
2-3 tbsp flour
3 tbsp butter
1 cooking apple, peeled, cored and diced
2 tbsp juniper berries, dried and crushed
50 ml/2 fl oz gin (optional)
300 ml/10 fl oz double cream

Serve with:
sauté or rosti potatoes (see recipe 410)
rowanberry jelly

1 Prepare the chops. Season with salt, pepper and four-spice. Coat the chops with the flour.

2 Melt 2 tbsp of the butter in a frying-pan and fry the chops on both sides in two batches. Add the apple and juniper berries. Fry the chops until red meat juice oozes from their upper sides. Place on a warm serving dish and keep warm.

3 Pour the gin, if using, into the frying-pan. Add the cream and simmer for a few minutes, while stirring. Taste the sauce, beat in the remaining butter and pour the sauce over the chops.

To drink
robust red wine

LEVEL OF DIFFICULTY
easy

PREPARATION TIME
30 minutes

PREPARE IN ADVANCE
no

ROAST VENISON WITH PINK PEPPER SAUCE

Serves 8

1 haunch venison
2 tbsp cooking oil
2 tsp salt
freshly ground black pepper

Sauce:
200 ml/7 fl oz boiling water
approximately 300 ml/10 fl oz beef stock
3 tbsp flour
200 ml/7 fl oz double cream
salt
freshly ground white pepper
3-4 tbsp pink peppercorns, crushed
2 slices goat's cheese
1 tbsp blackcurrant jelly
50 ml/2 fl oz dry white vermouth

Serve with:
baked cheese gratinée potatoes or Hasselback potatoes (see recipes 409 and 408)
broccoli timbales (see recipe 401)
rowanberry jam

1 Preheat the oven to 150° C/300° F, gas mark 3. Rub the meat with the oil. Place it on a wire rack over an oblong roasting tin and put in the oven.

2 Turn the meat after 1 hour, season with salt and black pepper. Insert a meat thermometer into the thickest part of the meat. Return to the oven and cook until the thermometer registers 70° C/158° F. The meat will then be slightly pink inside. Remove the joint from the oven and keep warm.

3 Make the sauce. Pour the boiling water into the roasting tin and stir to deglaze. Strain and make up to 600 ml/1 pint with stock. Pour into a saucepan and bring to the boil.

4 Mix the flour with a little cold water and stir into the gravy. Bring to the boil and continue boiling, stirring constantly, for 5 minutes. Add the cream. Season to taste with salt, white pepper and pink peppercorns. Stir in the cheese, blackcurrant jelly and vermouth. Make sure the sauce is thoroughly heated.

5 Place the joint on a carving board and carve at the table or cut into thin slices and place on a serving dish.

ROAST VENISON WITH PINK PEPPER SAUCE 268

TO DRINK
robust red wine

LEVEL OF DIFFICULTY easy
PREPARATION TIME 1 hr
PREPARE IN ADVANCE yes

SALT BEEF

Serves 6

1.5 kg/3¼ lb frozen beef e.g. topside, rump steak

Salt liquor:
1 litre/1¾ pints water
100 g/3½ oz coarse salt
2 tbsp sugar
3 cloves garlic, crushed (optional)

Serve with:
potato gratinée or mashed potatoes
pickled onions or pickles

1 The preparation should be done one day in advance of cooking. Preheat the oven to its lowest setting.

2 The meat should be thoroughly frozen. Take it directly from the freezer and place on a wire oven rack over a rectangular roasting tin. Place in the oven for 10-12 hours.

3 Next day, mix together the salt liquor ingredients. Place the warm meat in a tight-fitting container and pour over the liquor. Set aside to marinate in a cool place for 5 hours. Turn the meat occasionally.

4 Remove the meat and discard the salt liquor. Wrap the meat in foil and keep in the refrigerator.

5 Carve the meat in thin slices and serve as cold roast beef.

Variations:
There is another method which is quicker but requires more attention. Place the frozen meat in a small rectangular tin. Place in a cold oven and turn the oven on to 110° C/225° F, gas mark ¼. Insert a meat thermometer once the meat has thawed, after approximately 2 hours. Leave the meat in the oven until the thermometer registers 65° C/149° F. Boil the salt liquor ingredients together and pour over the warm meat. Set aside in a cool place for approximately 5 hours.

TO DRINK
red wine

LEVEL OF DIFFICULTY
easy

PREPARATION TIME
24 hrs

PREPARE IN ADVANCE
yes

KIDNEYS WITH MUSTARD SAUCE

Serves 4

600-700 g/1¼-1½ lb calves' kidneys
300 g/10½ oz flour
salt
freshly ground black pepper
4 tbsp butter

Sauce:
50 ml/2 fl oz brandy
2 tsp French mustard
300 ml/10 fl oz double cream
salt
2 tsp lemon juice
1 tbsp butter

Serve with:
boiled rice

1 Core the kidneys and remove the fat and membrane. Soak in cold water. Mix the flour with salt and pepper and coat the kidneys.

2 Melt half the butter and fry the kidneys for 2-3 minutes. They should be pink inside but not raw.

3 Remove the the kidneys from the pan and slice lengthwise.

4 Melt half the remaining butter in a frying-pan and add the kidneys without letting any blood that may have seeped on to the plate get into the pan. Fry the kidney slices for 2-3 minutes. Add a little pepper and turn the kidney slices over.

5 Pour over the brandy, warm slightly and set alight. Shake the pan gently until the flames die down.

6 Place the kidney slices on a serving dish and keep warm while you finish the sauce.

7 Stir the mustard into the frying-pan and add the cream. Bring to the boil and cook over high heat, stirring constantly, until it has thickened. Add the blood that was left on the plate to enhance the flavour. Lower the heat.

8 Season with salt and pepper and add lemon juice, to taste. Stir in the remaining butter without allowing the sauce to boil.

9 Pour the sauce over the kidney slices and serve immediately.

KIDNEYS WITH MUSTARD SAUCE 270

TO DRINK
robust red wine

LEVEL OF DIFFICULTY
medium difficult

PREPARATION TIME
30 mins

PREPARE IN ADVANCE
no

LIVER AND BACON

Serves 4

500 g/1 lb calves' liver
1-2 tbsp butter
salt
freshly ground black pepper
8 bacon slices, crisply fried
2 tbsp capers

Serve with:
boiled potatoes
tomato salad

1 Cut the liver into slices and remove any tough sinews.

2 Melt the butter in a frying-pan. Fry the liver slices for 2-3 minutes on each side. They should be cooked all the way through. Season with salt and pepper.

3 Place the liver on a serving plate, garnish with crispy bacon slices and capers.

Variations:
To make Paprika Liver, mix 3 tbsp flour with 1 tsp salt, 1/2 tsp white pepper and 1 tsp paprika. Coat the liver slices in the flour mixture and fry them in butter for 2-3 minutes each side. Remove the liver from the pan and stir in 150 ml/5 fl oz double cream. Pour the cream sauce over the liver slices. Garnish with rings of pepper.

TO DRINK
light red wine

LEVEL OF DIFFICULTY
easy

PREPARATION LEVEL
30 mins

PREPARE IN ADVANCE
no

BOILED TONGUE

Serves 8

1 kg/2¼ lb lightly salted ox tongue
water
1 onion
1 carrot
6 white peppercorns
5 allspice berries
1 bay leaf

Sauce:
3 tbsp butter
3 shallots, finely chopped
400 g/14 oz mushrooms, sliced
50 ml/2 fl oz ruby port or sherry
300 ml/10 fl oz stock
400 ml/14 fl oz double cream or crème fraîche
salt
freshly ground pepper

Serve with:
mashed potatoes, petit pois or butter-fried leaf spinach

1 Place the tongue in a saucepan and pour in enough cold water to cover. Bring to the boil and skim.

2 Slice the onion and carrot. Add them to the saucepan, together with the peppercorns, allspice and bay leaf. Cover and simmer for approximately 2½ hours. Remove the skin while the tongue is still warm.

3 Make the sauce. Melt the butter in a saucepan and sauté the shallots over low heat until soft. Add the mushrooms and simmer until the liquid has been absorbed. Add the wine, stock and cream or crème fraîche. Simmer for 5 minutes until the sauce has thickened. Season with salt and pepper to taste.

4 Cut the tongue into slices and place on a warm serving dish. Serve the sauce separately.

BOILED TONGUE 272

TO DRINK
medium dry white wine or light fresh red wine

LEVEL OF DIFFICULTY
easy

PREPARATION TIME
3 hrs

PREPARE IN ADVANCE
yes

BEEF PATTIES

Serves 4

2 tbsp breadcrumbs
100 ml/3$\frac{1}{2}$ fl oz
400 g/14 oz minced beef
1 tsp salt
freshly ground black pepper
1 tbsp cornflour
2 eggs
1 tbsp soya sauce
3 tbsp butter

Salad:
340 g/12 oz frozen French beans
2 tomatoes, diced
1 onion, finely chopped
1 tbsp wine vinegar
3 tbsp oil
salt
freshly ground white pepper

Stuffing:
1 x 50 g/1$\frac{3}{4}$ oz can anchovy fillets
1 egg yolk
1 tbsp French mustard
1 clove garlic, crushed
3 tbsp finely chopped parsley
$\frac{1}{2}$ tsp thyme

Serve with:
mashed or sauté potatoes

1 Make the salad. Cook the beans as instructed on the packet. Rinse in cold water. Mix the beans, tomatoes and onion in a bowl. Beat together the vinegar, oil, salt and pepper to make a dressing and pour over the salad. Toss lightly.

2 Make the patties. Mix the breadcrumbs and water and set aside for 5 minutes. Add the beef, salt, pepper, cornflour, egg and soya sauce. Work until the mixture is smooth.

3 Shape the mixture into 8 fairly large, thin patties.

4 Make the stuffing. Mash the anchovy fillets and mix thoroughly with the other stuffing ingredients.

5 Divide the filling between 4 of the patties. Place the remaining 4 patties on top of them and press the edges together to form 'sandwiches'. Melt the butter and fry them, turning once, until well browned and cooked through.

TO DRINK
lager or red wine

LEVEL OF DIFFICULTY
easy

PREPARATION TIME
1 hr

PREPARE IN ADVANCE
partly

STUFFED PEPPERS

Serves 4

2 tsp butter
2 large red or green peppers

Filling:
400 g/14 oz minced beef
1 onion, finely chopped
1 clove garlic, crushed (optional)
salt
freshly ground white pepper
1½ tsp dried basil
1 x 400 g/14 oz can chopped tomatoes
100 g/3½ oz strongly flavoured cheese, cubed
1 tbsp cornflour
2 tbsp melted butter

Serve with:
rice

1 Preheat the oven to 220° C/ 425° F, gas mark 7. Grease an ovenproof dish with the butter. Cut the peppers lengthways into halves, cutting right through the middle of the stalks. Remove the seeds but leave the stalks intact. Place the pepper halves on the prepared dish.

2 Make the minced beef filling. Mix together the beef, onion, garlic, if using, salt, pepper, and basil. Add half the tomatoes, the cheese cubes and cornflour. Mix well.

3 Spoon the mixture into the pepper halves. Press it down firmly with a spoon. Brush the tops with a little melted butter.

4 Bake the peppers for 15-20 minutes. Meanwhile, heat the remaining tomatoes. Arrange them around the peppers in the dish. Bake for further 5-10 minutes.

STUFFED PEPPERS 274

TO DRINK
red wine

LEVEL OF DIFFICULTY
easy
PREPARATION TIME
30 mins
PREPARE IN ADVANCE
yes

GREEK MARROW

Serves 4

2 marrows
salt
water
1 tbsp butter
75 g/2½ oz grated cheese

Filling:
2 tbsp butter or oil
1 small onion, finely chopped
250 g/9 oz minced beef
salt
freshly ground black pepper
1 tsp dried oregano or marjoram
1 clove garlic, crushed
150 ml/5 fl oz vegetable stock

Sauce:
2 tbsp butter
2-3 tbsp flour
400 ml/14 fl oz milk or milk and cream
50 g/1¾ oz strongly flavoured cheese, grated
salt
freshly ground black pepper
1 egg, lightly beaten

1 Cut the marrows in half lengthwise and place into lightly salted boiling water. Boil for 15-20 minutes until soft. Preheat the oven to 250° C/500° F, gas mark 10. Grease an ovenproof dish with 1 tsp of the butter.

2 To make the filling, melt the butter or heat the oil. Sauté the onion until soft without colouring. Add the beef and cook, stirring. Season with salt, pepper and add the oregano or marjoram and garlic. Add stock if the mixture is too dry.

3 Make the sauce. Melt the butter and stir in the flour. Gradually, stir in the milk or milk and cream. Bring to the boil, stirring. Simmer for 5 minutes. Remove the pan from the heat, stir in the grated cheese and season with salt and pepper to taste. Stir in the egg.

4 Remove the marrows and scrape out the seeds with a spoon. Place the marrows in the prepared dish and stuff them with the beef filling. Dot over the remaining butter and sprinkle over the grated cheese.

5 Bake in the oven for 10 minutes or until the marrows are thoroughly heated and the top is golden and bubbling.

TO DRINK
red wine, preferably Greek

LEVEL OF DIFFICULTY easy
PREPARATION TIME 1 hr
PREPARE IN ADVANCE yes

HAMBURGERS

Serves 4

500 g/1 lb minced beef
2 tbsp butter
salt
freshly ground pepper
4 hamburger buns
1 lettuce, shredded
1 onion, sliced
2 tomatoes

Sauce:
200 ml/7 fl. oz sour cream
2 tbsp chili sauce
2 tbsp French mustard
chopped cress (optional)

1 Mix together all the sauce ingredients in a bowl and set aside.

2 Shape the mince into 4 round burgers, slightly larger than the hamburger baps and 1 cm/½ inch thick. Melt the butter. Fry the burgers for ½-2 minutes each side, depending on how well done you like them. Season with salt and pepper after frying.

3 Place the burgers in the baps with the lettuce, onion, tomato and a little sauce.

Cheeseburger:
Shape the hamburgers as above and fry them on one side. Turn and place 1 slice of cheese on each burger. Allow the burger to cook and the cheese to melt before the burgers are placed in the baps and garnished as above.

Mexiburger:
More luxurious beefburgers with a hot taste. For 4 burgers, mix 500 g/1 lb minced beef with salt, 1 tsp chili powder and 1 crushed clove garlic. Form into burger shapes as above. Place the Mexiburgers in the baps with mild or hot taco sauce, lettuce and sliced avocado.

Hawaiiburger:
Cut bacon slices into strips. Place in a cold frying-pan and fry until crispy. Drain on kitchen paper. Fry the burgers as usual, place them in the baps together with 1 ring pineapple, the crisp bacon pieces, shredded lettuce and chili sauce.

TO DRINK
Coca Cola, lager or water

LEVEL OF DIFFICULTY
easy

PREPARATION TIME
30 mins

PREPARE IN ADVANCE
no

VEAL MEATBALLS WITH CREAM SAUCE

Serves 4-6

500 g/1 lb minced veal
85 g/3 oz white breadcrumbs
150 ml/5 fl. oz double cream
50 ml/2 fl. oz water
2 tbsp cornflour
1 egg
salt
freshly ground black pepper
2 tsp butter
100 g/3½ oz stoned prunes (optional)

Sauce:
2 tbsp butter
2 tbsp flour
300 ml/10 fl oz milk
150 ml/5 fl oz double cream
1 tbsp soya sauce
½ tsp salt
freshly ground white pepper

Serve with:
boiled potatoes, cauliflower, Brussels sprouts, pickled cucumber (see recipe 402) and cranberry sauce

1 Place the breadcrumbs in a bowl and add the cream and water. Set aside for 10 minutes. Add the veal, cornflour, egg, salt and pepper. Mix well.

2 Preheat the oven to 220° C/ 425° F, gas mark 7. Grease an ovenproof dish with the butter. Form oval balls of the veal mixture with your hands and a wet tablespoon. Press 1 prune, if using, into the centre of each ball and re-work so that the ball becomes smooth again. Place them in the prepared dish on a wire rack in the bottom of the oven and bake for 20 minutes.

3 Make the sauce. Melt the butter and stir in the flour. Gradually, stir in the milk and cream. Simmer for 5 minutes over low heat, stirring constantly. Add the soya sauce, salt, and a little white pepper to taste. Pour a little sauce over the meatballs and serve the remaining sauce separately.

VEAL MEATBALLS WITH CREAM SAUCE

TO DRINK
white or red wine, lager

LEVEL OF DIFFICULTY
easy
PREPARATION TIME
1 hr
PREPARE IN ADVANCE
yes

STUFFED CABBAGE LEAVES

Serves 4

40 g/1½ oz round grain rice
300 ml/10 fl oz milk
1 medium-sized white cabbage
1 onion, finely chopped
150 g/5 oz minced beef
150 g/5 oz minced pork
2 eggs
salt
freshly ground white pepper
4 tbsp butter
2 tbsp syrup
150 ml/5 fl oz stock
3-4 tbsp soya sauce
1 tsp arrowroot

Serve with:
mashed potatoes, salt gherkins or Grandma's cucumber (see recipe 416) and cranberry sauce

1 Boil the rice in 150 ml/5 fl oz milk until a thick 'porridge' results.

2 Discard the stalk and core of the cabbage head and blanch in boiling salted water. Separate the leaves and cut out the coarse central veins.

3 Melt the butter and sauté the onion. Mix together the minced meat, eggs, onions, the remaining milk, salt, pepper and rice.

4 Preheat the oven to 250° C/ 500° F, gas mark 10. Grease an ovenproof dish with a little of the butter. Place a generous tablespoon of the mixture on to each cabbage leaf. Fold and roll them into small parcels. Place the parcels, seam side down, closely together in the prepared dish. Melt the remaining butter. Spoon a little syrup and melted butter on top of the rolls.

5 Bake in the oven, turning them once during cooking so that they brown evenly.

6 After 30-40 minutes, add the stock mixed with a little soya sauce. Continue cooking for a further 30 minutes.

7 Transfer the cabbage rolls to a plate and keep warm. Pour the cooking liquid into a pan. Mix the arrowroot with a little cold water and pour into the pan. Heat, stirring, to make a thin sauce. Add salt, pepper and soya sauce to taste.

8 Place the parcels on plates and pour the sauce on top.

STUFFED CABBAGE LEAVES 278

TO DRINK
lager or beer

LEVEL OF DIFFICULTY
fairly easy

PREPARATION TIME
2 hrs

PREPARE IN ADVANCE
yes

MEATLOAF

Serves 4

500 g/1 lb finely minced good quality, lean beef (topside, fillet, or rump)
5 egg yolks
2 beef stock cubes, crumbled
salt
freshly ground black pepper
1 large cooked beetroot, peeled and chopped
1 large onion, finely chopped
3 tbsp chopped capers
3 tbsp butter

Serve with:
toast or butter-fried white bread
sliced tomatoes and raw onion rings

1 Mix the beef with the egg yolks, stock cubes, salt and pepper until smooth. Add the beetroot, onion and capers and mix well.

2 Shape the mixture into a loaf shape that will fit into the frying-pan. Melt the butter and fry the meatloaf until golden all over. It must not be burned on the outside and should be rare inside.

3 Cut the loaf into fairly thick slices and place on a serving dish. Garnish with toast or butter-fried white bread, sliced tomatoes and raw onion rings.

TO DRINK
lager or a robust red wine

LEVEL OF DIFFICULTY
easy

PREPARATION TIME
30 mins

PREPARE IN ADVANCE
partly

WALLENBERG'S VEAL BURGER

Serves 4

300 g/10½ oz finely minced veal
salt
freshly ground white pepper
½ tsp four spice (quatre-épices)
3 egg yolks
300 ml/10 fl. oz double cream
a85 g/3 oz white breadcrumbs
2-3 tbsp butter

Serve with:
mashed potatoes
petit pois
cranberry sauce

1 All the ingredients should be chilled. Mix the veal in a bowl placed inside a larger bowl half full of crushed ice. Using an electric mixer with dough hooks, work the mince on a low speed. First work the salt, pepper and four spice into the veal. Add the egg yolks, one at a time. Add the cream, a little at a time. It is important that each addition of cream is incorporated before adding more. The mixture will become fairly soft and moist.

2 Sprinkle half the breadcrumbs on to a work surface. Flatten out the veal mixture, using 2 spoons, to form 8-12 burgers. Sprinkle breadcrumbs on top and flatten with a wooden spatula.

3 Melt 2 tbsp of the butter in a frying-pan and fry the burgers slowly over a medium heat for approximately 4 minutes each side. Place the burgers on a warm serving dish. Melt a little more butter in the frying-pan and pour it over the burgers.

4 Serve with mashed potatoes, petit pois and cranberry sauce.

WALLENBERG'S VEAL BURGER 280

TO DRINK
dry white wine or light red wine

LEVEL OF DIFFICULTY
medium difficult

PREPARATION TIME
1 hr

PREPARE IN ADVANCE
partly

DUCK À L'ORANGE

Serves 6

7 oranges
85 g/3 oz sugar
300 ml/10 fl oz stock
100 g/3½ oz unsalted butter, chilled and diced
3 duck breasts
salt
freshly ground white pepper

Serve with:
mangetout
baby carrots
broccoli

1 First make the garnish. Scrub and dry the oranges and pare one of them very thinly with a potato peeler. Use only the orange peel, discarding any pith. Cut the peel into very thin strips. Boil them gently for a few minutes in water. Set aside to cool.

2 Squeeze the juice from 3 of the remaining oranges and reserve. Cut the 3 remaining oranges into wedges, making sure that they are free from any pith or membrane. Place the orange wedges on a dish.

3 Melt the sugar in a skillet with an ovenproof handle and stir until light brown. Add the orange juice and stock. Boil, stirring, until all the sugar has dissolved. Beat in the butter, a little at a time until the sauce has thickened. Remove from the heat and keep warm.

4 Preheat the oven to 170° C/ 325° F, gas mark 3. Score the duck skin with a sharp knife to make diamond shapes.

5 Place the skillet containing the sauce on high heat. Brown the duck breasts, skin side down, so that they become crispy. Lower the heat and brown on the other side. Place the skillet in the oven and bake for approximately 10-12 minutes. Add salt and pepper.

6 Warm the orange wedges in a little orange juice. Place the duck breasts on warm dinner plates. Pour over the sauce and garnish with orange wedges and strips of orange peel.

TO DRINK
a robust red wine or a dry white wine

LEVEL OF DIFFICULTY
medium difficult

PREPARATION TIME
1 hr

PREPARE IN ADVANCE
partly

CHICKEN IN DILL SAUCE

Serves 4

1 large or two small chickens
water
1 onion, cut into wedges
2 chicken stock cubes, crumbled
6 white peppercorns
1 bay leaf
dill sprigs

Sauce:
3 tbsp butter
3 tbsp flour
400-500 ml/14-17 fl oz stock
1 egg yolk
100 ml/3½ fl oz double cream
salt
freshly ground black pepper
juice of ½ lemon
1-2 tsp sugar (optional)
6 tbsp finely chopped dill

Serve with:
boiled potatoes
baby carrots

1 Rinse the chicken or chickens and trim the loose fat. Place the chicken in a snugly fitting saucepan and pour in enough water just to cover. Add the onions, stock cubes, peppercorns, bay leaf and dill sprigs. Bring to the boil and simmer, covered, over low heat for 30-40 minutes.

2 Remove the chicken from the saucepan. Skin and bone the chicken and cut the meat into bite-sized pieces. Strain and reserve the stock.

3 Make the sauce. Melt the butter and stir in the flour. Add the stock, a little at a time, stirring continuously. Simmer over low heat for approximately 15 minutes, stirring from time to time. Add a little more stock if the sauce becomes too thick. Beat together the egg yolk and cream. Lower the heat and stir the mixture into the sauce. Add salt, pepper, lemon juice and sugar, if using, to taste. Stir the chopped dill and chicken meat into the sauce.

4 Warm the chicken just before serving, but do not allow the sauce to boil as it may curdle.

TO DRINK
red wine, or medium dry or dry white wine

LEVEL OF DIFFICULTY
easy

PREPARATION TIME
1 hr

PREPARE IN ADVANCE
yes

PHEASANT BREAST

Serves 4-6

2 pheasants, drawn and plucked
2 tbsp butter

Stock:
1-2 tbsp butter
½ carrot, finely chopped
1 small stick celery
½ leek, cut into strips
1 small onion, chopped
2-3 juniper berries
400-500 ml/14-17 fl oz stock
100 ml/3½ fl oz dry white wine

Sauce:
2 tbsp butter
2 tbsp flour
300 ml/10 fl oz double cream
50 ml/2 fl oz brandy
salt
pepper

Serve with:
duchesse potatoes
petit pois
butter-fried mushrooms

1 Cut the breasts carefully from the birds. Skin the breasts and set aside. Reserve the carcass and giblets.

2 To make the stock, cut or break the carcass into pieces. Melt the butter and add the carcass and giblets. Add the carrot, celery, leek, onion and juniper berries and fry, stirring. Add the stock and wine, bring to the boil and simmer, covered, for 20-30 minutes. Add more stock if the consistency becomes too thick.

3 To make the sauce, strain the stock and boil until reduced to approximately 200 ml/7 fl oz. Knead together the butter and flour to make a *beurre manié*. Beat this into the sauce, a little at a time. Add the cream and brandy and simmer for 5 minutes. Season to taste.

4 Season the pheasant breasts with salt and black pepper. Melt the butter in a frying-pan and fry the breasts over medium heat for 3-4 minutes on each side.

5 Cut the warm pheasant breasts into thick diagonal slices. Place on a warm serving dish and spoon over a little sauce. Serve the remaining sauce in a separate bowl.

TO DRINK
red wine

LEVEL OF DIFFICULTY
medium difficult
PREPARATION TIME
1 hr
PREPARE IN ADVANCE
yes

ROAST STUFFED TURKEY

Serves 8-10

1 x 3 kg/2¼ lb turkey
½ lemon
salt
pepper
50 g/1¾ oz butter

Stuffing:
½ loaf white bread
50 g/1¾ oz butter
2 onions, chopped
½ tsp celery salt
freshly ground black pepper
½ tsp dried mixed herbs
1 clove garlic, crushed
200 ml/7 fl oz stock
2 tbsp sherry

Gravy:
400 ml/14 fl oz stock
3 tbsp flour
a little water
150 ml/5 fl oz white wine
200 ml/7 fl oz double cream
½-1 tsp dried tarragon

1 Preheat the oven to 170° C/ 325° F, gas mark 3. Make the stuffing. Remove the crusts and dice the bread. Melt half the butter and brown it. Dice the giblets. Melt the remaining butter and fry the giblets and the onion. Stir in the fried bread. Mix in salt, pepper, herbs, garlic, stock, and sherry.

2 Rub the turkey with the lemon. Season and stuff. Truss securely.

3 Melt the butter in a roasting tin and brush the turkey with it. Place on its side in the tin and roast for 30 minutes.

4 Remove the turkey from the oven and turn it over. Baste with the butter and roast for a further 30 minutes. Remove from the oven, baste and turn breast upwards. Roast for a further 30-60 minutes. Test with a metal skewer.

5 Remove the turkey and keep warm. Deglaze the tin with a little water. Strain and make up to 400 ml/14 fl oz with water mixed with stock cubes. Add the flour, mixed with a little water, stirring continuously. Add the wine, cream and tarragon. Simmer for 5 minutes, stirring. Carve the turkey, place on a warm serving dish and serve the gravy separately.

ROAST STUFFED TURKEY 284

TO DRINK
dry white wine or a light red wine

LEVEL OF DIFFICULTY fairly easy
PREPARATION TIME 2 hrs
PREPARE IN ADVANCE yes

FAGELFARS

Serves 8-10

500 g/1 lb diced chicken

Stock:
bird carcass and giblets
a few root vegetables
125 g/4 oz + 2 tsp flour
400 ml/14 fl oz water or stock
Mushroom sauce (see recipe 420)

Mould:
salt
black pepper
5 egg yolks
300 ml/10 fl oz double cream
1½ tsp cornflour
3-4 finely chopped parboiled morels
1 tbsp + 2 tsp butter
1 tbsp brandy
4 egg whites

Serve with:
boiled or croquette potatoes, French beans or mangetout

1 Place the giblets and carcass in a pan with a few root vegetables. Cover with water and simmer for 40 minutes.

2 To prepare the mould, boil together 120 g/4 oz of the flour and water or stock until thick. Leave to cool. Preheat the oven to 170° C/325° F, gas mark 3. Grease a 2-litre/3½ pint ring mould with 2 tsp butter and coat with the remaining flour.

3 Finely mince the meat. Season and stir into the flour mixture. Stir in the egg yolks, one at a time. Beat the cream and fold into the meat mixture. Add the cornflour.

4 Melt the remaining butter and fry the morels. Season, pour over the brandy and set alight. Stir into the meat mixture. Beat the egg whites until they form stiff peaks. Fold carefully into the meat mixture.

5 Place the meat mixture in the mould. Cover with greaseproof paper. Place in a roasting tin half filled with hot water. Bake for 1-1½ hours. Test with a skewer. Set aside for 5-10 minutes before turning it out.

6 Turn out the mould on to a serving dish. Spoon over a little warmed sauce and serve the remaining sauce separately.

TO DRINK
robust red wine

LEVEL OF DIFFICULTY
difficult

PREPARATION TIME
2-3 hrs

PREPARE IN ADVANCE
yes

GRETA'S CHICKEN

Serves 4

1 x 1.5 kg/3¼ lb chicken
2 chicken livers
1 bunch parsley, finely chopped
2 shallots, finely chopped
60 g/2 oz curd cheese
1 tsp paprika
½ tsp dried sage
½ tsp dried thyme
½ tsp dried rosemary
1 clove garlic, crushed
salt
freshly ground black pepper
2-4 tbsp butter
50 ml/2 fl oz brandy
3-4 tbsp dry white wine
300 ml/10 fl oz double cream

Serve with:
boiled new potatoes or rice
boiled seasonal vegetables
pickled fresh cucumber (see recipe 402)

1 Preheat the oven to 225° C/ 500° F, gas mark 10. Rinse the chicken and pat dry. Rub salt over the chicken, inside and out.

2 Purée the raw chicken livers and mix with the parsley, shallots, cheese, paprika, sage, thyme, rosemary, garlic and a little salt and pepper.

3 Fill the chicken cavity with the stuffing and truss securely. Melt half the butter in a flameproof casserole and brown the chicken all over. Pour over the brandy, warm slightly and set alight. Shake the pan gently until the flames die down.

4 Add the remaining butter, 2 tbsp of the wine and 200 ml/ 7 fl oz of the cream. Transfer the casserole, uncovered, to the oven and cook for 45 minutes. Do not baste the chicken but add the remaining wine and cream halfway through the cooking time. The chicken will be ready when the wings come away easily.

5 Strain the sauce into a saucepan. Keep the chicken warm. Bring the sauce to the boil, stirring constantly, and season to taste. A little wine, cream or stock may be used to thin it down if it becomes too thick.

GRETA'S CHICKEN 286

TO DRINK
red wine

LEVEL OF DIFFICULTY
medium difficult

PREPARATION TIME
1-2 hrs

PREPARE IN ADVANCE
yes

CHICKEN BREASTS IN VERMOUTH

Serves 4

6 chicken breasts
salt
freshly ground white pepper
1 tbsp butter
1 shallot, finely chopped
125 g/4½ oz thin strips of vegetables (carrot, celery and leeks)
1 chicken stock cube
50 ml/2 fl oz water
150 ml/5 fl oz dry vermouth
300 ml/10 fl oz double cream
1 tsp French mustard

Serve with:
mangetout, pommes châteaux (see recipe 405) or rice

1 Carefully flatten out the chicken breasts and season with salt and white pepper on both sides.

2 Melt the butter in a frying-pan. Add the vegetables and sauté over low heat without colouring.

3 Dissolve the stock cube in the water. Place the chicken breasts on top of the vegetables in the pan. Pour over the stock and add the vermouth. Simmer for 20 minutes, turning the chicken breasts after 10 minutes.

4 Place the chicken on a warm dish and cover with foil. Bring the stock and vegetables to the boil, add the cream and mustard and simmer, stirring constantly. Season with salt and pepper to taste.

5 Pour the sauce over the chicken breasts and serve immediately with boiled mangetout and pommes châteaux or rice.

TO DRINK
dry white wine or light red wine

LEVEL OF DIFFICULTY
easy

PREPARATION TIME
1 hr

PREPARE IN ADVANCE
partly

CHICKEN WITH BRANDY

Serves 4

1 large or 2 small chickens
2-3 tbsp butter
50 ml/2 fl oz brandy
150 ml/ 5 fl oz white wine
300 ml/10 fl oz double cream
4 tomatoes, peeled, seeded and chopped
1 apple, peeled, cored and diced
12-16 green olives
1 bay leaf
1 tsp curry powder
1 tsp thyme
1 tsp tarragon
12 whole, peeled, parboiled and lightly browned onions
20 butter-fried button mushrooms

Garnish:
1 tbsp chopped chives
1 tbsp chopped parsley

Serve with:
rice, pasta or boiled potatoes

1 Cut the chicken or chickens into pieces. Melt the butter in a heavy-based pan and brown the chicken pieces all over. Season with salt and pepper to taste. Pour off the fat. Pour over the brandy, heat gently and set alight. Shake the pan until the flames die down.

2 Add the white wine and cream, tomato, apple, olives, bay leaf, curry powder, thyme tarragon and the small browned onions.

3 Simmer over low heat for approximately 20 minutes, or until the chicken pieces are tender and cooked through. Add the mushrooms.

4 Sprinkle with chopped chives and parsley. Serve with rice, pasta or boiled potatoes.

CHICKEN WITH BRANDY 288

To drink
red wine

LEVEL OF DIFFICULTY
fairly easy

PREPARATION TIME
1 hr

PREPARE IN ADVANCE
yes

STUFFED CHICKEN BREASTS

Serves 4

8 boned chicken breasts
French mustard
salt
freshly ground black pepper
8 thin slices smoked ham
8 slices Emmental, Grève or Gruyère cheese
2-3 tbsp flour
112 g/4 oz butter
100 ml/3½ fl oz dry white wine or dry white vermouth
200 ml/7 fl oz double cream

Serve with:
wild rice
mangetout

1 Slit the chicken breasts lengthwise and flatten them with the back of a knife. Spread with a little mustard, salt and pepper. Top with a slice of ham and a slice of cheese. Fold or roll the breasts and secure with a cocktail stick, if necessary. Coat the rolls in plain flour.

2 Melt the butter in a frying-pan. Brown the rolls all over. Pour over the wine or vermouth and simmer over medium heat for approximately 20 minutes. Add more wine if required.

3 Remove the rolls from the pan and keep warm. Pour in the cream and simmer until a thin sauce is made. Season with salt and pepper to taste. Add the rolls to the sauce and allow to heat through thoroughly.

4 Serve with wild rice and boiled mangetout.

TO DRINK
dry white wine

LEVEL OF DIFFICULTY
medium difficult

PREPARATION TIME
1 hr

PREPARE IN ADVANCE
yes

LIGHTLY SALTED CHICKEN

Serves 4

1 x 1.5 kg/3¼ lb fresh chicken
2 tbsp salt

Sauce:
200-300 ml/7-10 fl oz crème fraîche
2-3 tbsp grated horseradish

Serve with:
boiled potatoes, boiled vegetables and tomato salad

1 Cut the chicken half and rub with salt. Place the two halves side by side, skin side down, in a plastic bag so that the liquid formed stays in the chicken halves. Set aside in the refrigerator for 24 hours. Do not turn the bag around during this time.

2 Boil enough water to cover the chicken. Add the chicken halves. Bring back to the boil and simmer for 40 minutes.

3 Remove the chicken halves, allow to cool and remove the skin and bones.

4 Cut the chicken meat into even-sized pieces and place on a serving dish, together with boiled vegetables.

5 Beat the crème fraîche and horseradish together. Serve the sauce separately.

Variations:
To make 'quick chicken', make a salt mixture of 2 litres/3½ pints water, 170 g/6 oz salt and 40 g/1½ oz sugar. Add the whole chicken and leave in the refrigerator for 48 hours. Remove the chicken from the refrigerator and boil as described above. Serve with the same vegetables.

LIGHTLY SALTED CHICKEN 290

TO DRINK
lager or dry white wine

LEVEL OF DIFFICULTY
easy

PREPARATION TIME
24-48 hrs

PREPARE IN ADVANCE
yes

ROAST PTARMIGAN OR GROUSE BREASTS

Serves 4

3-4 plucked and cleaned ptarmigan or grouse
3-4 thin slices of lard
salt
freshly ground white pepper
2 tbsp butter

Sauce:
10 tbsp mirepoix (2½ tbsp dried carrot, 2½ tbsp dried celery, 2½ tbsp dried onion, and 2½ tbsp dried leek)
2 parsley sprigs
1 tsp flour
500 ml/17 fl oz stock
100 ml/3½ fl oz red wine
50 ml/2 fl. oz calvados
200 ml/7 fl oz double cream
salt
freshly ground white pepper
2 tbsp butter
2 tbsp rowanberries or redcurrants
50 ml/2 fl oz water

1 Preheat the oven to 250° C/ 500° F, gas mark 10. Dry the birds. Truss and cover with thin slices of lard. Season.

2 Melt the butter in a roasting tin. Add the birds and roast. Lay them first on each leg side for 6 minutes and then on their backs for a further 6 minutes: 18 minutes. Remove the birds and set aside for 10 minutes.

3 Remove all the breast meat and keep warm. Cut off and chop the thigh meat.

4 Chop the carcass and return it to the roasting tin. Add the giblets, thigh meat, mirepoix and parsley. Fry for 2-3 minutes. Sprinkle over the flour and stir. Add the stock and red wine. Stir thoroughly to deglaze. Boil until the liquid has reduced to approximately 200 ml/7 fl oz.

5 Strain the liquid into a pan. Bring to the boil and add the cream and liqueur, stirring constantly. Boil until approximately 300 ml/10 fl oz liquid remains. Season to taste. Stir in the remaining butter.

6 Warm the rowanberries or redcurrants in the water.

7 Thinly slice the breasts diagonally and serve.

ROAST PTARMIGAN OR GROUSE BREASTS

To drink
red wine

LEVEL OF DIFFICULTY
medium difficult
PREPARATION TIME
2 hrs
PREPARE IN ADVANCE
yes

AUBERGINE AU GRATIN

Serves 6

3 aubergines
1 tbsp salt
250 g/8 oz smoked gammon, sliced
2 tsp butter

Tomato sauce:
2 x 400 g/14 oz cans chopped tomatoes
4 cloves garlic, crushed
1 tsp herb salt
freshly ground black pepper
2 bay leaves
1 tsp dried rosemary
1 tsp dried thyme

Cheese sauce:
2 tbsp butter
2 tbsp flour
250 ml/8 fl oz milk
120 g/4 oz grated Cheddar cheese
60 g/2 oz grated Parmesan cheese
½ tsp grated nutmeg

1 Slice the aubergines lengthwise and sprinkle with salt. Set aside for approximately 30 minutes to dégorge. Squeeze out the liquid and pat dry.

2 Make the tomato sauce. Pour the chopped tomatoes into a saucepan, add the garlic, herb salt, pepper, bay leaves, rosemary and thyme. Simmer for approximately 15 minutes. Preheat the oven to 200° C/ 400° F, gas mark 6. Grease an ovenproof dish with the butter.

3 Make the cheese sauce. Melt the butter and stir in the flour. Gradually, stir in the milk. Simmer over low heat, stirring, for 5 minutes. Stir in the cheese and allow to melt. Season with grated nutmeg.

4 Layer the aubergine slices with the gammon and tomato sauce in the prepared dish. Pour over the cheese sauce. Bake in the oven for 30-40 minutes until the aubergine slices are soft and the cheese is golden and bubbling. Test with a skewer.

AUBERGINE AU GRATIN 292

TO DRINK
mineral water

LEVEL OF DIFFICULTY
medium difficult

PREPARATION TIME
1½ hrs

PREPARE IN ADVANCE
yes

BEEF SALAD

Serves 6

500-600 g/1-1¼ lb roast beef or boiled fresh brisket
1 heart lettuce or shredded iceberg lettuce
12-14 potatoes, boiled, peeled and sliced
3-4 tomatoes
1 large fresh cooked beetroot, peeled and chopped
3 pickled gherkins, chopped
2-3 onions, finely chopped
2 peppers, sliced into rings
5 tbsp capers

Dressing:
2 tbsp wine vinegar
100 ml/3½ fl oz vegetable oil
1½ tsp French mustard
2 tsp grated horseradish
salt or herb salt
freshly ground white pepper
1 bunch chives, finely chopped

1 Make the dressing. Mix together the horseradish, mustard and vinegar. Stir in the oil. Season with salt and pepper to taste. Add the chives.

2 Carve the meat into thin slices, or thick strips, or dice it.

3 Cover a large serving dish with small lettuce leaves or shredded iceberg lettuce. Place the meat in the middle of the dish and arrange the remaining ingredients in decorative groups, separately, around the meat.

4 Pour over the dressing just before serving.

TO DRINK
red wine or lager

LEVEL OF DIFFICULTY
easy

PREPARATION TIME
30 mins

PREPARE IN ADVANCE
yes

CHEF'S CHICKEN SALAD

Serves 4

1 roast or grilled chicken
1 small can pineapple rings or chunks, drained
2 red onions, sliced
10 cm/4 inch piece fresh cucumber
8 slices bacon
1 iceberg lettuce or a mixture of several different types of salad leaves
170 g/6 oz canned sweetcorn, drained
200 g/7 oz frozen peas, cooked and cooled
1 red pepper, thinly sliced
1 large tart desert apple, cored and diced
1 tbsp parsley, finely chopped

Dressing:
200 ml/7 fl oz mayonnaise
100 ml/3½ fl oz sour cream
2-3 tbsp chili sauce
tabasco or cayenne pepper
salt
freshly ground black pepper

1 Remove all the chicken flesh from the bones and discard the skin. Dice the meat finely.

2 Cut the pineapple into small pieces, if necessary. Slice the onion into thin rings. Cut the cucumber in half lengthwise and chop into 5 mm/¼ inch thick pieces.

3 Fry the bacon slices until crispy and drain on kitchen paper.

4 Cut the salad leaves into pieces, if necessary, or shred the iceberg lettuce.

5 Place a layer of lettuce in the bottom of a salad bowl. Layer the remaining ingredients with the nicest pieces of chicken on the top. Alternatively, arrange all the ingredients in separate groups on the bed of lettuce. Sprinkle with finely chopped parsley. Keep cool until ready to serve.

6 Mix together all the ingredients for the dressing and serve in a separate bowl.

Variations:
The dressing can be seasoned with grated horseradish or crushed garlic.

CHEF'S CHICKEN SALAD 294

TO DRINK
rosé or dry white wine

LEVEL OF DIFFICULTY
easy

PREPARATION TIME
1 hr

PREPARE IN ADVANCE
yes

TOMATO QUICHE

Serves 4-6

Pastry:
90 g/3¼ oz flour
85 g/3 oz wholemeal flour
¼ tsp herb salt
125 g/4¼ oz butter
3 tbsp iced water

Filling:
2 x 400 g/14 oz cans plum tomatoes
1 large onion, chopped
1 clove garlic, crushed
1 tsp basil
2 eggs
200 ml/7 fl oz single cream or milk
120 g/6 oz grated cheese
salt
freshly ground white pepper

Garnish:
lightly boiled spring onions
sliced tomatoes

1 Make the pastry. Mix both types of flour together with the herb salt. Rub the flour and butter together until the mixture resembles fine breadcrumbs. Add the water and work the dough quickly. Set aside to rest in the refrigerator for at least one hour.

2 Meanwhile, make the filling. Put the tomatoes with their can juice into a saucepan and add the chopped onion, garlic and basil. Simmer until thick. Set aside to cool.

3 Beat the eggs with the cream or milk. Stir in the grated cheese and add the tomato mixture. Stir well. Season with salt and pepper to taste.

4 Roll out the dough thinly and place in a round pie dish approximately 25 cm/10 inches in diameter. Prick the base with a fork and press a strip of foil around the edges so that they do not collapse during cooking. Set the dish aside in the refrigerator for approximately 30 minutes. Preheat the oven to 200° C/ 400° F, gas mark 6.

5 Cook the pastry blind for 10 minutes. Remove the foil. Pour the filling into the pastry case and bake for further 20 minutes until the filling is fully cooked.

6 Garnish with spring onions and sliced tomatoes.

To drink
mineral water

LEVEL OF DIFFICULTY
fairly easy
PREPARATION TIME
1 hr + resting time
PREPARE IN ADVANCE
yes

PASTA WITH SEAFOOD SAUCE

Serves 4

400 g/14 oz pasta shells
water
salt
1-2 tbsp butter

Sauce:
300 g/10 oz white fish fillets
6 large mussels, cooked and cooled
200 g/7 oz cooked prawns
1 small can mussels in brine
3 tbsp butter
1 onion, finely chopped
1 clove garlic, crushed
2 tbsp flour
1 fish stock cube
300 ml/10 fl oz water
100 ml/3½ fl oz double cream
100 ml/3½ fl oz white wine
salt
freshly ground black pepper
1 tsp dried marjoram

Garnish:
smooth parsley leaves or fresh basil leaves

1 Cut the fish into bite-sized pieces. Take the large mussels out of their shells and cut into quarters. Peel and devein the prawns. Drain the canned mussels.

2 Melt the butter in a saucepan. Add the onion and garlic and fry over low heat for 2-3 minutes. Stir in the flour. Crumble the stock cube into the mixture. Add the water, cream and wine, a little at a time, stirring constantly. Simmer for 5 minutes, stirring constantly.

3 Lower the heat, Add the fish and large mussels. Simmer for 2-3 minutes. Add the prawns and canned mussels. Season with salt and pepper to taste and add the marjoram. Warm the sauce but do not allow it to boil. Keep warm.

4 Boil the pasta in plenty of salted water for 10 minutes, or until *al dente*. Drain well. Melt the butter in the saucepan and toss the pasta gently over low heat so that it becomes fully warmed and shiny.

5 Place the pasta on a serving dish and pour over the sauce. Garnish with smooth leaf parsley or fresh basil leaves.

PASTA WITH SEAFOOD SAUCE 296

TO DRINK
dry white wine

LEVEL OF DIFFICULTY
easy

PREPARATION TIME
1 hr

PREPARE IN ADVANCE
partly

PASTA PAELLA

Serves 4

1 x 1 kg/2¼ lb chicken
2-3 tbsp butter
salt
freshly ground black pepper
1 leek
½ head fennel
1 red pepper
300 g/10 oz cooked prawns
300 g/10 oz tagliatelle
water
50 g/1¾ oz butter
pinch saffron

1 Chop the chicken into pieces. Melt the butter in a large frying-pan and brown the chicken pieces all over. Season with salt and pepper. Cover and continue to cook over low heat for approximately 20 minutes.

2 Rinse and dry the leek, fennel and pepper. Cut into strips. Peel the prawns, reserving a few unpeeled for decoration.

3 Boil the pasta in plenty of salted water for 8-10 minutes, or until *al dente*. Drain the pasta well.

4 Melt the butter. Stir in the saffron and the vegetables and fry for 3-5 minutes. Stir in the prawns and fold in the pasta.

5 Place the pasta on a large dish. Add the chicken pieces and garnish with the reserved prawns. Serve immediately.

TO DRINK
red wine

LEVEL OF DIFFICULTY
easy

PREPARATION TIME
1 hr

PREPARE IN ADVANCE
partly

PASTA SPIRALS WITH WALNUT SAUCE

Serves 4

300 g/10 oz pasta spirals
water
salt
2 tbsp butter
1 x 340 g/12 oz can asparagus spears, drained

Sauce:
4 tbsp olive oil or walnut oil
2 cloves garlic, crushed
3 tbsp parsley, finely chopped
75 g/2¾ oz walnuts, finely chopped
50 g/1¾ oz pine nuts or cashew nuts, finely chopped
150 ml/5 fl oz boiling water
1 egg, lightly beaten
50 ml/2 fl oz single cream

Garnish:
walnut halves

1 First, make the sauce. Heat the oil in a frying-pan and fry the garlic and parsley for 1 minute. Add the nuts and fry gently over low heat for 3-4 minutes, stirring occasionally. Remove the pan from the heat. Beat together the egg, cream and water and pour the mixture into the frying-pan. Stir thoroughly. Keep the sauce warm.

2 Boil the pasta in plenty of salted water for 9-10 minutes, or until *al dente*. Drain the pasta, rinse with hot water and allow to drain thoroughly.

3 Melt the butter in a saucepan, add the pasta and toss lightly. Cut the asparagus in to pieces. Reserve the tips for the garnish and stir the rest into the pasta.

4 Place the pasta on a warmed serving dish. Pour over the warm sauce and garnish with asparagus tips and walnut halves.

PASTA SPIRALS WITH WALNUT SAUCE 298

TO DRINK
red wine

LEVEL OF DIFFICULTY
easy

PREPARATION TIME
30 mins

PREPARE IN ADVANCE
partly

TAGLIATELLE WITH A CHOICE OF SAUCES

Serves 6

450 g/1 lb tagliatelle
water
salt

Ham and cheese sauce:
100 g/3½ oz boiled ham
100 g/3½ oz smoked ham
3 tbsp butter
3 tbsp flour
400 ml/4 fl oz milk
400 ml/14 fl oz single cream
230 g/8 oz Emmental cheese, grated
100 g/3½ oz Parmesan cheese, grated
2 tsp Italian salad spice
2 tsp grated nutmeg
freshly ground black pepper

Gorgonzola sauce:
200 g/7 oz frozen chopped spinach, thawed
500 g/1 lb Gorgonzola
2 tbsp butter
120 g/4 oz leeks, thinly sliced
300 ml/10 fl oz single cream
200 ml/7 fl oz crème fraîche
85 g/3 oz chopped walnuts
herb salt or Italian salad spice

Serve with:
grated cheese

HAM AND CHEESE SAUCE

1 Dice the hams. Melt the butter and stir in the flour. Gradually add the milk, stirring constantly. Add the diced ham and simmer over low heat for approximately 5 minutes. Stir in the cream, grated cheese, salad spice and nutmeg. Season with pepper to taste.

GORGONZOLA SAUCE

1 Squeeze the water from the spinach. Slice the cheese.

2 Melt the butter and fry the leek low heat until soft. Stir in the cheese and allow to melt. Stir in the spinach, crème fraîche and cream. Add half the walnuts and the herb salt or salad spice. Use the remaining walnuts to garnish.

PASTA

1 Cook in plenty of boiling salted water for 8-10 minutes or until *al dente*. Drain and toss in the butter. Serve with your chosen sauce.

TO DRINK
red wine

LEVEL OF DIFFICULTY
easy

PREPARATION TIME
1 hr

PREPARE IN ADVANCE
yes

100 MAIN COURSE RECIPES

100 PUDDING & DESSERT RECIPES

CAMEMBERT À LA VIERGE
(Deep-fried Camembert)

Serves 4

1 egg
3 tbsp flour
25 g/1 oz fresh breadcrumbs
4 quarters Camembert
1 large bunch parsley
oil for deep-frying
salt

1 Lightly beat the egg. Place the flour and breadcrumbs on separate plates.

2 Coat each cheese quarter first in the flour, then in the beaten egg and finally in the bread-crumbs. It is most important that each cheese quarter is fully coated. Put the coated cheese in the refrigerator until ready to fry.

3 Wash the parsley, dry completely and remove the stalks. Heat the oil in a deep-fryer to 190° C/375° F or until a cube of stale bread turns golden in 30 seconds.

4 When the oil is hot, carefully put in the parsley. Remove with a perforated spoon after a couple of seconds. Drain on kitchen paper. Sprinkle over a pinch of salt.

5 Re-heat the oil. Carefully cook the cheese quarters for about 2 minutes until golden brown on the outside and soft and melted in the centre. When cooked, remove from the pan.

6 Serve the cheese quarters on individual plates and garnish with the parsley.

Variations:
This can also be served with warm cloudberry, cranberry or other sharp jams, jellies or sauces.

CAMEMBERT À LA VIERGE 300

TO DRINK:
full-bodied red wine

LEVEL OF DIFFICULTY
easy

PREPARATION TIME:
30 mins

PREPARE IN ADVANCE:
partly

CHEESE PASTIES

Serves 4

1 tsp butter or vegetable oil
300 g/10 oz frozen puff pastry, thawed
160 g/6 oz Västerbottenost or Emmental cheese
1 egg yolk to glaze

Garnish:
Celery sticks

1 Preheat the oven to 250° C/ 500° F, gas mark 10. Lightly grease a baking sheet.

2 Roll out the pastry to approximately 3 mm/½ inch thick. Cut into 12 cm/5 inch diameter circles.

3 Grate the cheese and form into four balls. Place one ball on half of each circle and brush with a little egg yolk. Fold the circles over to cover and press the edges down firmly with a fork to seal.

4 Brush the pasties with the remaining egg yolk to glaze. Place on the prepared baking sheet and bake for about 10 minutes, or until the dough has puffed up and turned golden brown.

5 When serving, cut each pasty towards the middle so that the melted cheese oozes out. Garnish with celery.

TO DRINK:
red wine

LEVEL OF DIFFICULTY:
medium difficult

PREPARATION TIME:
30 mins

PREPARE IN ADVANCE
partly

CHEESE BOARD

Allow 100-150 g/3½-5¼ oz cheese per person

Serve with:
white bread
pumpernickel
savoury biscuits (not salted or strongly spiced)
radishes
celery sticks
fresh peppers
endive

A piece of cheese is often appreciated after or even instead of dessert. It may be enough to serve just one sort: a substantial piece of Stilton, scooped out and filled with a little port and served with a spoon, or a strong-flavoured Cheddar cheese. A cheese board should offer a few, well-chosen, mature and well-flavoured cheeses which complement each other. Here follow a few examples of different types of cheese in their various categories. Choose two, three or maybe four kinds, one from each category.

PRESSED CHEESES
Emmental, Gruyère, Cheddar, Cheshire, Double Gloucester

WAX-RIND CHEESES
Vacherin, Port Salut, Bel Paese, Fontina, Havarti, Edam

SOFT CHEESES
Brie, Farmhouse Brie, Camembert, Munster, Feta, Pont-Évêque

VEINED CHEESES
Gorgonzola, Roquefort, Stilton, Danish Blue

WHITE AND BLUE CHEESES
Bavarian Blue, Blue Castello, Bresse Bleu, Cambozola.

Do not serve the cheese straight from the refrigerator. Keep the cheese at room temperature for approximately 1 hour before serving to allow the full flavour and consistency to develop.

CHEESE BOARD 302

To drink
Strong-flavoured cheeses, blue cheeses and Brie, Camembert and similar types demand a full-bodied red wine, preferably a finer wine than that served with the main course, or a ruby port. Dry white wines can be served with mild cheeses. Sweet white wines are well suited to blue cheese.

CHEESE SOUFFLÉ

Serves 4

50 g/10 oz flour
250 ml/8 fl oz milk
4 egg yolks
100 g/4 oz grated Emmental (or other strong-flavoured) cheese
pinch salt
pinch cayenne pepper
1 tbsp brandy (optional)
6 egg whites
1 tbsp cornflour

1 Preheat the oven to 180° C/ 350° F, gas mark 4. Put the flour in a saucepan, add the milk, bring to the boil and simmer for a few minutes, beating constantly. Remove from the heat and beat in the egg yolks and 1 tbsp butter.

2 Add the cheese, salt, cayenne pepper and brandy, if using. Allow to cool. Grease a soufflé dish or a deep straight-sided ovenproof dish with the remaining butter.

3 Beat the egg whites until stiff. Fold in the cornflour. Fold half the beaten egg whites into the cheese mixture. Stir thoroughly. Carefully fold in the remaining beaten egg whites. Do not over mix. Pour the mixture carefully into the prepared dish. Place in the bottom of the oven for 30-40 minutes. Do not open the oven door for the first 20 minutes as the soufflé will sink.

4 Serve immediately. Remember that guests should wait for the soufflé and not the other way around.

TO DRINK
red wine

LEVEL OF DIFFICULTY
medium to difficult

PREPARATION TIME
1 hr

PREPARE IN ADVANCE
partly

ORANGE SALAD

Serves 6

12 blood oranges
2 tbsp caster sugar
50 ml/2 fl oz Cointreau or Grand Marnier
2 tbsp chopped pistachio nuts or flaked almonds

Serve with:
Nutcakes (see recipe 442)

1 Wash the oranges. Thinly pare the rind with a potato peeler. Use only the peel, discarding any pith. Cut the peel into very fine strips. Boil in water for approximately 15 minutes and drain.

2 Put the orange peel in a saucepan, add the sugar and 4 tbsp water. Simmer on low heat for 45 minutes. Allow to cool.

3 Remove all the pith from the oranges. Segment them and remove the membrane with a sharp knife, reserving the juice. Put the oranges in a bowl. Add the reserved juice and the liqueur. Marinate in the refrigerator for 3 hours.

4 Turn the oranges into individual bowls or glasses and pour over the marinade. Sprinkle with the strips of peel and the chopped pistachio nuts or chopped almonds.

ORANGE SALAD 304

TO DRINK
sweet white wine or beer

LEVEL OF DIFFICULTY
easy

PREPARATION TIME:
1 hr + 3hrs marinating

PREPARE IN ADVANCE
yes

DESSERT PLATE

Serves 4

2 oranges
2 bananas
1 Ogen melon or honeydew melon
8-12 strawberries
1 bunch grapes
4 almond biscuits (florentines)
8-12 scoops of ice cream or sorbet

1 Peel the oranges and bananas. Cut into slices. Remove the rind and seeds from the melon and cut into large slices. Wash and hull the strawberries. Seed grapes.

2 Divide the fruits between 4 chilled plates, ensuring that they are arranged in an attractive way. Leave some space in the middle for the ice cream or sorbet.

3 Just before serving add the ice cream or sorbet to the middle of the arrangement. Garnish with the florentines and possibly a few green leaves.

Variations:
Vary the fruits and berries according to the season. Canned fruit, such as peaches, apricots, or pineapple may also be used. Other types of biscuits or cakes can be served as well as different flavours of ice cream or sorbet. Strawberries, grapes and pineapple slices can be dipped in a melted dark cooking chocolate and left to harden.

This delicious dessert plate can easily be made with whatever is available from the cupboard, refrigerator or freezer, or even from whatever the local corner shop has to offer !

TO DRINK
sweet white wine, port or sherry, depending on what fruit is served

LEVEL OF DIFFICULTY
easy

PREPARATION TIME:
30 mins

PREPARE IN ADVANCE
partly

GRAND DESSERT

Serves 1

1 large slice fresh pineapple
½ fresh fig
a few grapes
a slice of melon or papaya
kiwi slices
star fruit (carambola) slices
1-2 kumquats
small lychee
1 slice of chocolate cake (e.g. Chocolate Cake à la Varenne, (see recipe 338)
3 small scoops sorbet (see recipe 395) or ice cream

1 Wash and prepare the fruit. Peel if necessary. Cut into slices or quarters. Place in a bowl, cover with foil and chill in the refrigerator.

2 Arrange the different fruits on chilled plates and leave a space in the middle for a scoop of sorbet or ice cream. Add a small slice of cake.

3 Just before serving, add the sorbet or ice cream to the middle of each plate.

Variations:
A Grand Dessert plate can be made with endless variations. Select fruits that are in season. An type of of cake, biscuit, ice cream, sorbet or parfait can be served. Make chocolate truffles (see recipe 337) or ice cream truffles (see recipe 385). The most important consideration is that the plates should be beautifully arranged and the fruits fresh.

GRAND DESSERT 306

TO DRINK
sweet white wine, Champagne, port or Madeira, depending on the ingredients

LEVEL OF DIFFICULTY	easy
PREPARATION TIME	varied
PREPARE IN ADVANCE	partly

BAKED PINEAPPLE WITH PASSION FRUIT

Serves 4

450 g/1 lb strawberries
2 small pineapples

Marinade:
I orange
75 g/2½ oz castor sugar
75 ml/3 fl oz water
75 ml/3 fl oz Grand Marnier or Marsala

Passionfruit zabaglione:
4 passion fruit
4 egg yolks
4 tbsp castor sugar

1 First make the marinade. Pare the orange very thinly with a potato peeler. Slice the orange rind very thinly. Squeeze the juice. Boil the sugar and water until the sugar has dissolved. Add the liqueur and orange rind. Boil for about 5 minutes and set aside to cool. Add the orange juice.

2 Wash, hull and halve the strawberries. Add them to the marinade and chill in the refrigerator for 2 hours.

3 Cut the pineapples in half lengthwise. Remove the cores and cut the flesh into cubes. Keep the pineapple 'shells'. Put in the refrigerator.

4 Peel the passion fruit and remove the flesh. Strain and reserve the strawberries. Reserve the marinade. Put the egg yolks, sugar, marinade and passion fruit in a heatproof bowl and set over a pan of hot water. Beat the sauce until it becomes thick and frothy.

5 Preheat the grill. Put the pineapple halves on to heatproof serving plates. Fill with the pineapple cubes and marinated strawberries in layers. Pour over the sauce.

6 Heat under the grill for a few minutes until the sauce has a rich colour.

BAKED PINEAPPLE WITH PASSION FRUIT

TO DRINK
Marsala

LEVEL OF DIFFICULTY
medium to difficult

PREPARATION TIME
1 hr + marinating

PREPARE IN ADVANCE
partly

HONEYED BANANAS

Serves 4

1 large orange
200 ml /7 fl oz whipping cream
4 large firm bananas
100 g /3½ oz butter
100 ml/4 fl oz acacia honey
¼ tsp ground ginger
12 walnuts, chopped

1 Wash the orange and grate the rind. Squeeze the juice.

2 Whip the cream and add the grated orange rind. Set aside in the refrigerator.

3 Peel the bananas and cut in half lengthwise.

4 Melt the butter in a frying-pan. Add the honey and approximately 2 tbsp of the freshly squeezed orange juice. Set over low heat and simmer, stirring constantly, until the honey has melted and is well mixed. Add a further 2 tbsp orange juice and sprinkle over the ginger.

5 Add the bananas, cut side down. Lower the heat and simmer the bananas very slowly, uncovered, for about 10 minutes. Baste the bananas with the sauce occasionally.

6 Very carefully, transfer the bananas to a serving dish. Pour over the sauce and garnish with the chopped walnuts. Serve immediately with the ice cold orange cream.

HONEYED BANANAS 308

TO DRINK:
Sweet Madeira

LEVEL OF DIFFICULTY
easy

PREPARATION TIME
30 mins

PREPARE IN ADVANCE:
partly

ICY APPLES

Serves 6-8

425 g/15 oz sugar
175 ml/ 6 fl oz water
rind of 1 lemon
1 kg/2¼ lb cooking apples

Serve with:
crème fraîche or vanilla ice cream (see recipe 396)

1 Boil the sugar and water together until they have made a syrup. Add the lemon rind.

2 Peel and core the apples and cut them in very thin slices. Add to the syrup and boil for 2-2½ hours.

3 Rinse out a dish or plain mould with cold water and pour in the apple mixture. Place in the refrigerator for several hours, preferably overnight.

4 Turn the dessert out on to a serving plate and serve icy cold with crème fraîche or vanilla ice cream.

To drink:
Madeira or sweet white wine

LEVEL OF DIFFICULTY
easy

PREPARATION TIME
3 hrs + setting time

PREPARE IN ADVANCE
yes

HAGA STRAWBERRIES WITH ICE CREAM

Serves 4

450g /1 lb strawberries
100 ml/4 fl oz water
85 g/3 oz sugar
1 orange
100 ml/4 fl oz Grand Marnier
500 ml/17 fl oz vanilla ice cream
(see recipe 396)

1 Wash but do not hull the strawberries. Set aside to drain on kitchen paper.

2 Make a syrup by boiling together the water and sugar. Allow to cool.

3 Wash the oranges and pare the rind very thinly with a potato peeler. Discard any pith. Cut the rind into very fine strips. Boil in water for a few minutes until soft. Remove from the water and drain.

4 Squeeze the orange and pour the juice into the sugar syrup. Add the liqueur. Hull the strawberries and put them in a bowl. Pour over the sugar syrup and garnish with the orange rind. Set aside to marinate for 2 hours.

5 Serve with vanilla ice cream.

HAGA STRAWBERRIES WITH ICE CREAM 310

TO DRINK
sparkling red wine or
rosé wine

LEVEL OF DIFFICULTY
easy

PREPARATION TIME
30 mins + marination

PREPARE IN ADVANCE
yes

CINNAMON PEARS WITH ICE CREAM

Serves 4

4 firm pears
juice of 1 lemon
equal quantities sugar and water (to cover)
2 cinnamon sticks

Sauce:
85 g/3 oz sugar
40 g/1½ oz cocoa
100 ml/4 fl oz water

Serve with:
ice cream

1 Peel the pears, retaining the stalks. Brush them with lemon juice so that they do not discolour.

2 Make a syrup by boiling equal quantities of sugar and water. There should be enough to cover the pears completely. Add the cinnamon. Add the pears and simmer until soft. Test with a fork or skewer. Allow the pears to cool in the syrup.

3 To make the sauce, mix the sugar, cocoa and water in a pan. Bring to the boil, lower the heat and simmer until the sauce has thickened.

4 Place the pears on 4 individual serving plates, put ice cream around the pears and pour the hot chocolate sauce over the ice cream.

TO DRINK
sweet white wine

LEVEL OF DIFFICULTY
easy

PREPARATION TIME
1 hr

PREPARE IN ADVANCE
yes

APPLE MERINGUE

Serves 4

1 litre/1¾ pints water
85g /3 oz castor sugar
juice of ½ lemon
4 large, firm cooking apples

Meringue:
6 egg whites
250 g/8 oz castor sugar

Garnish:
hundreds and thousands

Serve with:
whipped cream or vanilla ice cream

1 Boil the water, sugar and lemon juice together to make a syrup. Preheat the oven to its lowest setting.

2 Peel and core the apples. Add them to the syrup and simmer until they are almost soft. Remove and drain the apples. Discard the syrup.

3 To make the meringue, beat the egg whites until they form stiff peaks. Add the sugar and continue beating until the meringue mixture is stiff and shiny.

4 Arrange the apples in an ovenproof dish and coat them with the meringue mixture, ensuring that they are fully covered. Garnish with hundreds and thousands.

5 Put the dish into the oven for 9-12 hours or overnight. If you are not serving the apples immediately, turn off the oven and leave them to cool down slowly. Before serving, preheat the oven to its lowest setting and re-cook the meringue apples for 15-20 minutes.

6 Serve the apples warm with ice cold cream or ice cream.

APPLE MERINGUE 312

TO DRINK
sweet white wine or ruby port

LEVEL OF DIFFICULTY
easy

PREPARATION TIME
1 hr + overnight cooking

PREPARE IN ADVANCE
yes

MELON WITH RASPBERRIES AND PORT

Serves 4

2 small Ogen or Galia melons
450 g/1 lb fresh or frozen and thawed raspberries
200 ml/7 fl oz white port

Garnish:
lemon or lime wedges

1 Cut the melons in half and remove the seeds.

2 Divide the raspberries between the melon halves.

3 Pour the port over the raspberries and place the filled melon halves on individual serving plates. Garnish with the lemon or lime wedges and serve with sugar in a separate bowl.

Variations:
Champagne or sparkling wine may be used instead of port.

TO DRINK
the wine used to flavour the dish

LEVEL OF DIFFICULTY
easy

PREPARATION TIME
30 mins

PREPARE IN ADVANCE
no

PEARS IN SAUTERNES

Serves 4

4 large pears
water
juice of 1/2 lemon

Syrup:
1 litre/1 3/4 pints water
85 g/3 oz caster sugar
2 tsp vanilla sugar

Sauce:
250 ml/8 fl oz Sauternes or other sweet white wine
150 ml/5 fl oz whipping cream
4 egg yolks
3 tbsp castor sugar

1 Peel the pears, retaining the stalks. Put the pears in a bowl and pour over the water and lemon juice to prevent discolouration.

2 To make the syrup, boil the water, sugar and vanilla sugar together. Add the pears and simmer over low heat for approximately 20-30 minutes, until the pears are soft. Test with a fork or skewer. When cooked, remove from the syrup, allow to cool and keep in the refrigerator.

3 To make the sauce, mix all the ingredients together in a pan. Simmer over very low heat, stirring constantly, until the sauce is thick and shiny. Allow the sauce to cool and transfer to the refrigerator.

4 Serve the pears on individual serving dishes and pour over the wine sauce.

To drink
Sauternes or other sweet white wine

LEVEL OF DIFFICULTY
fairly easy

PREPARATION TIME
1 hr

PREPARE IN ADVANCE
yes

RHUBARB MERINGUE

Serves 4

6-8 sticks rhubarb
1 tsp butter
85 g/3 oz castor sugar

Meringue:
4 egg whites
100 g/3½ oz castor sugar
flaked almonds (optional)

Serve with:
whipped cream

1 Preheat the oven to 220° C/425° F, gas mark 7. Rinse the rhubarb and cut into 2-3 cm/1 inch pieces. Lightly grease an ovenproof dish with the butter. Arrange the rhubarb in it, sprinkle over sugar and cover with foil. Bake for 20 minutes.

2 Beat the egg whites until they form stiff peaks. Add the sugar, beating constantly, until the meringue mixture is light and shiny.

3 Take the dish out of the oven and pour over the meringue mixture. Decorate with flaked almonds, if using. Return the dish to the oven and cook for approximately 5 minutes until the meringue is light golden.

TO DRINK
sweet white wine

LEVEL OF DIFFICULTY
easy

PREPARATION TIME
30 mins

PREPARE IN ADVANCE
partly

SWEDISH VEILED COUNTRY LASS

Serves 4-6

3-4 tbsp butter
60 g/2 oz dark breadcrumbs, such as rye bread
130 g/4 oz castor sugar
25 g/1 oz ground almonds
300 ml/10 fl oz whipping cream
200 ml/7 fl oz apple sauce or apple purée
100 g/4 oz dark cooking chocolate, grated

1 Melt the butter in a frying-pan. Add the breadcrumbs, sugar and ground almonds. Fry the mixture, stirring constantly, until crunchy. Allow to cool.

2 Whip the cream. Put half the apple sauce or purée in a glass bowl and cover with half the breadcrumb mixture. Cover with half the whipped cream and top with half the grated chocolate. Repeat these layers, finishing with a layer of grated chocolate.

3 Keep in the refrigerator for no longer than 1 hour before serving, or the bread mixture will loose its crispness.

SWEDISH VEILED COUNTRY LASS 316

TO DRINK:
sweet white wine

LEVEL OF DIFFICULTY
easy

PREPARATION TIME
30 mins

PREPARE IN ADVANCE
yes

BAKED APPLES WITH VANILLA SAUCE

Serves 4

4 apples
60 g/2 oz ground almonds
2 tbsp sugar
2 tbsp butter

Vanilla sauce:
200 ml/7 fl oz single cream
2-3 egg yolks
1½ tbsp castor sugar
1 tbsp cornflour
½ vanilla pod
100 ml/4 fl oz whipping cream

1 Preheat the oven to 220° C/425° F, gas mark 7 and core the apples. Place the apples on an ovenproof dish.

2 Mix the almonds and sugar together and pile this mixture into the centre of the apples, adding a slice of butter on the top. Bake for 20 minutes.

3 To make the vanilla sauce, beat together the single cream, egg yolks, sugar and cornflour in a pan. Cut the vanilla pod in half lengthwise and remove the seeds with a sharp knife. Add the seeds and pod to the cream mixture.

4 Put the saucepan over a low heat and simmer slowly, stirring constantly, until the sauce has thickened. It is important to beat or stir the sauce all the time, so that it does not stick or burn. Put the saucepan in cold water and stir occasionally until cool. Remove the vanilla pod. Beat the whipping cream and fold it into the sauce.

5 Serve the apples lukewarm with the cold sauce in a separate dish.

BAKED APPLES WITH VANILLA SAUCE

TO DRINK:
sweet white wine or ruby port

LEVEL OF DIFFICULTY
easy

PREPARATION TIME
1 hr

PREPARE IN ADVANCE
yes

ALMOND TOFFEE PEACHES

Serves 4-6

2 x 415 g/14.6 fl oz cans peach halves
1 tsp butter

Toffee mixture:
50 g/2 oz butter
43 g/1½ oz castor sugar
50 ml/2 fl oz whipping cream
1 tbsp flour
35g/1¼ oz flaked almonds

Serve with:
whipped cream or vanilla ice cream

1 Preheat the oven to 220° C/ 425 °F, gas mark 7. Lightly grease an ovenproof dish with the butter. Drain the peach halves and set aside to dry. When the peaches are dry, arrange them on the prepared dish, round sides upwards.

2 To make the toffee mixture, melt the butter in a small pan. Stir in all the remaining ingredients and simmer for a few minutes.

3 Pour the sauce over the peach halves. Bake in the oven for approximately 15 minutes or until the sauce has a rich colour. Allow to cool slightly before serving.

Variations:
The peach halves can be replaced by pears, apples or pineapple rings.

ALMOND TOFFEE PEACHES 318

To drink
ruby port

LEVEL OF DIFFICULTY
easy

PREPARATION TIME
30 mins

PREPARE IN ADVANCE
yes

TROPICAL FRUIT SALAD

Serves 8-10

1 Ogen melon
1 papaya
1 pineapple
2 bananas
3 kiwi fruit
3 peaches
2 oranges
4 fresh figs
20 grapes
1 pepino
230 g/8 oz strawberries
1-2 star fruit (carambola)
1 lime or 3 kumquats
8 lychees or cape gooseberries
3 passion fruit

Sauce:
100 ml/4 fl oz tropical nectar or the juice of 1 orange
100 ml/4 fl oz sparkling white wine

1 Halve the melon, remove the seeds, scoop out the flesh and cut into cubes. Do the same with the papaya. Cut the pineapple in half, remove the core and the flesh and cut the flesh into cubes.

2 Peel and slice the bananas and kiwi fruit. Peel, halve and stone the peaches and cut into slices. Peel the oranges and cut into slices. Cut the figs in half. Halve the grapes and remove the seeds. Cut the pepino into slices or cubes. Wash and hull the strawberries. Halve any large ones.

3 Arrange the fruit in layers in a bowl. Mix together the nectar or orange juice and wine to make the sauce and pour over the fruit salad. Keep in the refrigerator until ready to serve.

4 To garnish, slice the star fruit across so they make star shapes. Slice the lime and kumquats thinly. Peel the lychees or cape gooseberries. Cut the passion fruit into quarters.

Variations:
The ingredients consist mainly of tropical fruits that are easily available, though these are just suggestions. Select fruits to your own taste and try different combinations.

TO DRINK
sweet Champagne or other sparkling white wine

LEVEL OF DIFFICULTY
easy

PREPARATION TIME
1 hr

PREPARE IN ADVANCE
yes

WATERMELON BASKET

Serves 6-8

1 large watermelon
seasonal fruit and berries, such as bananas, kiwi fruit, pears, peaches, pineapple, cherries, raspberries and strawberries
juice of 2 lemons
3 tbsp icing sugar
50 ml/2 fl oz Cointreau (optional)

1 First make the watermelon basket. Mark the skin of the watermelon with a pencil or sharp knife in quarters, leaving a handle in the middle. Remove the skin with a sharp knife. Carefully cut out the flesh, removing as many seeds as possible. Cut the melon flesh into cubes or use a melon baller.

2 Clean, peel and stone or seed the seasonal fruits. Cut into slices or cubes. Mix all the fruits in a bowl, including the watermelon cubes. Mix the lemon juice with icing sugar and the liqueur, if using, and pour over the fruit. Cover with foil and chill in the refrigerator for approximately 1 hour. Refrigerate the reserved melon basket.

3 Just before serving, fill the melon basket with the fruit salad.

WATERMELON BASKET 320

TO DRINK
sweet white wine

LEVEL OF DIFFICULTY
easy

PREPARATION TIME
1 hr + chilling time

PREPARE IN ADVANCE
yes

ZABAGLIONE WITH BERRIES

Serves 4

6 egg yolks
100 g/3½ oz castor sugar
200 ml/7 fl oz Marsala, port or white wine

Serve with:
fresh or frozen berries, such as wild strawberries, raspberries, or blackberries

1 Beat the egg yolks, sugar and wine in a heatproof bowl until frothy. Place the bowl over a pan of hot, but not boiling water and gently heat the mixture, beating constantly until it is thick and light.

2 Serve the zabaglione warm or cold in individual glasses, together with the fruit. Cold zabaglione may be mixed together with 100 ml/4 fl oz whipped cream.

ZABAGLIONE WITH BERRIES 321

TO DRINK
Marsala, port or white wine

LEVEL OF DIFFICULTY
easy

PREPARATION TIME
30 mins

PREPARE IN ADVANCE
yes

BLUEBERRY PIE

Serves 4

Dough:
100 g/3½ fl oz butter
100 g/3½ fl oz sugar
2 eggs
25 ml/1 fl oz milk
200 g/7 oz flour

Filling:
250 g/9 oz blueberries
4 tbsp sugar
2 tsp cornflour

Serve with:
whipped cream or vanilla ice cream

1 First make the dough. Mix together the butter, sugar, 1 egg and the milk. Add the flour and work the dough quickly; it will become tough if handled for too long. Set the dough aside in the refrigerator to rest for approximately 1 hour.

2 Preheat the oven to 200° C/400° F, gas mark 6. Make the filling. Divide the blueberries between 4 individual ovenproof dishes. Mix the sugar and cornflour and sprinkle over the berries.

3 Roll our the dough to 3 mm/⅛ inch thick and cut out 4 lids to fit the dishes. Cover the dishes with the dough lids and smooth the edges. Beat the remaining egg and brush the dough lids. Sprinkle a little sugar on top. Bake in the oven for approximately 15 minutes.

Suggestion:
Leftover dough can be kept in a plastic bag in the refrigerator for a couple of days; it can also be frozen.

TO DRINK
coffee

LEVEL OF DIFFICULTY
easy

PREPARATION TIME
1 hr + resting

PREPARE IN ADVANCE
yes

LEMON MERINGUE PIE

Serves 6-8

Dough:
150 g/5 oz + 1 tsp butter, chilled
180 g/6 oz flour
2 tbsp iced water

Filling:
400 ml/14 fl oz water
85 g/3 oz castor sugar
80 g/2¾ oz cornflour
juice of 1 lemon
4 egg yolks
1 tbsp butter
grated rind of ½ lemon

Meringue:
4 egg whites
130 g/4½ oz castor sugar

1 Mix together 150 g/5 oz of the butter and the flour until the mixture resembles fine breadcrumbs. Add the water and work into the dough quickly. Set aside in the refrigerator to rest for 1 hour.

2 Grease a loose-based flan tin with the remaining butter. Roll out the dough and use it to line tin. Prick the base with a fork. Set aside in the refrigerator for approximately 30 minutes. Preheat the oven to 200° C/ 400° F, gas mark 6.

3 Bake the dough case for 15-20 minutes. Set aside to cool.

4 Make the filling. Mix the water, sugar, cornflour and lemon juice in a saucepan. Simmer for 3-4 minutes, stirring constantly. Remove the pan from the heat. Stir in the egg yolks and butter. Simmer over very gentle heat for a 2-4 minutes until thickened and mixed; do not allow to boil. Set the mixture aside to cool. Add the grated lemon rind. Preheat the oven to 150° C/ 300° F, gas mark 2.

5 Beat the egg whites until they form stiff peaks. Fold in the sugar.

6 Pour the lemon cream into the pastry case and spread the meringue mixture over the top. Bake for 8-10 minutes. Serve the pie after allowing it to cool slightly.

TO DRINK
sweet white wine

LEVEL OF DIFFICULTY
easy

PREPARATION TIME
1 hr + resting time

PREPARE IN ADVANCE
yes

FRUIT AND BERRY FLAN

Serves 6

Dough:
180 g/6 oz flour
2 tbsp sugar
150 g/5 oz + 1 tsp butter, chilled
2-3 tbsp iced water

Cream:
300 ml/10 fl oz single cream
3 egg yolks
2 tbsp castor sugar
1 tbsp cornflour
1 tsp vanilla essence

Jelly:
4 leaves gelatine
50 ml/2 fl oz water
1 tbsp castor sugar
200 ml/7 fl oz white wine

Garnish:
Seasonal fruits and berries

1 Make the dough. Mix the flour, sugar and 150 g/5 oz of the butter until the mixture resembles fine breadcrumbs. Add the water and work quickly into a dough. Set aside in the refrigerator to rest for 1 hour.

2 Meanwhile, mix together the cream, egg yolks, castor sugar, cornflour and vanilla essence in a pan. Bring to the boil, then simmer, stirring constantly, until thick and fluffy. Set aside to cool, stirring occasionally.

3 Preheat the oven to 200° C/ 400° F, gas mark 6. Grease a 25 cm/10 inch loose-based flan tin with the remaining butter. Roll out the dough. Line the tin with the dough and prick the base with a fork. Set aside in the refrigerator for 15-30 minutes. Bake blind in the bottom of the oven for 20-25 minutes. Set aside to cool.

4 Soak the gelatine leaves in cold water for 10 minutes to soften. Boil the water, sugar and gelatine leaves until the gelatine has melted. Add the wine. Chill in the refrigerator until the jelly has thickened.

5 Prepare the fruit and cut it into halves, slices or chunks.

6 Spread the cream evenly on the flan base. Arrange the fruit decoratively on top. Spoon over the jelly and put in the refrigerator until set.

FRUIT AND BERRY FLAN 324

TO DRINK:
sweet white wine

LEVEL OF DIFFICULTY
fairly easy

PREPARATION TIME
1 hr + resting & setting time

PREPARE IN ADVANCE:
yes

STRAWBERRY FLAN

Serves 6-8

Dough:
140 g/5 oz butter, softened
2 tbsp sugar
1 egg
1 tbsp cream
165 g/3/4 oz flour

Filling:
50 g/2 oz cooking chocolate
250 ml/9 fl oz single cream
4 tsp cornflour
40 g/1 1/2 oz castor sugar
3 egg yolks
1 cinnamon stick
100 ml/4 fl oz whipping cream
450 g/1 lb strawberries, hulled
1 tbsp icing sugar
1 tsp ground cinnamon

1 Make the dough. Beat 125 g/4 oz of the butter and the sugar. Beat in the egg and cream. Stir in the flour. Mix the dough and set aside in the refrigerator to rest for 1 hour.

2 Grease a loose-based flan tin with the remaining butter. Roll out the dough to 3 mm/1/8 inch thick and use to line the flan tin. Prick the base with a fork. Set aside in the refrigerator for 15-30 minutes. Preheat the oven to 200° C/400° F, gas mark 6.

3 Bake the flan case blind for 10 minutes. Remove the foil and bake for a further 15-20 minutes. Set aside to cool.

4 Melt the chocolate in a heatproof bowl over a pan of hot, but not boiling water. Brush melted chocolate evenly over the flan case.

5 Mix together the single cream, cornflour, sugar and egg yolks in a pan. Add the cinnamon stick. Simmer over very low heat, beating until thick. Remove the cinnamon stick. Set the cream aside to cool, stirring occasionally.

6 Halve the strawberries and arrange them on the flan base. Whip the cream and mix with the cinnamon cream. Spread over the strawberries.

7 Preheat the grill. Mix the icing sugar and cinnamon and sprinkle over the flan filling. Grill for 3-5 minutes. Keep in the refrigerator until ready to serve.

TO DRINK:
sweet white wine

LEVEL OF DIFFICULTY
fairly easy

PREPARATION TIME
1 hr + resting & cooling time

PREPARE IN ADVANCE
yes

STRAWBERRY CAKE

Serves 4-6

Dough:
120 g/4 oz flour
1 tsp castor sugar
pinch salt
100 g/3½ oz + 1 tsp butter, chilled
2 tbsp iced water

Filling:
150 g/5 oz almond paste
3 tbsp water
680 g/1½ lb strawberries

Glaze:
5 tbsp redcurrant jelly
5 tbsp blackcurrant juice

1 Make the dough. Mix together the flour, sugar, salt and 100 g /3½ oz butter until the mixture resembles fine breadcrumbs. Add the water and work into a dough quickly. Set aside in the refrigerator to rest for 1 hour.

2 Grease a 20 cm/8 inch loose-base cake tin with the remaining butter. Roll out the dough. Line the prepared tin with the dough, prick the base with a fork and set aside in the refrigerator for 15-30 minutes. Preheat the oven to 200° C/ 400° F, gas mark 6.

3 Bake for 15-30 minutes until the pastry is golden. Allow to cool slightly and transfer to a serving plate.

4 Grate the almond paste. Mix with the water to form a smooth paste. Spread over the dough base.

5 Wash and hull the strawberries and pile them on to the almond paste in a pyramid.

6 Melt the redcurrant jelly in a small saucepan and stir in the juice. Let the jelly thicken slightly and pour over the strawberries.

STRAWBERRY CAKE 326

TO DRINK
sweet white wine, Sauternes

LEVEL OF DIFFICULTY
easy

PREPARATION TIME
1 hr + resting time

PREPARE IN ADVANCE
yes

KIWI FRUIT FLAN

Serves 6

Dough:
240 g/8½ oz flour
85 g/3 oz castor sugar
¼ tsp vanilla essence
150 g/5 oz butter
1 egg, lightly beaten

Filling:
10 Kiwi fruit
4 eggs
250 ml/9 fl oz whipping cream
150 g/5 oz castor sugar
40 ml/1½ fl oz kirsch (optional)
25 g/1 oz soft brown sugar

1 Make the dough. Mix together the flour, sugar, and vanilla essence. Dice the butter and mix it in until the dough resembles fine breadcrumbs. Add the egg and quickly work into the dough. Put the mixture in a plastic bag and leave in the refrigerator to rest for 1 hour.

2 Roll out the dough and line a 28 cm/1 inch flan tin with a removable base. Prick the base with a fork and pinch strips of foil over the edges of the dough so that it does not collapse during baking. Set aside in the refrigerator for approximately 30 minutes. Preheat the oven to 200° C/400° F, gas mark 6.

3 Bake the dough shell for approximately 10 minutes. Remove the foil strips.

4 Peel and slice the kiwi fruit. Arrange evenly over the flan case.

5 Beat together the eggs, cream, sugar and kirsch, if using, in a bowl. Pour the egg mixture over the sliced kiwi fruit. Reduce the oven temperature to 180° C/350° F, gas mark 4 and bake for 20-25 minutes. Preheat the grill.

6 Sprinkle the brown sugar on top of the flan and set under the grill until the top is golden.

7 Transfer the flan to a serving dish. Allow to cool slightly before serving.

Variations:
Cherries, plums, peaches or other fruit may be used

KIWI FRUIT FLAN 327

TO DRINK
sweet white wine

LEVEL OF DIFFICULTY
medium difficult

PREPARATION TIME
1 hour + resting time

PREPARE IN ADVANCE
yes

PEAR PIE

Serves 6

Dough:
60 g/2 oz oat flakes
120 g/4 oz flour
150 g/5 oz butter, diced
2 tsp ice cold water
1 egg, lightly beaten

Filling:
5 large pears
500 ml/17 fl oz water
130 g/4½ oz castor sugar
a few cloves (optional)

Serve with:
whipped cream or vanilla ice cream

1 Mix the oat flakes and flour. Rub in the butter until the mixture resembles fine breadcrumbs. Add the water and work into the dough. Alternatively, make the dough in a food processor. Set the dough aside in the refrigerator to rest for 1 hour.

2 Peel the pears, cut into halves and remove the cores. Bring the water and sugar to the boil, stirring. Add the pears and allow to simmer until they are soft. Remove the pears and drain.

3 Preheat the oven to 200° C/ 400° F, gas mark 6. Place the pears, rounded side up, on a pie dish or ovenproof dish.

4 Roll out the dough and place a dough lid on top of the fruit. Cut out flowers or leaves from the leftover dough and decorate the lid with them. Brush with beaten egg. Bake in the middle of the oven for 20-25 minutes.

5 Serve the pie with whipped cream or vanilla ice cream.

PEAR PIE 328

To drink
sweet white wine

LEVEL OF DIFFICULTY
fairly easy

PREPARATION TIME
1 hr +resting time

PREPARE IN ADVANCE
yes

RHUBARB PIE

Serves 4-6

Dough:
180 g/6½ oz flour
2 tsp castor sugar
150 g cold butter, diced
1-2 tsp ice cold water

Filling:
6-7 rhubarb stalks
40 g/1½ oz cornflour
85 g/3 oz castor sugar
½ tsp vanilla sugar

Serve with:
vanilla sauce (see recipe 434), raw cream (see recipe 436) or whipped cream

1 Make the dough. Mix together the flour and sugar, add the butter and mix until the dough resembles fine breadcrumbs. Add the water and quickly work into the dough. Set the dough aside in the refrigerator to rest for 1 hour.

2 Preheat the oven to 200° C/ 400° F, gas mark 6. Roll out the dough and use to line a pie dish approximately 25 cm/10 inches in diameter. Prick the dough base with a fork.

3 Cut the rhubarb stalks in 3-cm/1-inch long pieces. Mix the cornflour, sugar and vanilla sugar. Arrange the rhubarb pieces on the dough and cover with the cornflour mixture.

4 Bake in the bottom of the oven for 25-30 minutes or until the dough has turned light gold and the rhubarb feels soft.

5 Serve the pie lukewarm with vanilla sauce, raw cream or whipped cream.

TO DRINK
sweet white wine

LEVEL OF DIFFICULTY
easy

PREPARATION TIME
1 hr + resting time

PREPARE IN ADVANCE
yes

CRÊPES SOUFFLÉS AU GRAND MARNIER

10-12 pancakes

Pancake mixture:
130 g/4½ oz flour
40 g/1½ oz castor sugar
3 eggs
300 ml/10 fl oz whipping cream
50 ml/2 fl oz Grand Marnier
pinch of salt
butter or oil for frying (½-1 tsp per pancake)

Soufflé filling:
100 g/3½ oz + 1 tsp butter
60 g/2¼ oz flour
150 ml/5 fl oz milk
150 ml/5 fl oz whipping cream
75 ml/3 fl oz Grand Marnier
85 g/3 oz castor sugar
8 eggs

1 Beat the pancake ingredients together. Heat the oil in a frying pan. Pour in a little batter and tilt the pan to spread it. Cook for 1 minute on each side, or until golden on both sides. Flip the pancakes over with a spatula. Stack the cooked pancakes interleaved with greaseproof paper. Preheat the oven to 250° C/500° F, gas mark 10. Grease an ovenproof dish with 1 tsp butter.

2 Make the soufflé mixture. Melt the butter. Stir in the milk, cream and liqueur. Add the sugar and remove the pan from the heat. Let the mixture cool slightly.

3 Separate the eggs and stir the egg yolks into the mixture.

4 Beat the egg whites until they form stiff peaks. Beat the soufflé mixture until frothy. Stir one quarter of the egg whites into the mixture and carefully fold in the remainder.

5 The parcels must be made quickly so that the soufflé mixture does not sink. Put one pancake at a time on to a plate and place a large helping of the soufflé mixture on top. Make a parcel by tuning over two sides of the pancake, then turn in the corners. Transfer to the prepared dish, folded sides down. Do the same with the remaining pancakes.

6 Bake in the oven for 12-14 minutes. Serve immediately.

CRÊPES SOUFFLÉS AU GRAND MARNIER 330

TO DRINK
Grand Marnier or Madeira

LEVEL OF DIFFICULTY
fairly difficult

PREPARATION TIME
1 hr

PREPARE IN ADVANCE
partly

MELT-IN-THE -MOUTH PANCAKES

Serves 4-6

Pancakes:
3 eggs
150 g/5 oz flour
pinch salt
600 ml/1 pint milk
2 tsp melted butter
butter or oil for frying

Filling:
500 ml-1 litre/17 fl oz-1¾ pints ice cream

Sauce:
450 g/1 lb strawberries
icing sugar to taste

Garnish:
whole strawberries

1 Purée the strawberries in a food processor or by rubbing through a wire strainer. Add icing sugar to taste. Keep cold in the refrigerator.

2 Make the pancake mixture and fry thin crêpes as described in recipe 330. Stack them on top of each other, interleaved with greaseproof paper and keep warm over a saucepan of simmering water or in a low oven.

3 Just before serving, put a large scoop of ice cream on top of each pancake and fold over the edges to make parcels. Sprinkle icing sugar over the warm pancakes and garnish with whole strawberries. Serve the sauce separately.

MELT-IN-THE-MOUTH PANCAKES

TO DRINK
white port or Madeira

LEVEL OF DIFFICULTY
easy

PREPARATION TIME
30 mins

PREPARE IN ADVANCE
partly

JAM OMELETTE

Serve 4

5 eggs, separated
300 ml/10 fl oz whipping cream
½ tsp castor sugar
1 tsp butter

Filling:
strawberry or raspberry jam

Garnish:
icing sugar

1 Preheat the oven to 250° C/500° F, gas mark 10. Beat the egg yolks together with the sugar and cream. Whisk the egg whites until they form stiff peaks and fold them into the mixture.

2 Melt the butter in a large frying-pan or skillet. Pour the omelette mixture into the pan and leave for a moment so that the base becomes coloured.

3 Put the omelette into the oven for a few minutes or until it is just cooked. Slide the omelette half on to a plate, cover with jam, and flip the other side over. Dust with sifted icing sugar. Serve immediately.

JAM OMELETTE 332

To drink
sweet white wine

LEVEL OF DIFFICULTY
medium difficult

PREPARATION TIME
30 mins

PREPARE IN ADVANCE:
no

CHOCOLATE WALNUT PANCAKES

Serves 4

Pancakes:
3 eggs
150 g/5 oz flour
pinch salt
600 ml/1 pint milk
2 tsp melted butter
butter for frying

Filling:
150 g/5 oz walnuts, ground
150 g/5 oz castor sugar
2 tsp dark rum
approximately 1 tbsp water
25 g/1 oz raisins

Sauce:
150 ml/5 fl oz water
170 g/6 oz castor sugar
80 g/2¾ oz cocoa powder

Garnish:
icing sugar

1 Make the pancakes and fry them as described in recipe 330. Keep warm. The mixture will make approximately 10 large pancakes.

2 Mix together the walnuts and the sugar. Stir in the rum and approximately 1 tbsp water. The filling should not be too runny. Add the raisins.

3 Divide the filling between the pancakes and either fold into quarters or roll them up.

4 Make the sauce. Boil the water and sugar until bubbling. Remove the pan from the heat and stir in the cocoa powder. This can be made in advance and re-heated.

5 Place the pancakes on a serving dish and sprinkle with icing sugar. Serve the sauce separately.

CHOCOLATE WALNUT PANCAKES 333

TO DRINK
chocolate or coffee liqueur

LEVEL OF DIFFICULTY easy
PREPARATION TIME 30 mins
PREPARE IN ADVANCE yes

THE WORLD'S BEST SCOTCH PANCAKES

Serves 4-6

100 g/3½ oz butter
100 g/3½ oz flour
300 ml/10 fl oz water
6 eggs separated
300 ml/10 fl oz whipping cream
½ tsp vanilla sugar

Serve with:
jam

1 Melt the butter and stir in the flour and water over a low heat until thick. Remove the pan from the heat and stir until the mixture has cooled slightly. Add the egg yolks, one at a time, stirring constantly.

2 Whip the cream until firm. Beat the egg whites until they form stiff peaks. Stir the whipped cream into the egg yolk mixture and fold in the egg whites. Add the vanilla sugar.

3 Cook the pancakes as described in recipe 330, but cook only one side. Sandwich the pancakes together in pairs with the uncooked sides towards each other. Place on an ovenproof dish. The pancakes can be kept like this for several hours or even until the next day. They can also be frozen, but must thaw for 1 hour before cooking.

4 Preheat the oven to 200° C/ 400° F, gas mark 6. Bake the pancakes for 7-10 minutes. They will rise like little soufflés. Quickly sprinkle the tops with a little icing sugar. Serve immediately with jam.

To drink
sweet white wine

LEVEL OF DIFFICULTY easy
PREPARATION TIME 1 hr
PREPARE IN ADVANCE yes

ORANGE TARTLETS

Serves 6

Dough:
150 g/5 oz butter
30 g/1 oz icing sugar
180 g/6 oz flour
40 g/1½ oz cornflour
1-2 tsp ice cold water

Custard:
200 ml/7 fl oz milk or single cream
1 tbsp plain flour
2 egg yolks
1-2 tbsp white sugar
2-3 tsp vanilla essence

Garnish:
5-6 oranges
200 ml/7 fl oz orange juice
3 gelatine leaves

1 Quickly work all the dough ingredients together, either by hand or in a food processor. Set the dough aside in the refrigerator to rest for 1 hour.

2 Make the custard. Beat together the milk or cream, flour, egg yolks and sugar over low heat. Simmer until thick. Allow to cool. Add vanilla essence to taste.

3 Preheat the oven to 200° C/400° F, gas mark 6. Roll out the dough and press it into tartlet tins. Prick the dough bases with a fork.

4 Bake the tartlets blind for 15 minutes or until they are cooked and light gold. Allow to cool slightly and then remove from the tins. Set aside to cool.

5 Soak the gelatine in water for 10-15 minutes. Peel the oranges and remove the pith. Cut into segments. Pour any juice from the oranges into a bowl.

6 Squeeze out the gelatine leaves and melt with a couple of drops of water over a low heat. Measure the orange juice. Make up to 200 ml/7 fl oz with water and add to the melted gelatine. Keep in the refrigerator until the jelly has slightly thickened but not set.

7 Divide the custard equally between the tartlets and arrange the orange segments on top. Carefully spoon over the jelly until the oranges are completely covered.

TO DRINK
sweet white wine

LEVEL OF DIFFICULTY
fairly easy

PREPARATION TIME
1 hour + setting time

PREPARE IN ADVANCE
yes

CHOCOLATE RATAFIAS

Makes approximately 25

Dough:
200 g/7 oz ground almonds
icing sugar
2 egg whites

Butter cream:
200 g/7 oz butter
150 g/5 oz icing sugar
200 ml/7 fl oz whipping cream
2 egg yolks
2 tsp cornflour
2 tbsp cocoa powder
few drops vanilla essence

Garnish:
100 g/3½ oz dark cooking chocolate
½ tsp butter (optional)

1 Preheat the oven to 200° C/400°F, gas mark 6. Line a baking sheet with greaseproof paper. Mix together the ground almonds and icing sugar. Stir in the egg whites and mix until smooth and flexible.

2 Using 2 teaspoons, put heaps of the mixture on the prepared baking sheet. With a floured hand, even the cakes out. Bake for approximately 10 minutes. Remove the cakes from the tray while still warm.

3 Make the butter cream. Cream the butter and sugar together until light and fluffy. Mix the remaining ingredients in a saucepan. Simmer slowly, beating constantly, until the cream has thickened. Do not allow it to boil. Set aside to cool. Stir in the butter and sugar mixture.

4 Spread the cream over the flat side of the cold cake bases. Keep in the refrigerator until the cream has set.

5 Melt the chocolate in a heatproof bowl over a pan of hot, but not boiling, water. Do not overheat or it will loose colour and gloss. It will be more workable if it is mixed with ½ tsp butter.

6 Dip the ratafias into the melted chocolate and set aside to harden. The chocolate can also be applied with a knife or brush.

CHOCOLATE RATAFIAS 336

To drink
coffee

LEVEL OF DIFFICULTY
fairly easy

PREPARATION TIME
1 hr

PREPARE IN ADVANCE
yes

CHOCOLATE TRUFFLES

Makes approximately 30

200 g/7 oz dark chocolate
1 tbsp butter
½ tbsp crème fraîche
1 tbsp strongly brewed coffee
90 g/3¼ oz icing sugar
1-3 tsp brandy or liqueur (optional)

Garnish:
100 g/3½ oz dark chocolate
40 g/1½ oz sifted cocoa powder

1 Melt the chocolate together with the butter in a heatproof bowl placed over a saucepan of hot, but not boiling water.

2 Mix the melted chocolate mixture, crème fraîche, coffee, icing sugar and liqueur, if using. Stir thoroughly and transfer the mixture to the refrigerator for 30 minutes until it has thickened and is workable.

3 Line a tray with greaseproof paper. Roll the mixture into small balls. Put them on the tray and stick each one with a cocktail stick. Put the tray in the refrigerator for approximately 2 hours.

4 To make the garnish, melt the chocolate. Coat the balls with a layer of melted chocolate, holding them by the cocktail sticks, and sift the cocoa powder over them to form a fairly thick covering.

5 Allow to set. Remove the cocktail sticks and keep in the refrigerator.

TO DRINK
coffee

LEVEL OF DIFFICULTY
easy

PREPARATION TIME
4 hrs including setting

PREPARE IN ADVANCE
yes

CHOCOLATE CAKE À LA VARENNE

Serves 6-8

100 ml/3½ fl oz strong coffee
250 g/8¾ oz dark cooking chocolate
250 g/8¾ oz unsalted butter
40 g/1½ oz castor sugar
4 eggs

Serve with:
whipped cream

1 Preheat the oven to 170° C/325° F, gas mark 3. Line a springform pan, approximately 20 cm/8 inches in diameter, with foil.

2 Pour the coffee into a heatproof bowl and set over a pan of hot, but not boiling water. Break the chocolate into pieces and add to the coffee. Stir until the chocolate has melted.

3 Add the butter and sugar alternately, a little at a time, stirring constantly, until the mixture is thoroughly combined.

4 Remove the bowl from the heat. Beat the eggs and stir them into the chocolate mixture.

5 Pour the mixture into the prepared pan and bake for approximately 1 hour. It will rise, then sink down and the top will become crispy. The cake should be a little sticky inside. Allow to cool and then put the cake, still in its pan, into the refrigerator until it has set.

6 Turn the cake out and serve with very lightly whipped cream.

CHOCOLATE CAKE À LA VARENNE 338

TO DRINK
sweet white wine or coffee

LEVEL OF DIFFICULTY
medium difficult

PREPARATION TIME
$1\frac{1}{2}$ hrs + setting time

PREPARE IN ADVANCE
yes

BLUEBERRY CAKE

Serves 4-6

Base:
200 g/7 oz almond paste
100 g/3½ oz + 1 tsp butter, softened
3 eggs, lightly beaten
60 g/2 oz breadcrumbs

Filling:
300 ml/10 fl oz whipping cream
350 g/12 oz blueberries

Glaze and garnish:
3 gelatine leaves
1 tbsp white sugar
200 ml/7 fl oz water
juice of ½ lemon
toasted, flaked almonds

1 Roughly grate the almond paste. Preheat the oven to 170° C/325° F, gas mark 3. Grease an ovenproof dish, 20 cm/8 inches in diameter, with 1 tsp of the butter.

2 Mix the almond paste, the remaining butter and the eggs to form a smooth batter. Pour the mixture into the prepared dish and cover with a layer of breadcrumbs. Bake the cake for 30-40 minutes. Test with a skewer.

3 Allow the cake to cool. Whip the cream stiffly and spread over the top and edges of the cake. Arrange the blueberries on top and put the cake in the refrigerator.

4 Soak the gelatine leaves in cold water for 10 minutes. Boil the sugar and water, stirring until the sugar has dissolved. Add the squeezed gelatine leaves and allow to melt. Add the lemon juice. Let the jelly cool down until slightly thickened. Spoon the jelly on top of the blueberries and allow to set on top of the cake. Sprinkle chopped or flaked almonds all around the edges of the cake.

TO DRINK
sweet white wine or white port

LEVEL OF DIFFICULTY
medium difficult

PREPARATION TIME
1 hr + setting time

PREPARE IN ADVANCE
yes

FILLED CONES

10-12 cones

2 tsp butter
90 g/3¼ oz + 1 tbsp flour
2 eggs
90 g/3¼ oz icing sugar, sifted

Filling:
300 ml/10 fl oz whipping cream
jam or lightly sugared berries

1 Preheat the oven to 200°C/400°F, gas mark 6. Grease 2 baking sheets with the butter and sprinkle them well with 1 tbsp of the flour. Mark 15 cm/6 inch diameter circles.

2 Lightly beat together the egg and sugar and mix in the remaining flour. Spread the mixture thinly over the marked-out circles on the baking sheets.

3 Bake in the middle of the oven until golden brown, about 3-4 minutes. Lift them carefully from the tray and make them into cones by shaping them round tall drinking glasses or Champagne flutes. If any of them sets before they have been made into cones, reheat in the oven for a couple of seconds to soften them. Allow to cool on the glasses so that they set in shape and then remove.

4 Whip the cream and mix in lightly sugared berries or jam to taste.

5 Fill the cones just before serving. Arrange them in a serving bowl and garnish with whole berries or few green leaves.

LEVEL OF DIFFICULTY
medium difficult

PREPARATION TIME
1 hr

PREPARE IN ADVANCE:
partly

CHOCOLATE CAKE

Serves 8

200 g/7 oz butter, softened
60 g/2 oz castor sugar
300 g/10½ oz flour
50 g/1¾ chocolate, melted

Filling:
3 egg yolks
60 g/2 oz castor sugar
1 tbsp flour
100 g/3½ oz chopped chocolate
200 ml/7 fl oz milk
100 ml/3½ fl oz whipping cream
3 tsp brandy (optional)

Icing:
100 g/3½ oz chocolate, broken into pieces
90 g/3¼ oz icing sugar
100 ml/3½ fl oz water

Garnish:
blanched almonds

1 Work the butter, sugar, flour and chocolate together to form a paste. Wrap and reserve.

2 Preheat the oven to 200° C/ 400° F, gas mark 6. Mark three circles, 23 cm/9 inches in diameter on greaseproof paper on a baking sheet. Divide the mixture into three equal quantities. Roll each to form a circle 23 cm/9 inches in diameter. Trim the edges.

3 Bake in the middle of the oven for 6-7 minutes. Cool on the paper.

4 Put all the filling ingredients, except the cream and brandy, in a pan. Simmer until thickened. Put the saucepan into cold water, stirring occasionally as the mixture cools. Whip the cream and stir into the mixture. Add the brandy, if using.

5 Spread half the filling on one layer of cake, place the second layer on top, spread with the remaining filling and top with the third cake layer.

6 Make the icing. Boil the water, sugar and chocolate, stirring constantly, until thickened, smooth and shiny. Test by putting a tiny bit into cold water; it should make a small ball. Allow to cool.

7 Spread the icing over the top of the cake and garnish with the blanched almonds. Keep in the refrigerator until serving.

TO DRINK:
sweet white wine or coffee

LEVEL OF DIFFICULTY
medium difficult

PREPARATION TIME
1 hr

PREPARE IN ADVANCE
yes

ALMOND CAKE WITH FRUIT

Serves 6-8

400 g/14 oz almond paste
2 egg whites
50 g/1¾ oz icing sugar
1 tsp melted butter

Garnish:
3 gelatine leaves
4 kiwi fruit
1 small can sliced pineapple in juice
1 small can peach halves
a few cocktail cherries

1 Preheat the oven to 200° C/400° F, gas mark 6. Grate the almond paste. Add the egg whites and icing sugar. Mix thoroughly until the consistency is smooth and even.

2 Draw a circle, 28 cm/11 inches in diameter, on a sheet of greaseproof paper. Brush the inside of the circle with melted butter. Spread half the almond mixture over it, without quite reaching the edges.

3 Put the rest of the almond mixture into a forcing bag and pipe the mixture straight across the circle four times, making 8 equal-sized triangles. Pipe the rest of the mixture around the edges, several times if there is enough.

4 Bake in the middle of the oven for 12-15 minutes or until the cake is golden. Set aside for 5 minutes before lifting from the paper, then leave to cool.

5 Soak the gelatine leaves in cold water for 10 minutes. Drain the canned fruits, reserving 200 ml/7 fl oz of the juice. Squeeze out the gelatine and melt in a pan with a small quantity of warm fruit juice. Stir into the remaining fruit juice and put into the refrigerator until it has started to thicken.

6 Peel and slice the kiwi fruit. Cut the pineapple into pieces. Cut the peach halves into quarters. Arrange the fruits alternately in the 8 triangles.

7 Glaze the fruit with the jelly in layers, allowing each layer to set before glazing another. Keep in the refrigerator until ready to serve. The cake base can be made in advance and can also be frozen.

ALMOND CAKE WITH FRUIT 342

TO DRINK
sweet white wine, preferably Sauternes

LEVEL OF DIFFICULTY
medium difficult

PREPARATION TIME
1 hr + setting time

PREPARE IN ADVANCE
yes

MARIA'S CREAM PUFFS

Makes 15

15 choux puffs - see recipe 349

Pastry:
120 g/4½ oz flour
1½ tbsp white sugar
75 g/2½ oz butter

Filling:
2 egg yolks
3 tsp castor sugar
3 tsp cornflour
300 ml/10 fl oz single cream
3 tsp vanilla sugar
100 ml/3½ fl oz whipping cream

Garnish:
icing sugar

1 Work all the ingredients for the pastry together to form a dough and set aside in the refrigerator to rest for 1 hour. Preheat the oven to 200° C/400° F, gas mark 6. Line a baking sheet with greaseproof paper.

2 Make the choux paste. Shape into balls and place on the prepared baking sheet. Do not put them too close together.

3 Roll out the pastry dough to 3 mm/⅛ inch thick and cut out circles with a 6 cm/2½ inch diameter cutter. Place one on each of the choux balls.

4 Bake in the bottom of the oven for 20-30 minutes until the choux puffs are pale gold and feel light.. Do not open the oven for the first 10 minutes. Allow to cool.

5 To make the filling, mix the egg yolks, sugar, cornflour and single cream in a saucepan. Simmer, beating constantly, until the cream has thickened. Allow to cool. Add the vanilla sugar. Beat the whipping cream and fold it into the mixture.

6 Cut a small opening in the base of the puffs and fill with the cream mixture. Close the opening and turn the puffs the right way up. Sprinkle with icing sugar.

Variations:
The puffs can also be filled with whipped cream or whipped cream mixed with puréed raspberries.

TO DRINK
sweet white wine, white or ruby port or coffee

LEVEL OF DIFFICULTY
medium to difficult

PREPARATION TIME
1 hour +resting time

PREPARE IN ADVANCE
yes

MERINGUE PYRAMID

Serves 4

16-20 small meringues (see recipe 397)
200 ml/7 fl oz whipping cream

Sauce:
40 g/1½ oz cocoa powder
85 g/3 oz castor sugar
½ tsp vanilla essence
100 ml/3½ fl oz water

1 Buy ready-made meringues or make them according to recipe 397; pipe 16-20 meringues on baking sheets and bake.

2 Make the sauce. Mix together the cocoa powder, sugar and vanilla essence in a saucepan. Add the water, stirring constantly. Boil until the sauce has thickened, beating constantly. Beat around the edges and base to ensure the sauce does not burn. Set aside to cool, stirring occasionally.

3 Whip the cream until frothy but not stiff.

4 Put some cream on a serving dish and make a pyramid by adding alternate layers of meringue and cream. Coil the chocolate sauce over the top.

MERINGUE PYRAMID 344

TO DRINK
sweet white wine

LEVEL OF DIFFICULTY
easy

PREPARATION TIME
30 mins

PREPARE IN ADVANCE
partly

PAVLOVA

Serves 8

5 egg whites
210 g/7½ oz castor sugar
2 drops vinegar spirit (optional - this is a highly concentrated vinegar used in cooking, pickling and making sweets)

Filling:
2 egg yolks
120 g/4¼ oz icing sugar
2 tsp vanilla sugar
400 ml/14 fl oz whipping cream

Garnish:
450 g/1 lb raspberries or other seasonal fruit
lemon balm leaves

1 Preheat the oven to 130° C/ 250° F, gas mark ½. Line a baking sheet with greaseproof paper. Beat the egg whites until stiff and frothy. Add the sugar and vinegar spirit, if using, and continue beating until the mixture is shiny and very stiff.

2 Spread some of this mixture to make a disc, 22 cm/9 inches in diameter, on the prepared baking sheet. Pipe the remaining mixture around the edge of the disc to make a basket.

3 Bake in the bottom of the oven for approximately 1 hour. Let the meringue cool down in the oven with the heat turned off or at room temperature.

4 Make the filling. Beat the egg yolks and icing sugar until fluffy. Add the vanilla sugar. Whip the cream and mix with the egg mixture.

5 Fill the cake with the vanilla cream just before serving. Garnish with the fruit and leaves.

PAVLOVA 345

To drink
white port

LEVEL OF DIFFICULTY medium difficult
PREPARATION TIME 1 - 1½ hrs
PREPARE IN ADVANCE yes

MERINGUE CAKE WITH CHOCOLATE MOUSSE

Serves 6

Base:
2 tsp butter
1 tbsp flour
1 egg white
85 g/3 oz castor sugar

Filling:
150 g/5¼ oz dark cooking chocolate
1 tbsp strong coffee
1 tsp brandy
1 egg yolk
300 ml/10 fl oz whipping cream

Garnish:
melted chocolate
whipped cream (optional)

1 Preheat the oven to 150° C/300° F, gas mark 2. Draw two circles 20 cm/8 inches in diameter on greaseproof paper. Grease the insides of the circles with the butter and sprinkle over the flour.

2 Beat the egg white very stiffly. Mix in the sugar and beat for a few more minutes. Spread the meringue mixture inside the circles. Bake near the bottom of the oven until the meringues feel firm. Remove from the paper and allow to cool on a wire rack.

3 Break the chocolate into pieces and melt together with the coffee in a saucepan. Remove from the heat and beat in the brandy and egg yolk. Set aside to cool.

4 Whip the cream fairly stiffly. Stir it into the chocolate mixture.

5 Put the meringue base in a loose-bottomed tin. Spread with half the chocolate mousse. Place the second meringue on top and cover with the rest of the chocolate mousse. Place in the freezer for 4-5 hours or overnight.

6 Remove the cake from the freezer 30 minutes before serving. Place the cake on a serving plate and coil the melted chocolate on top; garnish with piped whipped cream, if using.

MERINGUE CAKE WITH CHOCOLATE MOUSSE 346

To drink
coffee or sweet white wine

LEVEL OF DIFFICULTY
fairly easy

PREPARATION TIME
1 + freezing time

PREPARE IN ADVANCE
yes

NEAPOLITAN SLICE

8-10 slices

3 sheets frozen puff pastry, thawed

Filling:
250 ml/9 fl oz custard cream (see recipe 435)
100 ml/3½ fl oz whipping cream
150-200 ml/5¼-7 fl oz apple sauce or purée

Garnish:
½-1 tbsp redcurrant jelly, melted
60 g/2 oz icing sugar
3 tsp water

1 Roll out the puff pastry to form 3 rectangles 10 x 40 cm/ 4 x 16 inches. Put them on damp baking sheets, prick with a fork and set aside to rest. Preheat the oven to 250° C/ 500° F, gas mark 10.

2 Bake the pastry rectangles for approximately 10 minutes. Set aside to cool.

3 Make the vanilla cream. Allow to cool. Whip the cream and fold it into the vanilla cream.

4 Spread the apple sauce or purée over one of the pastry rectangles, add the next rectangle and spread with vanilla sauce. Add the last rectangle with the flat side up. Spread with melted jelly. Mix the icing sugar and water together and spread the icing on top of the jelly. Cut into slices with a very sharp knife.

NEAPOLITAN SLICE 347

To drink
sweet white wine or coffee

LEVEL OF DIFFICULTY fairly easy
PREPARATION TIME 1 hr
PREPARE IN ADVANCE yes

RICH NUTCAKE

Serves 8-10

Bases:
50 g/7¾ oz blanched almonds
50 g/7¾ oz hazelnuts
2 egg whites
40 g/1½ oz castor sugar
3 tsp flour

Filling:
200 ml/7 fl oz whipping cream
200 ml/7 fl oz crème fraîche
200 g/7 oz soft chocolate nougat
250 g/9 oz raspberries

Garnish:
raspberries
icing sugar

1 Preheat the oven to 130° C/250° F, gas mark ½. Chop the almonds and hazelnuts into fine pieces. Roast in the oven until golden.

2 Increase the oven temperature to 170° C/325° F, gas mark 3. Beat the egg whites until they form stiff peaks. Mix together the almonds, hazelnuts, sugar and flour. Fold in the egg whites.

3 You will require a loose-based cake tin, approximately 24 cm/10 inches in diameter. Draw 2 circles, the same size as the cake tin, on greaseproof paper. Spread the mixture evenly in the circles. Bake in the oven until the bases are brittle and have coloured slightly. Remove from the paper and set aside to cool.

4 Whip the cream. Whip the crème fraîche. Mix them together. Roughly grate the chocolate nougat and add it carefully to the cream mixture, together with the raspberries.

5 Place one of the nut circles in the cake tin. Spread the raspberry and nougat cream in a smooth layer on top and cover with the second nut circle. Keep in the refrigerator for a minimum of 3 hours before serving.

6 Garnish with raspberries and sprinkle icing sugar on top.

Variations:
The raspberries can be replaced with strawberries, blueberries or stoned cherries

RICH NUTCAKE 348

TO DRINK
sweet white wine

LEVEL OF DIFFICULTY
fairly easy

PREPARATION TIME
1 hr + setting time

PREPARE IN ADVANCE:
yes

PETITS CHOUX RING

Serves 6-8

Choux paste:
200 ml/7 fl oz water
100 g/3½ oz + 1 tsp butter
150 g/5¼ oz flour
4 eggs, lightly beaten

Cream:
2 eggs
2 tsp cornflour
1-2 tbsp castor sugar
500 ml/18 fl oz single or whipping cream
¼ tsp vanilla sugar

Filling:
450 g/1 lb strawberries, hulled and sliced

Icing:
120 g/4¼ oz icing sugar
¾-1 tbsp red fruit squash or water coloured with 2 drops of food colouring (optional)

1 To make the choux paste, bring the water and 100 g/3½ oz of the butter to the boil. Tip in the flour. Stir vigorously with a wooden spoon, until the mixture comes away from the sides of the pan. Remove from the heat. Stir for 2-3 more minutes. Allow to cool. Beat in 1 egg at a time.

2 Preheat the oven to 200° C/ 400° F, gas mark 6. Grease a baking sheet with the remaining butter and mark a circle, 20 cm/8 inches in diameter. Pipe small balls of the paste around the circle. Bake in the bottom of the oven for 30 minutes until the cake is a golden brown and feels dry and light.

3 Make the cream. Beat all the ingredients, except the vanilla sugar, in a saucepan. Simmer, beating vigorously, until it has turned thick and shiny. Allow to cool, stirring occasionally. Add vanilla sugar to taste.

4 Slice the choux ring in half to make a top and base. Sandwich the cream and strawberries between them.

5 Make the icing with icing sugar and the fruit squash or coloured water. Brush the icing over the top of the ring.

TO DRINK:
Sauternes

LEVEL OF DIFFICULTY medium difficult
PREPARATION TIME 1 hr
PREPARE IN ADVANCE yes

PINOCCHIO CAKE

Serves 6

Cake base:
3 egg yolks
85 g/3 oz castor sugar
40 ml/1½ fl oz single cream
2 tsp baking powder
90 g/3¼ flour
150 ml/5¼ fl oz melted butter

Meringue:
3 egg whites
170 g/6 oz castor sugar
1 tsp vanilla sugar
flaked almonds

Filling:
300 ml/10 fl oz whipping cream
230 g/8 oz raspberries, puréed

1 Preheat the oven to 200° C/400° F, gas mark 6. Beat the egg yolks and sugar until light and fluffy. Sift over the flour and baking powder and add the cream and melted butter. Mix until smooth.

2 Beat the egg whites until they form stiff peaks. Add the sugar and vanilla sugar and continue beating until stiff.

3 Line a cake or loaf tin with greaseproof paper. Pour in the sponge cake mixture and smooth the top. Spread the meringue mixture on top and sprinkle with flaked almonds.

4 Bake for 5 minutes. Lower the oven temperature to 170° C/325° F, gas mark 3. Bake for a further 20-30 minutes.

5 Allow the cake to cool. Whip the cream and mix with the raspberry purée. Slice the cake in half and cover one half with the cream and raspberry filling. Place the other slice on top.

Variations:
Other fruit purées or finely chopped fruit may be used instead of raspberries for the filling. Alternatively, the cake can be filled with custard cream (see recipe 435) instead of raspberry cream.

TO DRINK
sweet white wine, preferably Sauternes

LEVEL OF DIFFICULTY
medium difficult

PREPARATION TIME
1 hr

PREPARE IN ADVANCE
yes

PROFITEROLES WITH TOFFEE SAUCE

Serves 8-10

Choux paste:
200 ml/7 fl oz water
100 g/3½ oz + 1 tsp butter
150 g/3¼ oz plain flour
4 eggs

Filling:
vanilla ice cream

Toffee sauce:
400 ml/14 fl oz whipping cream
340 g/12 oz castor sugar
3 tsp cocoa powder
2 tbsp golden syrup
1 tbsp butter
1 tbsp vanilla sugar

1 Preheat the oven to 200° C/400° F, gas mark 6. Grease a baking sheet with 1 tsp of the butter. Make the choux dough as described in recipe 349. Put it into a forcing bag and pipe 30-40 small bun shapes on the prepared baking sheet. Bake in the middle of the oven for approximately 10 minutes or until the choux pastry has risen to more than double its size and is golden.

2 Make the sauce. Mix the cream, sugar, cocoa and syrup in a pan. Bring to the boil, stirring, then lower the heat, continue stirring and simmer for 20-30 minutes or until the sauce is thick and golden brown. Remove the saucepan from the heat. Stir in the butter and add vanilla sugar to taste. Stir occasionally while the sauce cools.

3 Cut a split in the profiteroles and fill each with vanilla ice cream. Stack them on a serving plate in a pyramid shape. Pour over the sauce. If there is any sauce left over, serve separately.

TO DRINK
sweet white wine

LEVEL OF DIFFICULTY
medium difficult

PREPARATION TIME
1 hour

PREPARE IN ADVANCE
yes

PEAR TARTLETS

Serves 6

Dough:
180 g/6½ oz flour
30 g/1 oz icing sugar
150 g/5¼ oz butter, chilled
1 egg yolk

Filling:
1 x 450 g/16 oz can pears in juice
300-400 ml/10-14 fl oz custard cream (see recipe 435)

Glaze:
2 gelatine leaves
lemon juice

1 First, make the pastry. Mix together the flour, icing sugar and butter until the mixture resembles fine breadcrumbs. Add the egg yolk and work quickly together to form a dough. Set aside in the refrigerator to rest for 1 hour.

2 Make the custard and allow to cool.

3 Roll out the dough and line 6 small fluted tart tins with removable bases. Prick the bases with a fork. Chill for 15-30 minutes. Preheat the oven to 200° C/400° F, gas mark 6.

4 Bake blind for 15-20 minutes or until golden. Set aside to cool.

5 Strain the pears and reserve 150 ml/5 fl oz of the juice. Cut the pears into thin quarters.

6 Soak the gelatine leaves in cold water for approximately 10 minutes. Squeeze out the water and melt the leaves in a little pear juice. Add lemon juice to taste. Keep in the refrigerator until the glaze starts to thicken.

7 Spread the custard over the base of the pastry moulds. Decorate with pear quarters and cover with the glaze. Place in the refrigerator until the glaze has set.

PEAR TARTLETS 352

TO DRINK
sweet white wine

LEVEL OF DIFFICULTY
fairly easy

PREPARATION TIME
1 hr + resting + setting time

PREPARE IN ADVANCE
yes

TOFFEE CREAM CAKE

Serves 6-8

Base:
1 tsp butter
2 tsp flour
4 egg whites
170 g/6 oz castor sugar
170 g/6 oz ground almonds

Toffee cream:
200 ml/7 fl oz whipping cream
85 g/3 oz castor sugar
50 ml/2 fl oz golden syrup
2 tsp butter
1 tsp vanilla sugar

Garnish:
250 ml/8½ fl oz whipping cream
½-1 tbsp cocoa powder

1 Preheat the oven to 170° C/325° F, gas mark 3. Using a plate as a template, draw a circle on greaseproof paper. Grease the circle with the butter, sprinkle over the flour and place the paper on a baking sheet.

2 Beat the egg whites until they form stiff peaks. Add the sugar, a little at a time, beating constantly. Fold in the almonds. Spread the mixture on the circle of greaseproof paper. Bake for 20-25 minutes. Set aside to cool.

3 Mix the sugar, syrup and cream in a heavy-based saucepan. Simmer over low heat, stirring constantly, until the cream has thickened. Remove from the heat and beat in the butter. Allow the sauce to cool almost completely and add the vanilla sugar. Spread the sauce over the top of the cake.

4 Beat the cream until stiff and spread over the top of the toffee cream. Sprinkle over the cocoa powder.

5 Keep the cake cold until ready to serve.

TOFFEE CREAM CAKE 353

TO DRINK
coffee or sweet white wine

LEVEL OF DIFFICULTY easy
PREPARATION TIME 1 hr
PREPARE IN ADVANCE yes

WILD STRAWBERRY TARTLETS

Makes 6-8

Dough:
90 g/3¼ oz flour
1 tbsp castor sugar
50 g/1¾ oz butter, chilled
3 tsp ice cold water

Filling:
150-200 ml/5-7 fl oz custard, cream (see recipe 435)
300 g/10 oz wild strawberries,
100 ml/3½ fl oz redcurrant jelly

1 Make the dough. Mix together the flour, sugar and butter until the mixture resembles fine breadcrumbs. Add the water and work the mixture together quickly. Set aside in the refrigerator to rest for 30 minutes.

2 Make the custard as in recipe 435. Preheat the oven to 200° C/400° F, gas mark 6.

3 Divide the dough into 6 or 8 equal portions, depending on the size of the tartlet tins. With floured fingers, press the dough into the tins or roll it out and line the tins.

4 Bake for 12-15 minutes. Set aside to cool.

5 Spoon the custard into the base of the moulds. Arrange the wild strawberries on top.

6 Melt the jelly in a pan over low heat. Allow to thicken slightly. Spoon it over the strawberries and allow to set.

Variation:
The tarts can be filled with other berries, such as raspberries, blackberries or blueberries.

WILD STRAWBERRY TARTLETS 354

To drink
sweet white wine

LEVEL OF DIFFICULTY
easy

PREPARATION TIME
1 hr +setting + resting time

PREPARE IN ADVANCE
yes

HAWAIIAN SANDWICH

Serves 4

2 sheets frozen puff pastry, partially thawed
1 egg, beaten
castor sugar

Filling:
½ pineapple
2 kiwi fruit
1 passion fruit
1 ripe mango
3 egg yolks
100 ml/3½ fl oz whipping cream
2 tsp plain flour

1 Preheat the oven to 200° C/ 400° F, gas mark 6. Line a baking sheet with greaseproof paper. Cut the pastry sheets in half and place them on the prepared baking sheet. Make a pattern of squares or diamonds with the back of a knife. Brush with the beaten egg and sprinkle over a little sugar.

2 Bake in the bottom of the oven for approximately 20 minutes until the pastry has puffed up and is golden. Cut the pastries in half lengthwise to make 4 bases and 4 tops.

3 Peel the pineapple and the kiwi fruit. Cut the passion fruit in half. Cut the mango with a sharp knife on both sides of the flat stone; cut the fruit in pieces and remove the peel, and loosen the fruit from around the stone.

4 Make a purée, in the food processor or food mill of 1 kiwi fruit, ¼ pineapple, ½ mango and the pulp of the passion fruit. Dice the remaining fruit. Strain the fruit purée, pour into a pan and bring to the boil.

5 Meanwhile, mix together the egg yolks, sugar and flour. Beat in the warm fruit purée. Transfer to a pan and simmer for 10 minutes, beating constantly. Set aside to cool.

6 Whip the cream and mix into the cold fruit purée mixture. Stir in the diced fruit.

7 Put the baked bases on individual serving plates. Add the fruit cream and cover with the square pastry tops.

8 Sprinkle the top with icing sugar, if desired, and serve immediately.

HAWAIIAN SANDWICH 355

TO DRINK
sweet white wine, semi-sweet Champagne

LEVEL OF DIFFICULTY
medium difficult

PREPARATION TIME
1 hr

PREPARE IN ADVANCE
yes

SOUFFLÉ CAKE

Serves 6-8

1 tbsp butter
6 egg whites
160 g/5½ oz castor sugar
35 g/1¼ oz cocoa

Garnish:
300 ml/10 fl oz whipping cream
3 tsp castor sugar
3 tsp rum
chocolate chips

1 Preheat the oven to its lowest setting. Grease a 2 litre/3½ pint loose-bottomed cake tin with the butter. Beat the egg whites to form stiff peaks. Mix in half the sugar. Beat until the mixture is stiff and shiny. Add the rest of the sugar and cocoa and beat a further 2 minutes.

2 Pour the mixture into the prepared tin. Bake for approximately 40 minutes. The cake will rise and then sink down again.

3 Let the cake cool in the tin. Whip the cream with sugar and rum to taste. Spread over the top of the cake while it is still in the tin and sprinkle with chocolate chips. Keep in the refrigerator overnight.

4 1 hour before serving, put the cake in the freezer. Serve directly from the freezer. Loosen the cake from the edges of the tin with a sharp knife and put on a serving plate.

SOUFFLÉ CAKE 356

TO DRINK:
sweet white wine

LEVEL OF DIFFICULTY
medium difficult

PREPARATION TIME
1 hr + setting + freezing time

PREPARE IN ADVANCE:
yes

GOLDEN CAKE

Serves 10-12

Dough:
150 g/5 oz flour
40 g/1½ castor sugar
½ tsp salt
1 tbsp vanilla sugar
40 g/1½ oz ground almonds
100 g/3½ oz butter
1 egg yolk

Filling:
3 eggs
500 g/1 lb curd cheese
grated rind of 1 lemon
210 g/7½ oz icing sugar
200 ml/7 fl oz crème fraîche
60 g/2 oz flour

Serve with:
raspberry or strawberry purée

1 Make the dough. Mix together all the ingredients, except the egg yolk, until the mixture resembles fine breadcrumbs. Add the egg yolk and quickly work into the dough. Set aside in the refrigerator to rest for at least 1 hour.

2 Preheat the oven to 200° C/ 400° F, gas mark 6. Roll out the dough and use to line a high-sided, loose-bottomed cake tin. Prick the base with a fork. Bake the dough shell blind for 10 minutes.

3 Make the filling. Separate the eggs. Press the curd cheese through a sieve.

4 Mix together all the ingredients, except the egg whites. Beat the egg whites to form stiff peaks and fold them into the mixture. Pour the filling into the dough shell.

5 Bake for approximately 40-50 minutes, until the mixture feels firm. Cover with foil if the top starts to brown before the filling has cooked.

6 Serve cold with a purée of strawberries or raspberries.

TO DRINK:
sweet white wine or white port

LEVEL OF DIFFICULTY medium difficult
PREPARATION TIME 1½ hrs + resting time
PREPARE IN ADVANCE yes

WALNUT CAKE WITH COFFEE CREAM

Serves 8-10

2 tsp butter
2 tsp flour

Base:
100 g/3½ oz walnuts
130 g/4½ oz castor sugar
4 egg whites

Coffee cream topping:
3 egg yolks
3 tbsp icing sugar
100 ml/4 fl oz strong coffee
75 g/2¾ oz dark chocolate, melted
50 ml/2 fl oz Madeira or port
300 ml/10 fl oz whipping cream

Garnish:
walnut halves
crystallized flowers, e.g. lilac, violets, mimosa

1 Preheat the oven to 170° C/ 325° F, gas mark 3. Grease and flour a round cake tin. Chop half the walnuts and grind the remainder. Mix with the sugar. Whisk the egg whites until they form stiff peaks and fold into the nut and sugar mixture. Turn into the prepared tin and bake for 15-20 minutes. Turn the cake on to a rack and allow to cool.

2 Make the coffee cream. Whisk the egg yolks and sugar in a heatproof bowl until light and creamy. Add the coffee and place the bowl over a pan of hot water. Beat the mixture until it has thickened. Beat in the chocolate. Stir in the Madeira or port. Allow to cool, stirring occasionally.

3 Whip the cream and mix it into the cold coffee mixture. Spread the cream over the cake. Put the cake in the freezer for 2 hours.

4 Take the cake out of the freezer shortly before serving and garnish with walnuts and crystallized flowers.

WALNUT CAKE WITH COFFEE CREAM 358

TO DRINK
coffee or coffee liqueur

LEVEL OF DIFFICULTY
fairly easy

PREPARATION TIME
1 hr + time in the freezer

PREPARE IN ADVANCE
yes

ZULEIKA CAKE

10-12 slices

2 tsp butter
2 tbsp fresh breadcrumbs

Base:
150 g/5 oz ground almonds
210 g/7 oz castor sugar
6 egg whites

Icing:
6 egg yolks
300 ml/10 fl oz whipping cream
130 g/4½ oz castor sugar
75 g/2½ oz butter

Garnish:
flaked roasted almonds

1 Grease a 28-cm/11-inch cake tin with a removable base with 2 tsp butter. Coat with the breadcrumbs. Preheat the oven to 200° C/400° F, gas mark 4. Mix the almonds with the sugar.

2 Beat the egg whites to form stiff peaks. Fold into the almond mixture. Pour the mixture into the prepared cake tin. Bake for 18-20 minutes in the bottom of the oven.

3 Mix all the ingredients for the icing in a saucepan. Simmer slowly over low heat until the cream has thickened. Add a little boiling water if the cream starts to separate or curdle.

4 Set aside to cool. Spread or pipe the cream on top of the cake base. Let the cake cool before serving, preferably overnight.

Variations:
Serve the cake with fruit salad made with fresh strawberries, pineapple pieces and sliced kiwi fruit.

TO DRINK
sweet white wine or white port

LEVEL OF DIFFICULTY	easy
PREPARATION TIME	1 hr
PREPARE IN ADVANCE	yes

APPLE DUMPLINGS WITH ALMONDS

Serves 4

4 medium-sized cooking apples
4 tbsp brandy
50 g/2 oz almonds, finely chopped
100 g/3½ oz almond paste
1 egg, beaten

Dough:
240 g/8½ oz flour
40 g/1½ oz castor sugar
150 g/5¼ oz butter, softened
1 small egg

Serve with:
lightly whipped cream, custard (see recipe 434) or ice cream

1 Line a baking sheet with greaseproof paper. Make the dough. Put all the dough ingredients into a bowl and work together into a smooth dough. Set aside in the refrigerator to rest for at least 1 hour.

2 Peel and core the apples. Prick the apples with a cocktail stick or needle. Brush with a little of the brandy and roll in the chopped almonds.

3 Grate the almond paste, add the remaining brandy and mix together until smooth.

4 Preheat the oven to 200° C/ 400° F, gas mark 6. Roll out the dough to form a square approximately 30 x 30 cm/ 12 x 12 inches. Cut the square into 4 pieces. Put one apple on each square. Fill the centres with the almond paste mixture. Brush the dough edges with beaten egg. Fold the four corners over the apples and pinch the edges together to form a parcel. Put the apple dumplings on the prepared baking sheet, brush with egg and sprinkle with the remaining chopped almonds. Bake for 20-25 minutes. Test with a fork or skewer to see if the apples are fully cooked; hard apples will take longer. Cover the dumplings with foil if they get too brown during baking.

APPLE DUMPLINGS WITH ALMONDS 360

TO DRINK
Sweet white wine or Madeira

LEVEL OF DIFFICULTY
fairly easy

PREPARATION TIME
1 hr + resting time

PREPARE IN ADVANCE
yes

CARAMEL CUSTARD

Serves 6

Glaze:
210 g/7½ oz castor sugar
3 tbsp boiling water

Custard:
600 ml/1 pint single cream
5 tsp castor sugar
4 eggs
1 egg yolk
3 blanched almonds, grated
1 tsp vanilla essence

Garnish:
a few blanched almonds, chopped

1 Glaze a 1-litre/1¾-pint mould. Put the sugar in a frying-pan and melt over low heat, stirring until an even light brown. Pour in the boiling water and stir until smooth. Pour instantly into a warm mould. Turn the mould around so the the caramel covers all the sides and base.

2 Preheat the oven to 170° C/ 325° F, gas mark 3. Bring the cream and sugar to the boil in the frying-pan that was used for the glazing mixture. Add the grated almonds and vanilla essence.

3 Beat the eggs and egg yolk together and pour on to the hot mixture, beating vigorously. Pour the mixture into the glazed mould. Cover with a lid or foil and secure the edges well.

4 Stand the mould in a roasting tin half filled with hot water and bake in the oven for approximately 45 minutes. Test with a skewer.

5 Allow the pudding to cool in the mould. Carefully turn out on to a serving dish and garnish with the chopped almonds.

To drink
sweet white wine or Madeira

LEVEL OF DIFFICULTY
medium difficult

PREPARATION TIME
1 hr

PREPARE IN ADVANCE
yes

CHARLOTTE RUSSE

Serves 8

4 gelatine leaves
3 eggs
4 tbsp castor sugar
300 ml/10 fl oz single cream
2 tbsp Cointreau or rum
250 ml/9 fl oz whipping cream
1 x 400 g/14 oz Swiss roll made with raspberry jam

1 Soak the gelatine leaves in cold water for 10 minutes to soften. Beat together the eggs and sugar until light and fluffy. Bring the single cream to the boil and pour into the egg mixture, beating constantly. Return the mixture to the pan and simmer over low heat until thickened. Put the saucepan into cold water and stir occasionally while the cream is cooling. Stir in the liqueur. Squeeze the gelatine leaves and melt over a low heat. Beat the gelatine into the cream. Whip the cream and add it to the mixture.

2 Line a 1.2-litre/2-pint plastic bowl or mould with clingfilm. Cut the Swiss roll into 1-cm/½-inch thick slices and arrange them as close together as possible all around the bowl or mould, ensuring they fit well at the base and edges.

3 Pour in the cold cream and place the pudding in the refrigerator until set.

4 Trim any edges that are higher than the filling. Loosen the pudding and invert on to a serving plate.

TO DRINK
sweet sherry

LEVEL OF DIFFICULTY
easy

PREPARATION TIME
1 hr + setting time

PREPARE IN ADVANCE
yes

HANNA'S FRENCH APPLE CAKE

Serves 6-8

6 cooking apples
75 ml/3 fl oz water
85 g/3 oz castor sugar

Dough:
100 g/3½ blanched almonds
100 g/3½ oz butter, softened
130 g/4½ oz castor sugar
2 eggs, separated
rind of ½ lemon, grated

Serve with:
custard (see recipe 434) or whipped cream

1 Peel the apples, cut into halves and remove the cores.

2 Bring the water and sugar to the boil. Add the apple pieces and simmer gently until soft. Set aside to cool.

3 Preheat the oven to 200° C/400° F, gas mark 6. Beat the butter and sugar until light and fluffy. Add the egg yolks, one at a time, then the almonds and lemon peel. Beat the egg whites until they form stiff peaks and fold carefully into the mixture.

4 Drain the apples and transfer to an ovenproof dish. Sprinkle over the almonds. Bake the apple cake for 15-20 minutes or until it is golden.

5 Serve the cake lukewarm or cold with custard or whipped cream.

HANNA'S FRENCH APPLE CAKE

TO DRINK:
ruby port

LEVEL OF DIFFICULTY
easy
PREPARATION TIME
1 hr
PREPARE IN ADVANCE
yes

CHEESECAKE

Serves 4

1 tsp butter
50 g/2 oz almonds
500 g/17½ oz curd cheese
1-2 tbsp castor sugar
2 eggs
4 tbsp plain flour
300 ml/10 fl oz milk

Serve with:
whole or puréed berries or jam

1 Lightly grease an ovenproof dish with the butter. Preheat the oven to 170° C/325° F, gas mark 3. Blanch and chop the almonds and mix them with the curd cheese and sugar.

2 Beat the eggs, flour and milk until smooth. Stir into the cheese mixture. Pour into the prepared dish and bake for 40-50 minutes until fully cooked.

3 Serve with fresh whole or puréed berries, or jam.

TO DRINK:
sweet white wine

LEVEL OF DIFFICULTY
easy

PREPARATION TIME
1 hr

PREPARE IN ADVANCE:
yes

PORTUGUESE ORANGE PUDDING

Serves 8

2 large oranges
8 eggs
castor sugar (the same weight as the eggs)

Glaze:
210 g/7½ oz castor sugar
3 tbsp boiling water

Garnish:
thin orange slices,
orange rind or small redcurrant bunches

Serve with:
whipped cream

1 First, glaze the dish or mould. Melt the sugar in a frying-pan over low heat, stirring constantly, until smooth and a light brown colour. Pour in the boiling water and stir until the glaze is smooth. Pour into a slightly warmed savarin mould or into small individual dishes. Turn the mould or dishes so that the mixture covers the base and sides evenly. Preheat the oven to 200° C/ 400° F, gas mark 6.

2 Grate the rind of both oranges and squeeze out the juice. Beat together the eggs and sugar. Add the grated orange rind and juice. Pour the mixture into the mould or dishes and cover with foil.

3 Place the mould or dishes in a roasting tin half filled with hot water and bake in the bottom of the oven for approximately 1 hour or until the pudding is cooked. Test with a knife. Allow to cool. Set aside in the refrigerator to set fully.

4 Invert on to a serving dish and garnish with thin orange slices and chopped orange rind or small bunches of redcurrants.

PORTUGUESE ORANGE PUDDING

To drink
sweet white wine

LEVEL OF DIFFICULTY fairly easy
PREPARATION TIME 1½ hrs + setting time
PREPARE IN ADVANCE yes

RIZ À L'IMPÉRATRICE

Serves 6-8

110 g/3¾ oz pudding rice
1¼ litres/2 pints milk
½ vanilla pod
60 g/2 oz caster sugar
4 gelatine leaves
2 tbsp warm water
300 ml/10 fl oz whipping cream

1 Rinse the rice and put into a saucepan with the milk. Cut the ½ vanilla pod into quarters; scrape the seeds into the pan and add the pieces of pod. Simmer for approximately 2 hours over very low heat until the rice is completely soft. Add more milk if necessary. Allow the mixture to cool. Remove the vanilla pod and stir in the sugar.

2 Soak the gelatine leaves in cold water for 10 minutes to soften. Melt them in 2 tbsp hot water. Mix the gelatine into the rice mixture.

3 Whip the cream until it forms stiff peaks and stir it into the rice mixture. Rinse a savarin mould or ring mould in cold water. Pour the rice mixture into the mould and place in the freezer for 3-4 hours or overnight.

4 Allow the dish or mould to stand at room temperature for approximately 20 minutes before serving. Turn out on to a serving dish and garnish as desired.

RIZ À L'IMPÉRATRICE 366

To drink
ruby port or sweet Madeira

LEVEL OF DIFFICULTY
easy

PREPARATION TIME
3 hrs + time in the freezer

PREPARE IN ADVANCE
yes

COFFEE CLOUD

Serves 6-8

200 ml/7 fl oz strong, cold coffee
50 ml/2 fl oz coffee liqueur, brandy or rum
4 eggs, separated
100 g/3½ oz sugar
400 g/14 oz curd cheese
2 tbsp crème fraîche
grated rind of 1 lemon
grated rind of 1 orange
20-24 ratafia biscuits
2-3 tbsp cocoa powder

1 Mix the coffee with the liqueur.

2 Beat the egg whites until they form stiff peaks. Beat the egg yolks with the sugar until light and foamy. Mix the cheese with the crème fraîche and stir in the beaten egg yolk mixture. Add the grated lemon and orange rind. Carefully fold in the egg whites.

3 Dip half the ratafias into the liqueur mixture, ensuring they are covered on both sides and arrange them in layers on the base of a serving dish. Cover with half of the cheese mixture. Dip the remaining ratafias in the liqueur mixture and arrange them on top. Spread the remaining cheese mixture over the top. Chill in the refrigerator for 2-3 hours or overnight.

4 Before serving, sprinkle with cocoa powder in an attractive pattern produced by sprinkling through a paper stencil or doyley.

TO DRINK
coffee liqueur or brandy

LEVEL OF DIFFICULTY
medium difficult

PREPARATION TIME
1 hr + setting time

PREPARE IN ADVANCE
yes

PINEAPPLE MOULD

Serves 6

300 ml/10 fl oz single cream
3 eggs, separated
200 ml/7 fl oz pineapple juice
1 tbsp cornflour
6 gelatine leaves
1 x 800 g/28 oz can sliced pineapple
300 ml/10 oz whipping cream

Garnish:
pineapple slices, halved, grapes, strawberries or other berries

1 Mix the single cream, egg yolks, cornflour and pineapple juice in a saucepan and simmer over low heat, beating until the mixture has thickened. Do not allow it to boil or it will curdle and separate. Set aside to cool.

2 Soak the gelatine leaves in cold water for 10 minutes to soften. Cut the pineapple slices into pieces, saving a few for the garnish.

3 Beat the whipping cream and set aside. Beat the egg whites until they form soft peaks. Strain the gelatine leaves and melt over low heat.

4 Stir the pineapple pieces and whipped cream into the egg yolk mixture. Add the melted gelatine in a fine stream and mix well. Fold in the egg whites.

5 Rinse a dish or mould with cold water. Pour in the mixture and chill in the refrigerator for at least 2-3 hours until firm.

6 Dip the dish in hot water and turn the pudding out on to a serving plate. Garnish with pineapple slices, grapes or strawberries.

PINEAPPLE MOULD 368

TO DRINK
sweet white wine

LEVEL OF DIFFICULTY
medium difficult

PREPARATION TIME
1 hr + setting time

PREPARE IN ADVANCE
yes

LEMON CHIFFON

Serves 6

6 gelatine leaves
3 eggs
85 g/3 oz castor sugar
300 ml/10 fl oz whipping cream
grated rind of 1 lemon
juice of ½-1 lemon

1 Soak the gelatine leaves in cold water for 10 minutes to soften.

2 Beat the egg yolks and sugar until light and fluffy. Beat the egg whites until foaming. Whip the cream.

3 Squeeze the gelatine leaves and melt them in a little water over low heat. Allow to cool slightly. Stir the gelatine in the egg yolk mixture. Stir in the lemon rind and juice. Mix in the whipped cream and fold in the egg whites. Rinse a dish or mould with cold water and pour in the mixture.

4 Place in the refrigerator for 2-3 hours until set. Loosen around the edges with a flat-bladed knife and turn out on to a serving plate. If the chiffon sticks, quickly dip the dish in warm water to loosen it from the mould. Garnish with fruit such as strawberries, grapes, or thin orange slices and whipped cream.

To drink
sweet white wine

LEVEL OF DIFFICULTY
easy

PREPARATION TIME
30 mins + setting time

PREPARE IN ADVANCE
yes

CHOCOLATE MOUSSE

Serves 6

150 g/5 oz dark cooking chocolate
3 tbsp brandy or fresh orange juice
1 tbsp instant coffee powder
1 egg yolk
1 tbsp icing sugar
300 ml/10 fl oz whipping cream

1 Break the chocolate into pieces and melt, together with the brandy or orange juice and coffee powder, in a heatproof bowl over a pan of hot, but not boiling water. Do not let the chocolate get too hot.

2 Remove the chocolate from the heat and stir until smooth. Mix in the egg yolk and icing sugar. Allow to cool.

3 Whip the cream until it has formed soft peaks. Do not over-beat or the mousse will turn grainy.

4 Stir the cream into the chocolate mixture.

5 Pour the mousse into dessert dishes, individual bowls or a large serving bowl. Set aside in a cool place or in the refrigerator for at least 2 hours before serving.

CHOCOLATE MOUSSE 370

TO DRINK
sweet white wine

LEVEL OF DIFFICULTY
easy

PREPARATION TIME
30 mins + setting time

PREPARE IN ADVANCE
yes

RASPBERRY MOUSSE

Serves 8

4½ leaves of gelatine
120 g/4 oz icing sugar
50 ml/2 fl oz water
2 egg yolks
450 g/1 lb raspberries
300 ml/10 fl oz whipping cream
2 egg whites

Garnish:
raspberries
star fruit (carambola) slices
(optional)

Serve with:
florentines (see recipe 440)

1 Soak the gelatine leaves in cold water for 10 minutes to soften.

2 Mix the icing sugar and water in a small saucepan and boil vigorously for 10 minutes. Strain the gelatine leaves and pour in a little of the hot sugar mixture. Stir well so that the gelatine melts.

3 Beat the egg yolks in a large bowl. Beating continuously, pour in the hot sugar mixture in a thin stream over the egg yolks. Work quickly, otherwise the mixture will become lumpy. Add the dissolved gelatine, mix thoroughly and set aside to cool.

4 Purée the raspberries in a food processor or by rubbing them through a wire strainer. Whip the cream. Stir the raspberry purée and the cream into the egg mixture. Beat the egg whites to form soft peaks and fold carefully into the raspberry mousse. Pour the raspberry mousse into a serving bowl or into separate dessert dishes. Place in the refrigerator for several hours or overnight to set.

5 Garnish just before serving.

TO DRINK:
sweet white wine

LEVEL OF DIFFICULTY
fairly easy

PREPARATION TIME
1 hr + setting time

PREPARE IN ADVANCE
yes

RASPBERRY SOUFFLÉ

Serves 8

2 tsp butter
85 g/3 oz + 1 tbsp sugar
400 g/14 oz raspberries
4 egg yolks
juice of ½ lemon
12 egg whites

Sauce:
300 g/10 oz raspberries
2-3 tbsp icing sugar
juice of 1 lemon

Garnish:
2 tsp icing sugar

1 First make the sauce. Purée the raspberries in a food processor or by rubbing them through a wire strainer. Stir in the icing sugar and the lemon juice. Add more sugar, if necessary.

2 Sieve the sauce to remove the pips. Keep cold.

3 Preheat the oven to 200° C/ 400° F, gas mark 6. Grease a soufflé dish or individual ramekins with the butter and coat with 1 tbsp of the sugar. Place on an baking sheet.

4 Mix the raspberries with half the remaining sugar and work in a food processor. Alternatively, purée the raspberries by rubbing them through a wire strainer and then stir in the sugar. Mix the purée with egg yolks and lemon juice.

5 Beat the egg white until they form stiff peaks. Beat in the remaining sugar. Beat until the mixture is stiff and shiny.

6 Carefully mix the raspberry purée with the beaten egg whites.

7 Spoon the soufflé mixture into the prepared dish or dishes. Smooth the top.

8 Place the tray in the bottom of the oven. Bake for 12 minutes until the soufflé has risen well.

9 Sprinkle over the icing sugar and serve immediately with the raspberry sauce.

RASPBERRY SOUFFLÉ 372

To drink:
sweet white wine

LEVEL OF DIFFICULTY
fairly easy
PREPARATION TIME
1 hr
PREPARE IN ADVANCE
yes

PRUNE SOUFFLÉ

Serves 4

2 tsp butter
225 g/8 oz stoned prunes, soaked in warm water
15-20 blanched almonds
5 egg whites
50 g/1¾ oz sugar

Serve with:
ice-cold single cream or soft vanilla ice cream

1 Preheat the oven to 170° C/ 325° F, gas mark 3. Grease a soufflé dish with the butter.

2 Chop the prunes into very fine pieces and roughly chop the almonds.

3 Beat the egg whites to form stiff peaks. Fold in the sugar and continue beating for a few minutes until the mixture is stiff and shiny. Mix in the prunes and chopped almonds. Put the mixture into the prepared dish.

4 Bake in the middle of the oven for approximately 30 minutes. Do not open the oven door during the first half of the baking time, otherwise the soufflé will sink and flatten out. Serve the soufflé straight from the oven.

Variation:
For apricot soufflé, substitute soaked dried apricots for the prunes.

PRUNE SOUFFLÉ 373

TO DRINK
ruby port or sweet white wine

LEVEL OF DIFFICULTY
easy

PREPARATION TIME
1 hr

PREPARE IN ADVANCE
yes

CHERRY MOULD

Serves 6

6 gelatine leaves
2 eggs, separated
1 x 450 g/1 lb jar cherry jam
300 ml/10 fl oz whipping cream

Garnish:
30 g/1 oz cooking chocolate, grated

Serve with:
almond ratafias (see recipe 441)

1 Soak the gelatine leaves into cold water for 10 minutes to soften.

2 Beat the egg yolks into the jam, mixing well.

3 Beat the egg whites until they form stiff peaks. Whip the cream.

4 Squeeze out the gelatine leaves and melt over a low heat. Stir the gelatine into the jam mixture.

5 Mix the whipped cream into the jam and egg mixture. Carefully fold in the egg whites.

6 Rinse a 500-ml/18-fl oz mould with cold water. Pour in the mixture and place in the refrigerator for 2-3 hours, until set.

7 Quickly dip the mould into hot water and invert on to a serving dish. Garnish with the chocolate and serve with small almond cakes.

CHERRY MOULD 374

TO DRINK
sweet white wine

LEVEL OF DIFFICULTY
easy

PREPARATION TIME
30 mins + setting time

PREPARE IN ADVANCE
yes

FLOATING ISLANDS

Serves 6

6 egg whites
175 g/6 oz sugar
1 tsp vanilla sugar
1 litre/1¾ pints milk
1 vanilla pod

Custard:
8 egg yolks
150 g/5 oz icing sugar
30 g/1 oz unsalted butter

Garnish:
2 tbsp castor sugar
1 tsp water

1 Beat the egg whites. When the eggs have started to thicken, add half the sugar. Beat until they form stiff peaks. Beat in the remaining sugar and the vanilla sugar. Continue beating until the mixture is very firm, stiff and shiny.

2 Pour the milk into a large saucepan. Cut the vanilla pod in half and scrape out the seeds with a sharp knife. Add the seeds and the pod to the milk and bring to the boil.

3 Scoop up balls of meringue mixture with a large spoon and poach them in the simmering milk. Simmer for a few minutes until the meringue balls have risen and stiffened slightly. Remove them with a perforated spoon and set aside to cool. Reserve 500 ml/17 fl oz of the milk.

4 Make the custard. Beat the egg yolks with sugar. Slowly pour over the reserved milk, beating constantly. Strain the sauce back into the pan.

5 Return the pan to the heat and beat until the sauce has thickened. Remove from the heat just before it boils and add the butter. Continue beating until the sauce has cooled down. Place in the refrigerator.

6 To make the garnish, dissolve the sugar in the water over low heat. Heat until a light brown caramel forms.

7 Pour the custard into deep plates, place a couple of 'islands' on top and pipe a little of the caramel over them.

TO DRINK
sweet white wine

LEVEL OF DIFFICULTY
fairly difficult

PREPARATION TIME
2 hrs

PREPARE IN ADVANCE
partly

WHITE CHOCOLATE MOUSSE AND KIWI SAUCE

Serves 4

Mousse:
1½ gelatine leaves
200 g/7 oz white chocolate
1 egg
1 egg yolk
1 tbsp Cointreau or Grand Marnier
300 ml/10 fl oz whipped cream

Sauce:
3 kiwi fruits
icing sugar

Garnish:
lemon leaves
sliced strawberries or kiwi fruit slices

1 Soak the gelatine leaves in cold water for 10 minutes to soften. Melt the chocolate in a heatproof bowl over a pan of hot, but not boiling water. Allow to cool but not to set.

2 Beat the egg and egg yolk in a stainless steel bowl over a pan of hot, but not boiling water until thickened. Squeeze the gelatine leaves and stir into the warm egg mixture until melted. Allow to cool while still beating.

3 Add the melted chocolate to the mixture, a little at a time, until the mixture is smooth and even. Stir in the liqueur.

4 Whip the cream until thick and carefully fold into the chocolate mixture.

5 Put the mousse in the refrigerator for 2 hours, until it has set.

6 Meanwhile, make the sauce. Peel the kiwi fruits and purée them in a mixer or food processor. Add icing sugar to taste, if required. Keep the sauce cold until ready to serve.

7 Pour a little sauce on 4 individual dishes. Shape the mousse into egg-shaped balls, using two warm tablespoons, and place them on top of the sauce.

8 Garnish with a few lemon leaves, sliced strawberries or slices of kiwi fruit.

WHITE CHOCOLATE MOUSSE AND KIWI SAUCE 376

TO DRINK
sweet white wine

LEVEL OF DIFFICULTY
medium difficult

PREPARATION TIME
1 hr + setting time

PREPARE IN ADVANCE
yes

ORANGE PARFAIT

Serves 4

4 oranges
4 egg yolks
4 tbsp white sugar
300 ml/10 fl oz whipping cream

Meringue:
2-3 egg whites
2-3 tbsp white sugar

1 Scrub the oranges in warm water.

2 Cut a lid from each orange and scoop out the fruit and juice. Remove the pips and pith and reserve the juice.

3 Beat the egg yolks with the sugar until light and fluffy.

4 Whip the cream, mix with the egg mixture and stir in 75 ml/3 fl oz orange juice.

5 Fill the oranges with the mixture. Place in the freezer for 3-4 hours or longer.

6 Take the oranges out of the freezer and allow to stand for 15-20 minutes at room temperature. Make the meringue lids. Preheat the oven to 250° C/ 500° F, gas mark 10.

7 Beat the egg whites until they form stiff peaks. Add 1 tbsp sugar per egg white and continue beating until the mixture is firm and shiny.

8 Pipe the meringue mixture on to the top of the filled oranges. Bake in the oven for 1-2 minutes until the meringue has turned golden.

To drink
sweet white wine

LEVEL OF DIFFICULTY
easy

PREPARATION TIME
30 mins + freezing time

PREPARE IN ADVANCE
yes

'DIME' BAR ICE CREAM

Serves 4-6

1 litre/1¾ pints old-fashioned vanilla ice cream
5 large 'Dime' bars

Garnish:

chopped 'Dime' bar
grated plain chocolate

1 Chop the 'Dime' bars with a sharp carving knife.

2 Stir the ice cream until it is soft and mix in the chopped 'Dime' bars.

3 Keep the ice cream in the freezer until ready to serve.

4 Place scoops of ice cream in a bowl or individual dessert glasses. Garnish with a little chopped 'Dime' bar and a little grated chocolate.

'DIME' BAR ICE CREAM 378

TO DRINK:
sweet white wine

LEVEL OF DIFFICULTY
easy

PREPARATION TIME
30 mins + freezing time

PREPARE IN ADVANCE
yes

ICE CREAM SANDWICHES

Serves 6

For the base and top:
12 almond ratafias (see recipe 441)

Filling:
1 litre/1¾ pints vanilla ice cream

Sauce:
225 ml/8 fl oz water
250 g/8 oz castor sugar
120 g/4 oz cocoa powder

1 Bake the almond ratafias as instructed in recipe 441, but make them a larger (1 large tablespoon per ratafia).

2 Make the sauce. Boil together the water and sugar until bubbling vigorously. Remove from the heat and beat in the cocoa powder. This can be made in advance and re-heated before serving.

3 Place half the ratafias on a serving dish. Add a scoop of ice cream to each. Place another ratafia on top. If the ratafias are too small, make the bases and covers from two or three biscuits. Pour over a little chocolate sauce, allowing it to drip over the edges. Serve the remaining sauce separately.

TO DRINK:
sweet white wine

LEVEL OF DIFFICULTY
easy

PREPARATION TIME
1 hr

PREPARE IN ADVANCE
partly

FROZEN LEMON CAKE

Serves 6

1 lemon
150 ml/5 fl oz whipping cream
2 egg yolks
85 g/3 oz castor sugar
150 ml/5 fl oz crème fraîche
2 egg whites
15 blanched almonds, finely chopped

Sauce:
4 passion fruit
50 ml/2 fl oz water
40 g/1½ oz castor sugar

Garnish:
mint or lemon leaves

1 Wash the lemon well. Grate the peel and squeeze the juice.

2 Whip the cream. Beat the egg yolks with the sugar until fluffy. Add the lemon peel and juice, whipped cream and crème fraîche.

3 Whisk the egg whites until they form stiff peaks. Carefully fold into the mixture, together with the almonds.

4 Rinse a loose-bottomed cake tin, 23 cm/9 inches in diameter, with cold water. Transfer the mixture to the tin. Keep the cake in the freezer for at least 2 hours.

5 Scoop the pulp from the passion fruit. Mix the water and sugar and boil for a few minutes. Add the fruit from the passion fruit. Remove from the heat and set aside to cool.

6 Garnish the cake with passion fruit sauce and mint or lemon leaves.

FROZEN LEMON CAKE 380

TO DRINK:
sweet Madeira

LEVEL OF DIFFICULTY
medium difficult

PREPARATION TIME
30 mins + freezing time

MADE IN ADVANCE:
yes

BAKED ALASKA

Serves 6

2 sponge cakes the size of the ice cream block (ready-made cakes can be used)
4-5 tbsp whisky, brandy, rum or fruit juice
1 litre/1¾ pints vanilla ice cream

Meringue:
4 egg whites
5-6 tbsp castor sugar

Garnish:
Canned fruit, e.g. peaches, apricots, pineapple, or thawed frozen berries, such as raspberries, strawberries or blackberries

1 Preheat the oven to 250° C/ 500° F, gas mark 10. Soak the cake bases in the spirit or fruit juice and put one of them on an ovenproof dish.

2 Beat the egg whites until they form stiff peaks. Add the sugar and beat until the whites are very stiff.

3 Take the ice cream out of the freezer and place on top of the sponge base in the dish. Place the other sponge on top of the ice cream.

4 Pipe or spread the meringue mixture over the ice cream ensuring that it is completely covered, including the edges.

5 Place the dish in the oven and bake for 5 minutes, until the meringue has tuned light gold. Check that it is not browning too quickly. Garnish with fruit and serve immediately.

TO DRINK
sweet Madeira

LEVEL OF DIFFICULTY
easy

PREPARATION TIME
30 mins

PREPARE IN ADVANCE
no

ICE CREAM RATAFIA MELBA

Serves 4

8 orange ratafias (see recipe 439)
500 ml/18 fl oz vanilla ice cream
4 canned peach halves

Sauce:
200 g/7 oz raspberries
icing sugar to taste

Garnish:
50 g/2 oz almond paste
icing sugar
2 drops green food colouring

1 First make the garnish. Knead the almond paste with a little icing sugar coloured with a couple of drops of the food colouring. Roll out on an icing sugar coated surface. Cut out 4 star or circle shapes with a biscuit cutter. Roll out the trimmings and make 4 'stalks'.

2 To make the sauce, purée the raspberries in a food processor or by rubbing them through a wire strainer and add icing sugar to taste. Sieve the sauce to remove any pips.

3 Place 4 orange ratafias on a plate and top each with a large scoop of ice cream. Place another ratafia on top. Place a peach half on each one. Cover with almond paste shapes and add the almond paste stalk. Carefully pour the raspberry sauce around the base. Serve immediately.

ICE CREAM RATAFIA MELBA 382

TO DRINK
sweet white wine

LEVEL OF DIFFICULTY
easy

PREPARATION TIME
30 mins

PREPARE IN ADVANCE
partly

ICE CREAM BOMBE

Serves 8-10

1 litre/1¾ pints hard vanilla ice cream
1 litre/1¾ pints orange ice cream or sorbet
1 litre/1¾ pints raspberry sorbet
100-150 ml/4-5 fl oz whipping cream

Garnish:
100 g/3½ oz cooking chocolate
6 slices pineapple
15-20 strawberries

1 Make the bombe in a 3-litre/5-pint bowl with a rounded base or bombe mould. Stir the vanilla ice cream until smooth and spread an even thick layer around the inside of the bowl. The sides of the bowl should be covered. Put the bowl in the freezer and leave until the ice cream is hard.

2 Stir the orange ice cream or sorbet until soft enough to spread. Press over the vanilla ice cream in the bowl, covering it completely. Freeze again.

3 When this layer is frozen, press the raspberry sorbet over the orange ice cream or sorbet. Freeze again. If the bombe is not full, top up with whipped cream. Put the bombe back in the freezer for 3-4 hours.

4 Prepare the garnish while the ice cream is in the freezer. Melt the chocolate in a heatproof bowl set over a pan of hot, but not boiling water. Cut the pineapple rings into halves. Partly dip the pineapple and strawberries into the chocolate sauce. Set aside to let the chocolate harden on the fruits.

5 Transfer the ice cream bombe to the refrigerator 30 minutes before serving.

6 Dip the bowl quickly into hot water and turn the bombe out on to a serving dish. Garnish with the chocolate dipped fruits.

ICE CREAM BOMBE 383

TO DRINK
sweet white wine

LEVEL OF DIFFICULTY
fairly difficult

PREPARATION TIME
5-6 hrs freezing

PREPARE IN ADVANCE
yes

ICE CREAM MERINGUE

Serves 6

3 egg whites
120 g/4 oz + 2 tsp icing sugar

Filling:
600 ml/1 pint vanilla ice cream

Garnish:
hundreds and thousands (optional)

1 Preheat the oven to its lowest setting. Line a baking sheet with greaseproof paper. Beat the egg whites until they form stiff peaks. Add 120 g/4 oz sugar, beating continuously, until the mixture is stiff and shiny.

2 Form the mixture into egg shapes with 2 spoons. Put the meringues on the prepared baking sheet and sprinkle over a little sugar.

3 Bake the meringues for 1 hour. Make a hollow for the ice cream in the bases of each meringue by pressing lightly with the back of a spoon. Allow the meringues to cool.

4 Just before serving, sandwich together with the ice cream.

ICE CREAM MERINGUE 384

To drink
sweet white wine

LEVEL OF DIFFICULTY
medium difficult

PREPARATION TIME
2 hrs

PREPARE IN ADVANCE
yes

ICE CREAM TRUFFLES

Serves 8

500 ml/18 fl oz vanilla ice cream
500 ml/18 fl oz chocolate ice cream
100 g/3½ oz dark chocolate
60 g/2 oz coconut butter
100 g/3½ oz white chocolate

1 Using a 25 mm/1 inch ice cream scoop or 2 teaspoons, make ice cream balls as evenly shaped as possible. Place them on a plate, cover with cling film and put in the freezer.

2 Melt the dark chocolate with half the coconut butter in a heatproof bowl over a pan of hot, but not boiling water. Melt the white chocolate with the remaining coconut butter in a separate bowl in the same way.

3 Remove the ice cream balls from the freezer. Dip the vanilla ones into the dark chocolate, and the chocolate ones into the white chocolate. Make sure that they are fully coated. Do this very quickly or the ice cream will melt. Put straight back into the freezer until serving.

To drink
coffee

LEVEL OF DIFFICULTY
easy

PREPARATION TIME
1 hr + freezing time

PREPARE IN ADVANCE
yes

GRAPEFRUIT PARFAIT WITH TOFFEE SAUCE

Serves 6-8

Parfait:
4 egg yolks
60 g/2 oz icing sugar
juice and grated rind from
1 grapefruit
½ vanilla pod
400 ml/14 fl oz whipping cream

For the mould:
1 grapefruit

Toffee sauce:
50 g/1¾ oz cocoa powder
100 g/3½ sugar
500 ml/18 fl oz whipping cream

1 Mix the egg yolks, icing sugar and grapefruit juice in a heatproof bowl. Cut the vanilla pod lengthwise. Scrape the seeds into the saucepan and add the pod. Place the bowl over a pan of hot, but not boiling water and beat the mixture until thick and fluffy. Remove from the heat. Allow the mixture to cool, still beating. Remove the vanilla pod.

2 Whip the cream. Mix with the egg mixture and add the grated fruit rind.

3 Peel the other grapefruit and cut the fruit into thin slices. Line an oblong dish with the slices. Pour in the parfait mixture and place in the freezer for 4-5 hours.

4 Make the toffee sauce. Mix the cocoa powder and sugar in a saucepan. Add the cream. Stir over low heat until the sauce has thickened.

5 Remove the parfait from the freezer. Cut into slices and place in a serving dish. Serve the sauce in a separate bowl.

GRAPEFRUIT PARFAIT WITH TOFFEE SAUCE 386

TO DRINK:
sweet white wine

LEVEL OF DIFFICULTY
medium difficult

PREPARATION TIME
1 hr + freezing time

PREPARE IN ADVANCE
yes

QUICK RASPBERRY ICE CREAM

Serves 4

250 g/8 oz frozen raspberries
1 egg
2-3 tbsp icing sugar
100 ml/4 fl oz whipping cream

Garnish:
whole raspberries
wafers

1 Put the frozen raspberries in a food processor, add the icing sugar and the egg. Start the machine. Pour in the cream and process for 30 seconds.

2 Spoon the ice cream into individual glasses and serve immediately garnished with whole raspberries and wafers.

Variations:
This quick ice cream can be made with all kinds of berries. The quantity of sugar will vary depending on how sweet the berries are.

QUICK RASPBERRY ICE CREAM 387

To Drink:
sweet white wine

LEVEL OF DIFFICULTY
easy

PREPARATION TIME
10 mins

PREPARE IN ADVANCE
no

CLOUDBERRY PARFAIT CAKE

Serves 6-8

Cake base:
1 tbsp butter
2 tbsp fresh breadcrumbs
5 egg whites
200 g/7 oz icing sugar
150 g/5 oz ground almonds

Parfait:
3 gelatine leaves
4 egg yolks
85 g/3 oz sugar
100 ml/3½ fl oz water
400 ml/14 fl oz whipping cream
150 g/5 oz cloudberries, loganberries, blackberries or raspberries

Garnish:
toasted, flaked almonds
whole cloudberries, loganberries, blackberries or raspberries

1 Preheat the oven to 170° C/ 325° F, gas mark 3. Grease a springform pan with the butter and coat with the breadcrumbs. Soak the gelatine in cold water for 10 minutes for the parfait.

2 Beat the egg whites with the icing sugar until they form stiff peaks. Mix in the ground almonds. Pour the mixture into the prepared pan. Bake in the middle of the oven for 15 minutes. Allow to cool in the tin.

3 To make the parfait, beat the egg yolks, sugar and water over low heat until the mixture has thickened. Remove the pan from the heat and set aside to cool, stirring occasionally.

4 Squeeze the gelatine leaves and melt over low heat. If needed, add a few drops of water. Pour the gelatine into the custard in a fine stream, beating constantly.

5 Whip the cream and mix into the custard. Stir in the cloudberries or other fruit.

6 Spread the parfait on top of the almond base still in the tin. Place in the freezer for at least 2-3 hours.

7 Remove from freezer 30-40 minutes before serving. Garnish with lightly flaked almonds and whole berries.

CLOUDBERRY PARFAIT CAKE 388

TO DRINK:
sweet white wine

LEVEL OF DIFFICULTY
medium difficult

PREPARATION TIME
1 hr + freezing time

PREPARE IN ADVANCE:
yes

ITALIAN ICE CREAM

Serves 8

½ vanilla pod
350 ml/12 fl oz single cream
8 egg yolks
100 g/3½ oz icing sugar
100 g/3½ oz dark cooking chocolate
400 ml/14 fl oz double cream
75 g/2½ oz chopped walnuts

1 Cut the vanilla pod lengthwise, scrape the seeds into the single cream and add the pod. Bring to the boil and simmer until the cream has thickened, stirring occasionally.

2 Beat the egg yolks and icing sugar together until light and fluffy. Remove the vanilla pod from the vanilla cream and pour it in a fine stream into the egg mixture, beating constantly. Pour the mixture into a heatproof bowl.

3 Melt the chocolate in a heatproof bowl over pan of hot, but not boiling water. Warm 100 ml/ 3½ fl oz of the double cream and mix thoroughly with the melted chocolate. Stir in the remaining double cream.

4 Set the egg and vanilla cream mixture over a pan of hot, but not boiling water. Beat constantly until it becomes thick and fluffy.

5 Stir the chocolate into the egg mixture, a little at a time. Add half the chopped walnuts and mix well.

6 Put the bowl into ice cold water and beat until the mixture has cooled. Pour into a mould or dish and put in the freezer. Stir a couple of times during freezing before the mixture has hardened. Freeze for 3-4 hours.

7 Remove from the freezer 15 minutes before serving. Scoop into glasses or bowls and garnish with the remaining chopped walnuts.

TO DRINK
Marsala

LEVEL OF DIFFICULTY
medium difficult

PREPARATION TIME
2 hrs + freezing time

PREPARE IN ADVANCE
yes

CINNAMON PARFAIT WITH APPLE SAUCE

Serves 6-8

Parfait:
4 egg yolks
90 g/3 oz icing sugar
½ vanilla pod
400 ml/14 fl oz whipping cream
1 tsp ground cinnamon

Sauce:
400 ml/14 fl oz apple juice
1 tbsp arrowroot

Garnish:
75 ml/3 fl oz water
85 g/3 oz sugar
3 cooking apples

1 Put the egg yolks and icing sugar in a heatproof bowl. Cut the vanilla pod in half lengthwise, scrape the seeds into the egg mixture and add the rest of the pod. Set the bowl over a pan of hot, not boiling water and beat until the mixture is thick and fluffy. Remove from the heat and allow to cool, stirring constantly. Remove the vanilla pod.

2 Whip the cream. Mix together the egg mixture, cinnamon and whipped cream. Pour the parfait mixture into a long, narrow, oblong dish or mould and put in the freezer for 4-5 hours.

3 To make the garnish, bring the water and sugar to the boil, stirring until the sugar has dissolved. Peel and core the apples. Simmer in the caramel mixture until soft. Leave to cool.

4 Make the sauce. Dilute the apple juice with water if it is very concentrated and bring to the boil. Mix the arrowroot with a little water and beat into the apple juice. Keep stirring over the heat until it has thickened. Remove from heat. When cool, add the apple balls to the mixture.

5 Take the parfait out of the freezer. Cut into slices and place on a serving dish. Serve the sauce separately. Alternatively, arrange the sauce and apple balls in individual dishes, adding the parfait slices on top.

CINNAMON PARFAIT WITH APPLE SAUCE 390

TO DRINK
white or ruby port or sweet Madeira

LEVEL OF DIFFICULTY
fairly easy

PREPARATION TIME
1 hr + freezing time

PREPARE IN ADVANCE
yes

KNICKERBOCKER GLORY

Serves 4

2 large peaches, stoned and sliced
2 bananas, peeled and sliced
2 kiwi fruit, peeled and sliced
500 ml/18 fl oz vanilla ice cream
150 ml/5 fl oz whipping cream
50 g/1¾ oz finely chopped hazelnuts
4 cocktail cherries

Sauce:
225 g/8 oz frozen raspberries, thawed
2-4 tbsp icing sugar

1 Start to make the raspberry sauce. Purée the raspberries by rubbing through a wire strainer or in a food processor. Add icing sugar to taste. Remove the pips by straining the sauce through a sieve.

2 Divide half the raspberry sauce between 4 tall glasses. Arrange the peaches, bananas and kiwi slices in layers and put the ice cream on top. Whip the cream and divide between the glasses. Sprinkle over the chopped nuts and top with the remaining raspberry sauce. Finally, place a cocktail cherry on top of each.

Variations:
Use strawberry ice cream and strawberry jam instead of vanilla ice cream and raspberry purée. Other fruit may also be used, according to season.

TO DRINK
sweet Madeira or white wine

LEVEL OF DIFFICULTY
easy

PREPARATION TIME
30 mins

PREPARE IN ADVANCE
partly

LINGONBERRY PARFAIT

Serves 6-8

500 g/18 oz lingonberries or cranberries
250 g/8 oz castor sugar
3 egg yolks
60 g/2 oz icing sugar
400 ml/14 fl oz whipping cream

Serve with:
almond biscuits (see recipe 440)

1 Boil the berries with the castor sugar until soft. Set aside to cool.

2 Whip the cream until firm.

3 Purée the berries in a food processor or by rubbing through a wire strainer.

4 Beat the egg yolks with the icing sugar until light and fluffy. Mix in the fruit purée and fold in the cream.

5 Pour the mixture into a bowl and place in the freezer for 3-4 hours.

6 Using an ice cream scoop or two spoons arrange balls of parfait in a serving bowl.

LINGONBERRY PARFAIT 392

TO DRINK
herbal tea

LEVEL OF DIFFICULTY
easy

PREPARATION TIME
½-1 hr + freezing time

PREPARE IN ADVANCE
yes

MANGO PARFAIT WITH STRAWBERRY SAUCE

Serves 6

4 ripe bananas
400 ml/14 fl oz whipping cream
150 g/5 oz icing sugar

Sauce:
400 g/14 oz strawberries
100 g/3½ oz icing sugar

Serve with:
walnut flake biscuits (see recipe 443)

1 Cut the mangoes in half and remove the stones. Remove the peel and chop the pulp roughly. The fruit is difficult to handle if peeled first. Remove any fruit that sticks to the stone. Pureé the mango in a food processor or blender.

2 Whip the cream, add the mango purée and icing sugar and mix well. Pour into a bowl and freeze for 4-5 hours.

3 Make the sauce. Purée the strawberries in a food processor or by rubbing through a wire strainer. Add icing sugar to taste.

4 Scoop the parfait on to a serving dish with an ice cream scoop or two spoons. Pipe a little strawberry sauce on top and serve the rest of the sauce separately.

MANGO PARFAIT WITH STRAWBERRY SAUCE

TO DRINK
sparkling red wine or
Sauternes

LEVEL OF DIFFICULTY
easy

PREPARATION TIME
30 mins + freezing time

PREPARE IN ADVANCE
yes

SPARKLING ELDERFLOWER SORBET

Serves 4

200 ml/7 fl oz elderflower juice
150 ml/5 fl oz water
1 egg white
1 bottle sparkling white wine or elderflower wine

Garnish:
lemon leaves (optional)

Serve with:
florentines (see recipe 440)

1 Mix the juice and water. Beat the egg whites until they form stiff peaks, then mix them into the juice. It does not matter if the egg whites float to the top. Leave in the freezer for 2 hours.

2 Meanwhile cool the wine. Remove the sorbet from the freezer. Beat until frothy. Leave to stand at room temperature if the sorbet has frozen too hard. Return the sorbet to the freezer for a further 2 hours, stirring once or twice during this time.

3 Half fill 4 large wine glasses with the chilled wine, spoon the sorbet on top, and serve immediately while the wine is still sparkling and before the sorbet melts. Garnish with lemon leaves if using.

TO DRINK:
sparkling white wine

LEVEL OF DIFFICULTY
easy

PREPARATION TIME
30 mins + freezing time

PREPARE IN ADVANCE
yes

BLACKCURRANT SORBET IN ALMOND BASKETS

Serves 4-6

Sorbet:
85 g/3 oz + 1 tbsp castor sugar
100 ml/3½ fl oz water
210 g/7½ oz blackcurrants
2 egg whites

For greasing:
1 tbsp butter
1 tbsp flour

Almond baskets:
60 g/2 oz butter
100 g/3½ oz castor sugar
2 egg whites
2 drops almond essence
50 g/1¾ oz flour
1 tsp ground almonds
½ tsp vanilla essence

1 To make the sorbet, boil 85 g/3 oz of the sugar with the water for approximately 5 minutes, stirring constantly, until the sugar has dissolved. Allow to cool. Purée the blackcurrants in the food processor.

2 Mix the puréed fruit with the syrup and freeze for 1-1½ hours, until semi-frozen.

3 Beat the egg whites until they form stiff peaks. Fold in the remaining sugar and beat into the semi-frozen mixture.

4 Freeze for a further 2 hours. Beat or stir occasionally during this time so that the sorbet becomes smooth.

5 Meanwhile, make the almond baskets. Preheat the oven to 170° C/325° F, gas mark 3. Grease and flour several baking sheets. Cream together the butter and sugar. Mix in the remaining ingredients.

6 Spoon the mixture on to the prepared baking sheets and spread out into circles approximately 10 cm/4 inches in diameter. Bake for 10 minutes until golden. While they are still warm, lay them over upturned coffee cups to form baskets. If reshaping is required, reheat in the oven for a moment. Allow the baskets to cool completely.

7 Remove the sorbet from the freezer just before serving. Spoon or scoop sorbet into the baskets and serve immediately.

BLACKCURRANT SORBET IN ALMOND BASKETS 395

TO DRINK
Sauternes

LEVEL OF DIFFICULTY
medium difficult

PREPARATION TIME
1 hr + freezing time

PREPARE IN ADVANCE
yes

ICE CREAM WITH WINE POACHED APPLES

Serves 6

Ice cream:
6 egg yolks
255 g/9 oz castor sugar
1 vanilla pod
500 ml/17 fl oz milk
250 ml/9 fl oz whipping cream

Apples in red wine:
750 ml/26 fl oz full-bodied red wine
1 cinnamon stick
190 g/6½ oz castor sugar
6 firm apples

1 Put the egg yolks and sugar in a bowl. Cut the vanilla pod lengthwise and scrape the seeds into the bowl. Beat until the mixture is light and fluffy.

2 Boil the milk with the remainder of the vanilla pod. Beat in the egg mixture. Stand the saucepan in a basin of cold water, beating until the mixture has cooled. Remove the vanilla pod. Whip the cream and add it to the mixture. Place in the freezer for 3-4 hours, stirring occasionally.

3 To cook the apples, boil the wine together with the sugar and cinnamon stick, until reduced by half.

4 Peel and core the apples. Simmer the apples in the wine for 8-10 minutes. Set aside to cool in the wine. They can be kept in the refrigerator before serving for up to four days.

5 Scoop the ice cream into a serving bowl and arrange the apples with the wine sauce around the sides.

ICE CREAM WITH WINE POACHED APPLES 396

TO DRINK:
Madeira

LEVEL OF DIFFICULTY
medium difficult

PREPARATION TIME
1 hr + freezing time

PREPARE IN ADVANCE:
yes

VANILLA PARFAIT WITH RASPBERRY SAUCE

Serves 6

Parfait:
1 vanilla pod
4 egg yolks
90 g/3 oz icing sugar
300 ml/10 fl oz whipping cream

Meringue:
4 egg whites
210 g/7½ oz castor sugar

Sauce:
400 g/14 oz raspberries
icing sugar to taste

Garnish:
3 kiwi fruit, peeled and sliced

1 First make the parfait. Cut the vanilla pod lengthwise and scrape out the seeds into a heatproof bowl. Add the egg yolks and icing sugar. Place the bowl over a pan of hot, but not boiling water. Beat the mixture until light and airy. Set the bowl over a basin of cold water and continue beating until the mixture has cooled.

2 Whip the cream stiffly and mix with the custard. Spoon into small moulds and put in the freezer for 3-4 hours.

3 Make the meringues. Preheat the oven to its lowest setting. Line a baking sheet with greaseproof paper. Whisk the egg whites until they form stiff peaks. Add half the sugar. Continue whisking until the whites are very stiff and shiny. Add the remaining sugar and whisk for a few more minutes. Pipe 6 meringue bases and 6 tops, the same size as the parfait moulds, on to the prepared baking sheet. Bake for 2 hours or until the meringues have dried out.

4 Make the sauce. Purée the raspberries in a food processor or by rubbing them through a wire strainer. Strain to remove the seeds. Add the icing sugar.

5 Remove the parfait from the freezer 30 minutes before serving. Put a meringue base on each of 6 plates. Place a parfait on each base and cover with the meringue top. Pour the raspberry sauce around and garnish with kiwi slices.

TO DRINK
ruby port or sweet white wine

LEVEL OF DIFFICULTY
medium difficult

PREPARATION TIME
2 hrs + freezing time

PREPARE IN ADVANCE
yes

WARM APPLES WITH CINNAMON ICE CREAM

Serves 4

6 apples
75 g/2¾ oz butter
85 g/3 oz castor sugar

Ice cream:
300 ml/10 fl oz whipping cream
2 egg yolks
4 tbsp icing sugar
4 tbsp ground cinnamon

1 To make the ice cream, whip the cream, and stir in the egg yolks, sugar and cinnamon. Put the ice cream in the freezer for approximately 3 hours or until frozen.

2 Peel and core the apples. Cut them into equal-sized wedges. Melt the butter in a frying-pan. Add the sugar and apple wedges and simmer over very low heat until softened.

3 Serve the apples warm with ice cream. Sprinkle a pinch of cinnamon over the ice cream.

Note:
Instead of homemade cinnamon ice cream, you can use 500 ml/18 fl oz vanilla ice cream and stir in 2 tbsp ground cinnamon.

WARM APPLES WITH CINNAMON ICE CREAM 398

TO DRINK
Madeira

LEVEL OF DIFFICULTY
easy

PREPARATION TIME
30 mins + freezing time

PREPARE IN ADVANCE
yes

SPECIAL COFFEES

Irish Coffee

40 ml/1½ fl oz Irish whiskey
150 ml/5 fl oz strong, hot coffee
2 tsp demerara sugar
2 tbsp lightly whipped cream

Pour the whiskey into a warm glass. Pour in the hot coffee and stir in the sugar so that it dissolves. Pour the cream over the back of a spoon on to the top of the coffee so that it floats.

Variations:

Café Grand Marnier

substitute Grand Marnier for the whiskey and sugar

Café Bénédictine

As above, but use Bénédictine liqueur

Café Normande

As above, but use calvados and 2 tsp icing sugar

Café Créole

100 ml/3½ fl oz water
40 g/½ oz cocoa powder
140 g/5 oz demerara sugar
hot, strong coffee

Mix the water, cocoa and sugar and boil until the mixture is thick and creamy. Put 2 spoons of this mixture into each glass and fill with coffee. Top with whipped cream, if liked.

Spiced Oriental Coffee

Serves 4

1 orange
6 cloves
1 cinnamon stick
2 tsp sugar
600 ml/1 pint water
60 g/2 oz dark roasted ground coffee
150 ml/5 fl oz whipped cream

Wash the orange, grate the rind and cut the flesh into wedges, removing the pith. Put the rind, cloves, cinnamon and sugar into a saucepan. Add the water and bring to the boil. Simmer for 5 minutes. Pour the coffee into cups, top with whipped cream and garnish with the orange wedges.

100 PUDDING & DESSERT RECIPES

100
SOUP &
STARTER
RECIPES

COCKTAIL SELECTION

SALMON PINWHEELS:
Cut white bread lengthwise into thin slices. It is easier to do this with frozen bread that has not completely thawed. Remove the crusts and place the bread on damp greaseproof paper. Spread the slices with a thin coating of softened butter. Cover with thin slices of gravad lax, or slightly salted or smoked salmon. Sprinkle over finely chopped dill. Roll up the slices, Swiss roll fashion, from the shorter side. Wrap the roll in clingfilm and keep in the refrigerator for a couple of hours. Slice the roll into thin 'pinwheels' just before serving.

CUCUMBER BOATS:
Slice a fresh cucumber lengthwise. Scrape away the pips with a spoon. Cut into 4 cm/1½ inch lengths and fill them with black caviar or lumpfish roe. Garnish with a thin wedge of lemon.

TIGER BEEF:
Cut out small circles of white bread with a pastry cutter and spread with butter. Cover with finely minced raw beef to make miniature steak tartare. Grind over a little white pepper, add a spoon of lumpfish roe and garnish with finely chopped onion.

CHEESE BALLS:
Mix together equal quantities of blue cheese and a grated hard cheese, such as Cheddar, adding a little cream or crème fraîche to make a smooth mixture. Add paprika and brandy to taste. Leave the mixture to cool and set slightly. Shape into balls and roll in finely chopped parsley. Decorate each with a walnut half and keep refrigerated until ready to serve.

COCKTAIL SELECTION 100

TO DRINK
still or sparkling white wine

LEVEL OF DIFFICULTY
easy

PREPARATION TIME
varied

PREPARE IN ADVANCE
partly

CANAPÉS

To start a dinner party with extra special sandwiches is both appetizing and practical. Vary the toppings and choose them to complement the main course. The bases consist of white or brown bread cut out to form circles, squares or triangles. The crusts should be removed and the slices should not be too thick. Spread with ordinary or herb butter.

Suggestions for toppings:

- Prawns, sliced hard-boiled egg, mayonnaise and dill sprigs
- A thin slice of smoked salmon or gravad lax, lettuce and a small dill sprig
- Spread out a few slices of rare roast beef slightly overlapping. Spread with butter mixed with grated horseradish. Roll up, Swiss roll style, and chill. Cut into slices, place 2-3 slices on each piece of bread and garnish with parsley
- Russian caviar on butter-fried white bread
- Lobster slices, mayonnaise and dill sprigs
- Smoked eel with scrambled egg
- Trout or lumpfish roe and finely chopped red onion or leeks cut into thin strips
- Smoked salmon with cream of horseradish.
- Black or red lumpfish roe with lemon or dill
- Chive butter, sliced hard-boiled egg, anchovy fillets, red pepper strips or tomato wedge and dill sprigs
- 2 thin slices of boiled new potatoes, sliced pickled herring, crème fraîche or soured cream and chives
- Goose or chicken liver pâté, sliced mushrooms or gherkins
- Liver pâté mixed with a little cream and brandy and spiced with crushed pink peppercorns and gherkins sliced lengthwise
- Sliced, boiled tongue with asparagus tips, a dash of mayonnaise and sliced olives
- Roast beef, lettuce leaf, grated horseradish, pickles, parsley and curry mayonnaise
- Puréed blue cheese with sliced radishes or whole walnuts

TO DRINK
Champagne, dry white wine or lager

LEVEL OF DIFFICULTY easy
PREPARATION TIME varied
PREPARE IN ADVANCE yes

CRUDITÉS WITH DIPS

Fresh raw vegetables:
carrots
cauliflower
broccoli
celery sticks
courgettes
cucumber
baby corn cobs
small button mushrooms
radishes
red, green and yellow pepper
fennel
cherry tomatoes

Serve with:
sour cream mixed with a ready-made dip
Roquefort cheese dip
anchovy dip

1 Mix the dips and chill before serving.

2 Rinse and prepare the vegetables. Cut the cauliflower and broccoli into florets. Cut the remaining vegetables into thin strips. Tomatoes, mushrooms and radishes should be served whole.

3 Place the vegetables in separate groups on a serving dish. Serve with one or more dips.

Roquefort Dip:
Purée 100 g/3½ oz Roquefort cheese with 300 ml/10 fl oz sour cream or crème fraîche in a food processor. Add a few dashes of tabasco sauce and, if wished, crushed garlic.

Anchovy Dip:
Purée approximately 150 g/5¼ oz anchovies (3 cans), 1 tbsp dried thyme, 1 tbsp dried basil, 1½ tbsp French mustard, 1-2 tbsp red wine vinegar and ½ tsp freshly ground white pepper in a food processor. Work the mixture for only a few seconds. Scrape the purée from the sides of the food processor and switch on again. Drizzle 100-150 ml/3½-5 fl oz olive oil slowly through the tube while the machine is on.

TO DRINK
dry white wine

LEVEL OF DIFFICULTY
easy
PREPARATION TIME
30 mins
PREPARE IN ADVANCE
yes

MINI CRUSTADES

A handy alternative to sandwiches, crustades can be bought ready made and the fillings can be varied.

A few suggestions for fillings:

• A thin slice of smoked salmon or gravad lax, shaped into a rose, and a dill sprig
• Kipper pâté, mixed with a little cream and an olive slice
• Puréed kipper mixed with mayonnaise and chopped capers, finely chopped chives
• Anchovy mousse, (see recipe 129)
• Caviar cream, finely chopped chives
• Purée of avocado, seasoned with herb salt and lemon juice, 1-2 cooked, peeled prawns
• Crème fraîche or soured cream, bleak (ablette), lumpfish or trout roe, leeks in fine strips
• Sour cream, black caviar, a sliver of lemon
• A warm morel or mushroom sauce, chopped parsley
• Chopped chicken meat, curry mayonnaise, red pepper cut into strips

The fillings can be prepared well in advance.

Fill the crustades just before serving, otherwise, if left too long, the fillings will seep into the bread.

TO DRINK
dry white wine or lager

LEVEL OF DIFFICULTY
easy

PREPARATION TIME
30 mins

PREPARE IN ADVANCE
partly

SAVOURY PETITS CHOUX

30-40 petits choux

Pastry:
200 ml/7 fl oz water
100 g/3½ oz butter
150 g/5¼ oz flour
4 eggs

Salmon filling:
150 g/5¼ oz smoked salmon
3-4 hard-boiled eggs, chopped
100 ml/3½ fl oz mayonnaise
50 ml/2 fl oz sour cream
freshly ground white pepper
2 tbsp finely chopped dill

Caviar filling:
1 x 60 g/2 oz can black caviar
200 ml/7 fl oz double cream, beaten
1 tbsp lemon juice
½ tbsp grated onion
dill sprigs

Prawn filling:
100 ml/3½ fl oz mayonnaise
100 ml/3½ fl oz whipping cream, beaten
75-100 g/2½-3½ oz cooked prawns, finely chopped
3 tbsp finely chopped dill

Egg and anchovy filling:
3 hard-boiled eggs, chopped
6-8 anchovy fillets, chopped
3 tbsp mayonnaise
¼ tsp paprika
1 tbsp finely chopped chives
freshly ground white pepper

Caviar cream:
250 ml/8 fl oz double cream, beaten
60 g/2 oz cream cheese
60 g/2 oz lumpfish roe
1-2 tbsp finely chopped onion

1 Preheat the oven to 200° C/ 400° F, gas mark 6. Make the choux pastry, (see recipe 349). Pipe or shape the mixture into small balls and place on a greased baking sheet. Bake for approximately 10 minutes until they have doubled in size and are golden.

2 Cut a lid off the choux pastries and make a gash in the middle of the bottom half. Fill them with a spoonful of crème fraîche and caviar or black roe or one of the other fillings.

SAVOURY PETITS CHOUX 104

To drink
lager, schnapps or dry white wine

LEVEL OF DIFFICULTY
medium difficult

PREPARATION TIME
1 hr

PREPARE IN ADVANCE
partly

PIROSHKIS
(Russian Pastries)

Serves 4
Approximately 20 pastries

Rice filling:
300 ml/10 fl oz water
2 tbsp butter
125 g/4½ oz round grain rice
700 ml/1¼ pints milk
salt

Pastry:
200 ml/7 fl oz water
2 tsp salt
350 g/12 oz rye flour
2tbsp melted butter or water

Egg butter:
2 hard-boiled eggs, chopped
100 g/3½ oz butter

Serve with:
trout or lumpfish roe, anchovy fillets or gravad lax

1 Make the rice filling. Bring the water and butter to the boil and add the rice. Simmer over low heat until the rice has absorbed all the water. Add the milk. Simmer, covered, over very low heat for approximately 30 minutes, stirring occasionally. Season with salt to taste and allow to cool.

2 Mix the water, salt and rye flour to make a smooth dough. Make the dough into a roll and cut into 20 pieces. Roll out each piece into a thin circle, 14 cm/5½ inches in diameter. Stack the circles on top of each other, sprinkling flour between them to stop them sticking.

3 Preheat the oven to 250° C/ 500 °F, gas mark 10. Brush the flour from the dough circles and place 2 tbsp rice filling in the middle of each. Fold up and pinch the edges all around with the thumb and forefinger.

4 Place the piroshkis on a lined baking sheet and bake for approximately 10 minutes. Brush with melted butter or water.

5 Make the egg butter by mixing the creamed butter with the chopped hard-boiled eggs.

6 Serve warm with egg butter and something flavoursome, such as anchovy fillets, gravad lax, trout or lumpfish roe, or black caviar.

TO DRINK
lager, vodka, or schnapps

LEVEL OF DIFFICULTY
medium difficult
PREPARATION TIME
1 hr
PREPARE IN ADVANCE
yes

KAJSA'S APPETIZERS WITH MUSHROOM CAPS

Serves 4

KAJSA'S APPETIZERS
8 slices white bread
150 g/5¼ oz soft cheese
100 g/3½ oz black caviar or lumpfish roe
60 g/2 oz butter

1 Cut the crusts off the bread and cut each slice into 4 pieces or circles. Spread plenty of cheese on half the bread pieces. Add a layer of caviar or lumpfish roe and cover with the remaining bread. Press together lightly so that the caviar or roe is pressed into the cheese.

2 Fry the sandwiches in butter on both sides until they are golden. Serve immediately.

FILLED MUSHROOM CAPS
100 g/3½ oz curd cheese
10-12 anchovy fillets
1 clove garlic, crushed
16 large mushrooms

1 Beat the cheese until smooth. Purée the anchovy fillets in a blender or by pounding in a mortar. Mix the cheese with the anchovies and garlic, to taste.

2 Twist the mushroom stems to remove them. Fill the caps with the cheese mixture and place them, filled side up, on a dish. Chill before serving.

Variations:
The cheese can be flavoured in a variety of ways. Here are a few suggestions.
Mix 100 g/3½ oz curd cheese with one of the following mixtures:
1 tbsp chopped cress, 1 tbsp chopped chives, ½ tsp grated onion
50 g/1¾ oz finely chopped or minced smoked salmon and a few drops lemon juice
50 g/1¾ oz finely chopped smoked meat and 2-3 tbsp grated horseradish
50 g/1¾ oz finely chopped walnuts

KAJSA'S APPETIZERS WITH MUSHROOM CAPS 106

TO DRINK
cocktails or dry white wine

LEVEL OF DIFFICULTY
easy

PREPARATION TIME
30 mins

PREPARE IN ADVANCE
partly

CHESSBOARD CAKE

25 mini open sandwiches

1 loaf white bread
soft cheese or softened butter
finely chopped dill
24 large cooked peeled prawns
100 g/3½ oz black caviar or lumpfish roe
dill sprigs
a few thin slices lemon or lime

1 Cut the bread lengthwise and remove the crusts. Cut 5 bread strips, 20 cm/8 inches long and 4 cm/1½ inches wide. Place them on top of each other and cut 5 strips at the same time to make 5 equal squares; in this way you will end up with 25 pieces of bread. Each piece should be 4 cm/1½ inches square.

2 Spread the pieces of bread with soft cheese or butter. Dip 12 of the pieces in chopped dill and place 2 peeled prawns on each. Cover the remaining pieces with caviar or lumpfish roe.

3 Arrange the open sandwiches in line, in alternating order, to make a square 'cake'. Garnish the prawns with small sprigs of dill and the caviar or lumpfish roe with slivers of sliced lemon or lime.

4 Keep the 'cake' cold until ready to serve.

TO DRINK
white wine or lager

LEVEL OF DIFFICULTY
easy

PREPARATION TIME
1 hr

PREPARE IN ADVANCE
yes

AVOCADO SOUP

Serves 4

2 large ripe avocados
500 ml/17 fl oz chicken or vegetable stock
200 ml/7 fl oz crème fraîche
salt
freshly ground black or white pepper

Garnish:
4 lemon slices
50-100 g/1¾-3½ oz red lumpfish roe
1 tbsp finely chopped chives

1 Cut the avocado pears in half. Scoop out the flesh. Purée by rubbing through a wire strainer or in a food processor.

2 Stir in the stock and crème fraîche. Season with salt and pepper to taste.

3 Divide the soup between 4 soup bowls. Place a thin slice of lemon on top and a dash of roe. Sprinkle over a little finely chopped chives.

Variations:
This soup can be served both warm and cold. It can also be garnished with avocado wedges.

AVOCADO SOUP 108

TO DRINK
dry white wine

LEVEL OF DIFFICULTY
easy

PREPARATION TIME
30 mins

PREPARE IN ADVANCE
partly

BOUILLON WITH CHEESE PASTRY

Serves 10

Bouillon:
2½ litres/4½ pints beef stock
150 ml/5 fl oz sherry

Pastry:
100 g/3½ oz butter, chilled
125 g/4½ oz flour
1-2 tbsp iced water

Filling:
50 g/1¾ oz blue cheese
100 ml/3½ fl oz double cream
100 ml/3½ fl oz milk
2 eggs
75 g/2½ oz Gruyère, grated
¼ tsp freshly ground black pepper
pinch cayenne pepper

1 Make the dough. Rub the butter into the flour until the mixture resembles fine breadcrumbs. Add the water and work the dough together quickly. Set aside to rest in the refrigerator for about 1 hour.

2 Make the filling. Mash the blue cheese. Stir in the cream, a little at a time, until smooth.

3 Beat together the milk, eggs, grated cheese, black and cayenne peppers and beat into the cheese and cream mixture.

4 Preheat the oven to 200° C/400° F, gas mark 6. Roll out the dough thinly between 2 layers of clingfilm. Line 10 dariole moulds with the dough.

5 Divide the filling between the moulds. Bake in the middle of the oven for approximately 15-20 minutes, until they have risen and are golden on top. Let the pastries cool in the moulds so that they keep their shape. Remove from the moulds when cool. (Disposable foil moulds are easiest.)

6 Just before serving, warm the pastries in the oven, preheated to 200° C/400 °F, gas mark 6, for approximately 5 minutes. At the same time, make the bouillon, by heating the stock and stirring in the sherry. Pour the hot bouillon into bouillon cups, soup bowls or a soup tureen and serve the pastries on small side plates.

TO DRINK
dry sherry or Madeira

LEVEL OF DIFFICULTY
easy

PREPARATION TIME
1 hr + resting time

PREPARE IN ADVANCE
yes

CRÈME NINON (SPARKLING PEA SOUP)

Serves 6

1 tbsp butter
1 small onion, finely chopped
450 g/1 lb frozen green peas, thawed
½ small carrot
½ tsp thyme
salt
600 ml/1 pint beef stock
1 tbsp soya sauce
1 tsp lemon juice
100 ml/3½ fl oz + 2 tbsp sherry
2 tsp arrowroot
150 ml/5 fl oz double cream, whipped
½ bottle sparkling dry white wine

Serve with:
cheese sticks (see recipe 438)

1 Melt the butter in a saucepan and sauté the onion. Add the peas, carrot, thyme and 1 tsp salt. Pour in enough water so that it almost covers the peas. Bring to the boil and simmer slowly for approximately 30 minutes.

2 Bring the stock to the boil and add the soya sauce and 100 ml/3½ fl oz of the sherry.

3 Drain the peas from the water and remove the carrot. Purée the peas in a food processor or blender, or rub them through a wire strainer.

4 Mix the purée and stock and bring to the boil. Add a little lemon juice and salt to taste. Stir the arrowroot into the remaining sherry and add to the soup, while stirring. If the colour is too pale, one or two drops of green food colouring may be added.

5 Heat the soup and carefully stir in the whipped cream. Do not mix too vigorously; the soup should have a swirl of cream in it. Pour into a warm soup tureen.

6 Carry the hot soup to the table. Open the wine and pour the sparkling wine into the soup. Stir carefully so that the bubbles do not disappear. Serve immediately in warm bowls.

CRÈME NINON 110

TO DRINK
the wine used in the soup

LEVEL OF DIFFICULTY
easy
PREPARATION TIME
1 hr
PREPARE IN ADVANCE
partly

VICHYSSOISE

Serves 4

1 onion
4 medium leeks
1½ tbsp butter
1 litre/1¾ pints stock
4 potatoes, peeled
3 parsley sprigs
1 bay leaf
1 thyme sprig
100 ml/3½ fl oz double cream
salt
freshly ground pepper

Garnish:
1 bunch chives, finely chopped

1 Cut the onion and the pale section of the leeks into thin slices. Melt the butter and fry the onion and leek over low heat until soft but not coloured.

2 Add the stock. Dice the potatoes and add to the stock. Make a herb bouquet from the green of the leeks, parsley, bay leaf and thyme and tie together with string. Add to the saucepan. Simmer the soup until the potatoes have broken up.

3 Remove the herb bouquet. Rub the soup through a strainer or purée in a food processor. Pour the soup back into the saucepan, add the double cream and bring back to the boil. Season with salt and pepper to taste.

4 Serve the soup, piping hot or ice cold, depending on the season, sprinkled with finely chopped chives.

TO DRINK
white wine

LEVEL OF DIFFICULTY
easy

PREPARATION TIME
1 hr

PREPARE IN ADVANCE
yes

FRENCH ONION SOUP

Serves 4

6 medium onions
3-4 tbsp butter
1 litre/1¾ pints beef stock
200 ml/7 fl oz dry white wine
1 bay leaf
½ tsp dried thyme
freshly ground black pepper
salt
4 slices French bread
300 g/10½ oz Emmental cheese, grated
50 g/1¾ oz Parmesan cheese, grated

1 Peel the onions and cut them into very thin slices. Preheat the oven to 250° C/500° F, gas mark 10.

2 Melt the butter in a large saucepan. Add the sliced onion and fry, stirring, over low heat for approximately 10 minutes until golden, shiny and transparent but not browned.

3 Pour over the stock and add the wine, bay leaf, thyme, black pepper, and salt to taste. Bring back to the boil and simmer slowly for 20-30 minutes.

4 Place the bread slices on a baking sheet and brown them lightly in the oven.

5 Divide the soup between 4 ovenproof individual bowls. Place the browned slices of bread on top of the soup. Mix the two cheeses together and sprinkle over the bread.

6 Stand the bowls in a roasting tin and place in the oven for approximately 5 minutes until the cheese has melted and is golden.

To drink
red wine

LEVEL OF DIFFICULTY
easy
PREPARATION TIME
1 hr
PREPARE IN ADVANCE
yes

FISH AND SEAFOOD SOUP

Serves 8

10-12 cooked crayfish
½ carrot
100 g/3½ oz celery
1 large leek
4 tbsp vegetable oil
2½ litres/4½ pints water
3 tbsp tomato purée
300 ml/10 fl oz dry white wine
1 litre/1¾ pints double cream
3 tbsp butter
3 tbsp flour
salt
freshly ground white pepper
500-600 g/1-1¼ lb fish fillets
fresh leaf spinach or chives,
roughly chopped

1 Peel the crayfish tails and cut in half. Keep in the refrigerator.

2 Chop the carrot, celery and leek. Heat the oil and fry the vegetables. Add the crayfish trimmings and fry them for a few minutes. Pour over the water and bring to the boil. Boil for 20 minutes.

3 Strain the stock and pour into a clean saucepan. Bring to the boil and boil until reduced by about half. Reserve 200 ml/7 fl oz .

4 Add the tomato purée, wine and double cream to the remaining stock. Mix the butter and flour to make a *beurre manié*. Stir into the stock, a little at a time. Boil for 20-30 minutes, stirring occasionally. Season to taste. Add more wine, if desired.

5 Cut the fish fillets into small pieces and poach them quickly in the reserved fish stock. Warm the crayfish tails in the stock but do not allow it to boil. Using a slotted spoon, remove the fish and crayfish tails and strain the stock into the soup saucepan.

6 Pour the soup into a warm tureen or into warm soup bowls. Garnish with the poached fish fillets, crayfish tails and spinach or chives.

TO DRINK
dry white wine

LEVEL OF DIFFICULTY medium difficult
PREPARATION TIME 1-1½ hrs
PREPARE IN ADVANCE yes

SPARKLING CUCUMBER SOUP

Serves 4

1 onion
1 tbsp butter
6 tbsp chopped parsley
1 tsp basil
1 cucumber
500 ml/17 fl oz vegetable stock
100 ml/3½ fl oz double cream
salt
freshly ground black pepper
200 ml/7 fl oz sparkling white wine

Radish Cream:
1 bunch radishes, finely chopped
100 ml/3½ fl oz crème fraîche
2 cloves garlic, crushed

1 Peel and chop the onion. Melt the butter in a saucepan and fry the onion, parsley and basil.

2 Cut the cucumber into slices and reserve ¼ for garnish. Pour the stock over the fried onion and add the cucumber. Simmer for 10 minutes.

3 Strain the stock into a saucepan. Put the cucumber and onion mixture into a food processor or blender and purée. Mix the purée with the stock and cream. Season with salt and pepper to taste.

4 Quickly bring the soup to the boil again and garnish with the reserved sliced cucumber. Add the wine just before serving.

5 Mix the ingredients for the radish cream together and serve in a separate bowl.

SPARKLING CUCUMBER SOUP 114

TO DRINK
sparkling white wine

LEVEL OF DIFFICULTY
easy

PREPARATION TIME
30 mins

PREPARE IN ADVANCE
partly

MOREL SOUP WITH SMOKED SALMON

Serves 6

80 g/3 oz dried morels or other mushrooms, soaked
1 onion, finely chopped
60 g/2 oz butter
1 chicken stock, crumbled
600 ml/1 pint Madeira
1 litre/1¾ pint double cream
salt
freshly ground white pepper
120 g/4¼ oz smoked salmon, cut into fine strips

Garnish:
cress

1 Wipe the mushrooms and chop them roughly. Finely chop the onion.

2 Melt the butter and fry the onion and mushrooms, without colouring. Add the stock cube, wine and cream.

3 Simmer until it has reached the right consistency and season with salt and pepper to taste.

4 Warm the soup just before serving and pour into a tureen or individual soup bowls. Add the strips of smoked salmon. Garnish with cress.

To drink
dry white wine

LEVEL OF DIFFICULTY
easy

PREPARATION TIME
30 mins

PREPARE IN ADVANCE
yes

MUSSEL SOUP

Serves 4

24 large fresh mussels
100 ml/3½ fl oz fish stock
200 ml/7 fl oz dry white wine
1 tbsp finely chopped onion
½ stalk celery, finely chopped
1 bunch parsley, leaves and stalks separated
400 ml/14 fl oz double cream
salt
freshly ground pepper
pinch cayenne pepper

Serve with:
cheese sticks (see recipe 438)

1 Scrub the mussels under cold, running water. Discard any mussels which do not open when sharply tapped.

2 Bring the stock and wine to the boil in a large saucepan. Add the mussels, onion, celery and parsley stalks. Simmer, covered, for approximately 5 minutes or until the mussels have opened. Discard any mussels which do not open.

3 Remove the mussels with a slotted spoon. They are not used in the soup, so may be either discarded, used in another dish, or frozen. Strain the stock and boil until reduced by one-third. Add the cream and simmer for further 3-5 minutes stirring constantly. Season with salt, ground pepper and cayenne pepper to taste.

4 Pour the soup into warm, individual soup bowls and sprinkle over a little chopped parsley.

Variations:
Like many other soups, this one can also be served chilled, which is refreshing on a hot summer's day.

To drink
dry white wine or dry sherry

LEVEL OF DIFFICULTY
medium difficult

PREPARATION TIME
1 hr

PREPARE IN ADVANCE
yes

PRAWN SOUP

Serves 6

1½ litres/2½ pints fish stock
400 g/14 oz cooked prawns
½ carrot
2 stalks celery
½ leek
1½ tsp butter
1 tbsp finely chopped onion
1 tbsp finely chopped shallots
1 tbsp flour
100 ml/3½ fl oz white wine
1 tbsp tomato purée
2 dill sprigs
salt (optional)
freshly ground black pepper
pinch cayenne pepper
2 egg yolks
3 tbsp brandy
1 tbsp double cream

Garnish:
dill sprigs

Serve with:
cheese sticks (see recipe 438)

1 Bring the fish stock to the boil. Peel and devein the prawns. Rinse the prawn shells and allow to dry in the oven on very low heat.

2 Finely chop the carrot and celery and cut the leek into thin strips.

3 Melt the butter in a large frying-pan. Add the prawn shells, onion, shallots, carrot, celery and leek. Fry, stirring. Sprinkle over the flour and stir thoroughly. Add the fish stock, white wine, tomato purée and the dill. Simmer for 20-30 minutes.

4 Rub the mixture through a fine strainer. Press out as much liquid as possible from the prawn shells. Season the soup with salt, pepper and a little cayenne pepper to taste.

5 Beat the egg yolks together with the brandy. Beat the egg mixture into the soup just before serving. Simmer the soup, beating constantly. Add the peeled prawns to warm but do not allow to boil.

6 Pour the soup into a heated tureen or individual soup bowls, swirl a little cream on the top, and sprinkle with dill.

TO DRINK
mineral water or dry white

LEVEL OF DIFFICULTY
fairly easy
PREPARATION TIME
1 hr
PREPARE IN ADVANCE
yes

CHANTERELLE SOUP

Serves 6

90 g/3 oz dried chanterelles
800 ml/1½ pints water
3 vegetable stock cubes
2-3 tbsp butter
6 tbsp flour
5 tsp tomato purée
50 g /¾ oz Roquefort
300 ml/10 fl oz crème fraîche
2 tsp lemon juice
salt
freshly ground white pepper
finely chopped parsley

1 Roughly crush the dried chanterelles by hand. Place in a bowl, cover with water and allow to soak for at least 1 hour. Drain the mushrooms and reserve the liquid.

2 Warm the mushroom soaking liquid, water and stock cubes in a large saucepan.

3 Melt the butter in a frying-pan and fry the mushrooms over low heat for approximately 5-10 minutes. Sprinkle over the flour and stir well. Stir in the stock, a little at a time. Stir in the tomato purée and the cheese and simmer for approximately 10 minutes.

4 Add the crème fraîche, lemon juice and salt and pepper to taste.

5 Just before serving, sprinkle with chopped parsley.

CHANTERELLE SOUP 118

To drink
light red wine

LEVEL OF DIFFICULTY
easy

PREPARATION TIME
30 mins + soaking time

PREPARE IN ADVANCE
yes

BROCCOLI QUICHE

Serves 6

Pastry:
180 g/6¼ oz flour
150 g/5¼ oz butter, chilled
2-3 tbsp iced water

Filling:
200 g/7 oz broccoli
2 small red and green peppers
2 eggs
200 ml/7 fl oz milk or single cream
150 g/5¼ oz strongly flavoured cheese, grated
salt
freshly ground black pepper

1 Make the pastry. Rub together the flour and butter until the mixture resembles fine breadcrumbs. Add the water and work the pastry together quickly. Set aside in the refrigerator to rest for about 1 hour.

2 Roll out the dough and use to line a loose-based pie dish, approximately 23 cm/9 inches in diameter. Prick the base with a fork. Rest in the refrigerator for at least 15 minutes. Preheat the oven to 200° C/400° F, gas mark 6. Bake the flan base for 10-15 minutes.

3 Cook the broccoli in boiling, salted water, drain and rinse under cold water. Separate the stalks and the heads and reserve both. Seed the peppers and cut into thin rings.

4 Beat together the eggs, milk or cream and three-quarters of the grated cheese. Season with salt and pepper to taste.

5 Sprinkle the remaining cheese on to the pastry. Add the broccoli stalks and pour over the egg mixture. Arrange the broccoli heads around the edges and the sliced red and green peppers in an attractive pattern in the centre. Bake the flan for 30-40 minutes until the filling has risen and the flan is golden.

6 The flan can be made in advance and warmed just before serving.

Variations:
Serve the flan as a main course with smoked sliced ham and a salad.

TO DRINK
mineral water

LEVEL OF DIFFICULTY
easy

PREPARATION TIME
1 hr + resting time

PREPARE IN ADVANCE
yes

SALMON QUICHE

Serves 6-8

Pastry:
150 g/5¼ oz butter, chilled
200 g/7 oz flour
2-3 tbsp iced water

Filling:
1 large onion
1 leek
2-3 tbsp butter
300 g/10 oz smoked salmon
3 eggs
300 ml/10 fl oz single cream
75 g/2¾ oz Gruyère cheese, grated
¼ tsp paprika
freshly ground black pepper
1 bunch dill, finely chopped
salt

1 Make the pastry. Rub the butter into the flour until the mixture resembles fine breadcrumbs. Add the water and work the pastry together quickly. Set aside in the refrigerator to rest for approximately 1 hour.

2 Peel and chop the onion. Rinse and slice the leek. Melt the butter in a frying-pan and sauté the onion and leek over low heat until soft and transparent. Allow to cool.

3 Roll out the dough and use to line a loose-based flan dish. Pinch strips of foil around the inside edges of the dough so that they do not collapse during cooking. Prick the dough base with a fork. Leave the base in the refrigerator for at least 15 minutes. Meanwhile, preheat the oven to 200° C/400° F, gas mark 6.

4 Cook the pastry base blind for 10 minutes.

5 Meanwhile, dice the salmon. Beat together the eggs and milk. Add the salmon, the onion mixture, grated cheese, paprika, pepper, and dill. Season with a little salt.

6 Remove the foil strips from the flan case and pour the filling into the pastry base. Bake for 20-30 minutes or until the filling has risen and is golden.

Variations:
Gravad lax can be substituted for smoked salmon.

SALMON QUICHE 120

TO DRINK
dry white wine or lager

LEVEL OF DIFFICULTY
easy

PREPARATION TIME
1 hr + resting time

PREPARE IN ADVANCE
yes

ONION TART

Serves 6-8

Pastry:
175 g/6 oz flour
150 g/5¼ oz butter, chilled
2-3 tbsp iced water

Filling:
3 tbsp butter
4 large onions, sliced
3 eggs
300 ml/10 fl oz single cream
200 g/7 oz strongly flavoured cheese, grated
salt or herb salt
freshly ground black pepper
cayenne pepper

Garnish:
leek cut into fine strips
lumpfish roe

1 Make the pastry. Rub the butter into the flour until the mixture resembles fine breadcrumbs. Add the water and work the dough together quickly. Set the pastry aside in the refrigerator to rest for approximately 1 hour.

2 Melt the butter in a saucepan. Add the onion and sweat over very low heat for 20-30 minutes until soft. Remove from the heat and allow to cool.

3 Roll out the dough. Line a 25 cm/10 inch diameter loose-based flan tin with the dough and prick the base with a fork. Crimp foil around the inside edges of the dough so that it does not collapse during baking. Set aside in the refrigerator for at least 15 minutes.

4 Meanwhile, preheat the oven to 200° C/400° F, gas mark 6. Beat together the eggs and cream. Add the grated cheese, salt, black pepper and cayenne pepper to taste. Stir in the onion.

5 Bake the dough case blind for 10 minutes. Remove the foil. Pour the filling into the pastry case and bake for a further 20-25 minutes or until the filling is golden.

6 Place the tart on a dish and garnish with the leek strips. Serve the roe separately.

Variations:
Instead of one large tart, you can make several small tartlets in small, loose-based tartlet tins.

TO DRINK
lager or white wine

LEVEL OF DIFFICULTY
easy

PREPARATION TIME
1 hr + resting time

PREPARE IN ADVANCE
yes

CHEESE FLAN

Serves 6-8

Pastry:
150 g/3¼ oz butter, chilled
175 g/6 oz flour
2-3 tbsp iced water

Filling:
300 ml/10 fl oz double cream
3 egg yolks
2 tbsp flour
200 g/7 oz strong-flavoured cheese, grated
salt
freshly ground black pepper
¼ tsp grated nutmeg
1 tbsp brandy (optional)
1 tbsp Madeira (optional)

1 Make the pastry. Rub the butter into the flour until the mixture resembles fine breadcrumbs. Add the water and work the pastry quickly together. Set the pastry aside in the refrigerator to rest for approximately 1 hour.

2 Make the filling. Beat the cream until frothy, add the egg yolks and sift in the flour. Mix well. Stir in the cheese and season with salt, pepper, and nutmeg. Add the brandy and Madeira, if using.

3 Roll our the dough fairly thinly and line a loose-based tin, approximately 25 cm/10 inches in diameter. Prick the dough base with a fork. Set aside in the refrigerator for 15-30 minutes. Preheat the oven to 200° C/400° F, gas mark 6.

4 Bake the dough case blind for 10 minutes. Pour in the filling and bake for a further 20-25 minutes or until the filling has risen and is golden.

Variations:
This flan may be served for lunch or supper, with thinly sliced smoked ham and a green salad. This will be enough to serve 4-5. It can also be served in small slices between meals as a snack, or at the end of a meal instead of a cheese board or other cheese dish.

CHEESE FLAN 122

To drink
red wine

LEVEL OF DIFFICULTY
easy

PREPARATION TIME
1 hr + resting time

PREPARE IN ADVANCE
yes

CHEESE PÂTÉ

Serves 8-10

250 g/8¾ oz fresh or frozen and thawed broccoli
2 tsp butter
2 tbsp breadcrumbs
5 eggs
300 ml/10 fl oz milk or single cream
500 g/1 lb strong-flavoured cheese, grated
2 tbsp cornflour
salt
freshly ground pepper
¼ tsp dried thyme

Serve with:
Nobi sauce (see recipe 431) and a green salad

1 Drain the broccoli, if frozen. Cut it into small pieces. Grease a rectangular 1.5 litre/2¾ pint dish with the butter and sprinkle with breadcrumbs. Preheat the oven to 170° C/325° F, gas mark 3.

2 Beat the eggs and add milk or cream. Add the cheese and cornflour. Season with salt, pepper and thyme.

3 Pour approximately half the mixture into the dish and add the drained broccoli pieces. Pour the remaining mixture on top. Alternatively, the broccoli may be stirred into the mixture.

4 Bake in the bottom of the oven for 1-1½ hours. Test with a skewer. Set aside to cool in the dish.

TO DRINK
red wine

LEVEL OF DIFFICULTY medium difficult
PREPARATION TIME 1½ hrs + cooling time
PREPARE IN ADVANCE yes

CRAB FLAN WITH WHITE SAUCE

Serves 4-6

Pastry:
175 g/6 oz flour
150 g/5¼ oz butter, chilled
2-3 tbsp iced water

Filling:
3 tbsp butter
3 tbsp flour
2-3 cloves garlic, crushed
200 ml/7 fl oz double cream
200 ml/7 fl oz crème fraîche
2-3 tsp paprika
2 tsp tomato purée
2 tbsp sherry
salt
freshly ground black pepper
cayenne pepper
225 g/8 oz cooked crabmeat

1 Make the pastry. Rub the butter into the flour until the mixture resembles fine breadcrumbs. Add the water and work the dough together quickly. Set aside in the refrigerator to rest for approximately 1 hour.

2 Roll out the dough and use it to line a loose-based tin. Prick the base with a fork. Pinch foil strips inside the inner edges to stop the pastry collapsing during baking. Set aside in the refrigerator for approximately 30 minutes. Preheat the oven to 200° C/400° F, gas mark 6.

3 Bake the pastry case blind for approximately 10 minutes. Remove the foil strips and bake for a further 15-20 minutes until the dough is lightly golden.

4 Meanwhile, make the filling. Melt the butter in a saucepan and stir in the flour and garlic. Gradually add the cream and crème fraîche, stirring constantly. Stir in the paprika, tomato purée and sherry. Simmer for approximately 5 minutes. Season with salt, black pepper and cayenne pepper to taste.

5 Cut crabmeat into small pieces and stir into the filling.

6 Warm the pastry base in the oven if it has been baked in advance. Heat up the filling and pour into the pastry base.

CRAB FLAN WITH WHITE SAUCE 124

TO DRINK
dry white wine

LEVEL OF DIFFICULTY
easy

PREPARATION TIME
1 hr + resting time

PREPARE IN ADVANCE
yes

SCOTCH EGGS

Serves 4

4 eggs

Meat mixture:
60 g/2 oz breadcrumbs
50 ml/2 fl oz single cream
50 ml/2 fl oz water
250 g/8¾ oz minced beef or lamb
1 egg yolk
1 tbsp melted butter
½ tsp salt
freshly ground white pepper

oil for deep-frying

Coating:
1 egg white, lightly beaten
125 g/4½ oz breadcrumbs

Garnish:
lettuce leaves
tomato wedges

1 Hard boil the eggs and allow them to cool. Remove the shells.

2 Mix together the breadcrumbs, cream and water and set aside for approximately 10 minutes. Add the minced meat, egg yolk, melted butter, salt and pepper. Work the mixture until smooth.

3 Divide the mixture into 4 equal portions and flatten each portion on a work surface. Lay one egg on each and roll the egg into the mixture. Make sure the eggs are well covered.

4 Brush the outsides with beaten egg white and roll in breadcrumbs.

5 Heat the oil in a deep-fryer until it registers 190°C /275° F, or a cube of stale bread turns golden within 30 seconds. Fry the scotch eggs for approximately 10 minutes until they are golden brown and crunchy outside. Drain on kitchen paper.

6 Cut into halves or into wedges and serve warm or cold with lettuce leaves and tomato wedges.

SCOTCH EGGS 125

TO DRINK
lager

LEVEL OF DIFFICULTY
fairly easy
PREPARATION TIME
30 mins
PREPARE IN ADVANCE
yes

EGGS BENEDICT

Serves 4

200 ml/7 fl oz Béarnaise sauce (see recipe 419)
4 eggs
1 litre/1¾ pints water
salt
1 tsp vinegar
4 slices white bread
60 g/2 oz butter
4 slices boiled ham

Garnish:
asparagus spears

1 Make the Béarnaise sauce. Stand the saucepan in tepid water until the sauce is going to be served.

2 Poach the eggs. Bring the water to the boil in a saucepan and add the salt and vinegar. Break each egg separately into a cup and slide them, one by one, into the simmering water. Remove the eggs with a slotted spoon after 3-4 minutes. Tidy up any broken edges on the egg white and place them in tepid water until ready to use.

3 Remove the crusts from the bread. Melt the butter and fry the bread slices until golden yellow. Place on dinner plates and add one slice of boiled ham to each slice of bread. Top with a poached egg and spoon over the Béarnaise sauce. Garnish with asparagus.

To drink
mineral water

LEVEL OF DIFFICULTY
easy
PREPARATION TIME
30 mins
PREPARE IN ADVANCE
partly

OEUFS EN COCOTTE

Serves 4

150 g/5¼ oz smoked salmon
4 tbsp finely chopped dill
freshly ground black pepper
1 tbsp butter
4 eggs
4-6 tbsp double cream

Garnish:
dill sprigs

1 Preheat the oven to 170° C/325° F, gas mark 3. Cut the salmon into strips. Mix the salmon, dill and pepper to taste.

2 Grease 4 individual ramekin dishes with the butter. Place the salmon and dill mixture in the bases of the dishes. Break the eggs, one at a time, into cups to ensure that they are fresh and that the yolks remain whole. Carefully pour one egg into each dish. Add 3-5 tsp double cream to each egg.

3 Place the ramekins in a roasting tin half filled with hot water. Bake in the oven for approximately 10 minutes or until the egg white has set but the yolk is still runny.

4 Garnish the cocottes with dill and serve immediately.

Variations:
Oeufs en cocotte can be made in various ways. Use one of the following recipes instead of the salmon and dill base:

- Sliced butter-fried mushrooms
- Drained canned asparagus tips.
- 2 anchovy fillets and 1 tsp lightly fried onion
- Butter-fried leaf spinach spiced with 1 tbsp nutmeg
- 1 tbsp of mushrooms in white sauce

TO DRINK
mineral water

LEVEL OF DIFFICULTY easy
PREPARATION TIME 30 mins
PREPARE IN ADVANCE yes

EGG AND ANCHOVY SALAD

Serves 6

3 tsp French mustard
1 large clove garlic, crushed
1 tbsp vinegar
200 ml/7 fl oz olive oil
2 x 125 g/4½ oz cans anchovy fillets
juice of ½ lemon
1 tsp dried tarragon
freshly ground black pepper
salt
6 hard-boiled eggs
6 large boiled potatoes
iceberg or round lettuce
capers

Serve with:
toast or crispbread and butter

1 Mix the mustard, garlic, vinegar and oil. Drain and reserve the oil from one can of anchovies and chop the anchovies. Add the anchovy oil, a little lemon juice, tarragon and pepper to the dressing. The dressing is inclined to separate; this does not matter. Mix the chopped anchovies into the dressing. Add salt and more lemon juice, to taste. Set the dressing aside in the refrigerator for approximately 2 hours so that the flavours mingle.

2 Shell the eggs. Separate the yolks and whites. Wrap the yolks in clingfilm and set aside in the refrigerator. Roughly chop the egg whites. Dice the potatoes and mix them with the chopped egg whites. Pour the dressing over them. Toss well. Cover with clingfilm and set aside in the refrigerator for several hours or overnight.

3 Cut the remaining anchovy fillets lengthwise. Taste the salad and add a little more anchovy oil if the taste is not strong enough. Mash the egg yolks.

4 Arrange the lettuce leaves or shredded iceberg lettuce in the base of a deep bowl. Place the marinated salad in the middle. Cover with the mashed egg yolks and arrange the anchovy fillets in a decorative pattern on top. Garnish with capers.

EGG AND ANCHOVY SALAD

TO DRINK
lager or beer

LEVEL OF DIFFICULTY
easy

PREPARATION TIME
12 hrs

PREPARE IN ADVANCE
yes

ANCHOVY MOUSSE

Serves 6-8

1 x 125 g/4½ oz can anchovy fillets
3 gelatine leaves
300 ml/10 fl oz double cream
1 tbsp brandy
2 tbsp dill, finely chopped
3 tbsp onion, finely chopped

Garnish:
1 x 125 g/4½ oz can anchovy fillets
8 stuffed olives

1 Drain the anchovy fillets and reserve the liquid. Mash the fillets in a mortar or a food processor.

2 Soak the gelatine leaves in cold water for approximately 10 minutes. Squeeze out the water and allow the gelatine to melt over low heat.

3 Beat the cream and stir in the mashed anchovy fillets, reserved liquid, brandy, dill, chopped onion and gelatine. Mix well.

4 Rinse a 500 ml/17 fl oz dish with cold water. Pour the mixture into it, cover and set the mousse aside to set in the refrigerator for several hours.

5 Dip the dish quickly in warm water and turn out on to a serving dish. Garnish with anchovy fillets cut lengthwise, arranged in a lattice pattern, and sliced stuffed olives.

6 Serve with crispbread, toast or small salted cheese biscuits. Alternatively, fill small mini crustades with the mousse and decorate with one olive slice and a little dill.

TO DRINK
dry vermouth or lager

LEVEL OF DIFFICULTY
easy

PREPARATION TIME
30 mins + setting time

PREPARE IN ADVANCE
yes

ANCHOVY ROLL

Serves 6-8

50 g/1¾ oz butter
60 g/2 oz flour
300 ml/10 fl oz milk
200 ml/7 fl oz single cream
3 eggs
½ tsp baking powder

Filling:
3 tbsp butter
3 large onions, finely chopped
1 x 125 g/4½ oz can anchovy fillets, drained with 2 tsp can oil reserved
6 tbsp finely chopped parsley
170 g/6 oz cheese, grated

1 Preheat the oven to 250° C/500° F, gas mark 10. Make the dough. Melt the butter and stir in the flour. Gradually stir in the milk and cream. Allow to cool slightly, stirring constantly. Add the reserved oil. Remove the pan from the heat.

2 Separate the eggs. Stir the yolks and baking powder into the mixture. Beat the egg whites until they form stiff peaks and fold into the mixture.

3 Line a rectangular baking tin, approximately 30 x 40 cm/12 x 16 inches, with greaseproof paper. Spread the mixture in the tin. Bake for approximately 20 minutes. Allow to cool slightly; place another sheet of greaseproof paper over the top and invert the pastry base.

4 Grease a baking sheet with a little butter. Make the filling. Melt the remaining butter and fry the onions. Chop the anchovies. Sprinkle the onions, anchovies, parsley and two-thirds of the grated cheese over the pastry base. Roll up, Swiss role style, and place the roll, seam side down, on the baking sheet.

5 Sprinkle over the remaining grated cheese just before serving and return to the oven for 8-10 minutes until the cheese has melted.

Variations:
Anchovy can be replaced by fine strips of smoked ham, or chopped prawns and chopped dill in hollandaise sauce.

ANCHOVY ROLL 130

TO DRINK
lager or schnapps

LEVEL OF DIFFICULTY
easy

PREPARATION TIME
1 hr

PREPARE IN ADVANCE
partly

BLINIS

Serves 4-6

200 ml/7 fl oz milk
1 egg
10 g/½ oz yeast
60 g/2 oz flour
60 g/2 oz self-raising flour
½ tsp salt
2 tbsp double cream or sour cream
2 tbsp butter

Serve with:
Russian caviar, which is the traditional complement, or lumpfish roe, finely chopped onion and sour cream

1 Warm the milk to 37° C/ 98° F (blood heat). Separate the egg. Pour a little of the milk into a bowl and stir in the yeast.

2 Add both types of flour, the egg yolk and remaining milk. Beat until the mixture is smooth and season with salt to taste. Cover and set aside to rise for 2 hours.

3 Beat the egg white until it forms stiff peaks. Stir the cream or soured cream into the mixture and carefully fold in the egg whites.

4 Heat a skillet and melt 1 tsp of the butter. Add enough mixture to cook one blini. Cook on both sides, slide out of the pan and continue making blinis in the same way until the mixture is used up, making 4-6 blinis.

5 Serve them piping hot, direct from the pan, with the accompaniments in separate bowls.

TO DRINK
vodka, Champagne or lager

LEVEL OF DIFFICULTY
fairly easy

PREPARATION TIME
30 mins + rising time

PREPARE IN ADVANCE
partly

SWEDISH BLOATERS

Serves 4

1 tbsp butter
8-10 bloaters, filleted
freshly ground black or white pepper
6 tbsp finely chopped dill
1 tbsp finely chopped parsley
3 tbsp finely chopped chives
150-200 ml/5-7 fl oz double cream
2 tbsp butter

1 Preheat the oven to 220° C/ 425° F, gas mark 7.

2 Grease an ovenproof dish with 2 tsp of the butter. Arrange the bloaters in the dish and sprinkle over a little pepper. Cover with dill, parsley and chives. Pour over enough cream almost to cover the fish. Dot with the remaining butter.

3 Bake for approximately 10-15 minutes until the cream has thickened and is pale golden in colour.

Variations:
The bloaters can be replaced with other types of smoked fish, such as kippers, mackerel or trout. Allow 1 fillet per person. The dish is less fattening if the double cream is replaced with a mixture of 1 egg and 150 ml/ 5 fl oz milk or single cream.

TO DRINK
beer

LEVEL OF DIFFICULTY
easy

PREPARATION TIME
30 mins

PREPARE IN ADVANCE
yes

LEMON FOURRÉ

Serves 4

4 lemons
4-6 canned sardines
8 black or green olives
1 tsp French mustard
2 tbsp crème fraîche
salt
freshly ground pepper

Garnish:
black caviar or lumpfish roe
parsley

1 Cut slices from the top of the lemons to make lids. Scrape out the flesh with a small sharp knife and a spoon and reserve. Cut a thin slice from the base of each lemon to make a flat surface, so that the lemons will stand upright.

2 Mash the sardines and finely chop the olives. Mix together the sardines, olives, mustard, crème fraîche and a little of the lemon flesh. Season with salt and pepper to taste.

3 Fill the lemons with the mixture. Top with black caviar or lumpfish roe and place the lemon lids on top. Decorate with a little parsley.

Variations:
Canned tuna fish in oil or brine can be substituted for the sardines.

TO DRINK
white wine or lager

LEVEL OF DIFFICULTY
easy

PREPARATION TIME
30 mins

PREPARE IN ADVANCE
yes

MATJES HERRING MOULD

Serves 6-8

300 ml/10 fl oz double cream
2 cans Matjes herrings
200 ml/7 fl oz crème fraîche
1 bunch chives, finely chopped
freshly ground black pepper

Garnish:
radishes
lemon slices
dill sprigs

Serve with:
boiled new potatoes

1 Beat the cream until smooth and thick.

2 Drain the herrings and chop finely.

3 Mix together the cream, crème fraîche, chopped herring and chives. Season with black pepper to taste.

4 Rinse a ring mould with cold water. Pour in the herring mixture, cover with foil and put the mould in the freezer for at least 4 hours, preferably overnight.

5 Leave the mould at room temperature for a short while before turning out. If the ring does not come away easily from the mould, quickly dip in lukewarm water.

MATJES HERRING MOULD 134

To drink
lager or schnapps

LEVEL OF DIFFICULTY
easy

PREPARATION TIME
30 mins + setting time

PREPARE IN ADVANCE
yes

PICKLED BALTIC HERRING

Serves 6-8

1 kg/2¼ lb Baltic herring

Marinade:
1 litre/1¾ pints water
100 ml/3½ fl oz vinegar
2 tbsp salt

Sauce:
200 ml/7 fl oz mayonnaise
200 ml/7 fl oz sour cream or crème fraîche
2 tbsp mustard
1 clove garlic, crushed

Garnish:
finely chopped dill

Serve with:
boiled potatoes
bread and butter

1 Fillet the herrings and remove the skin. Mix the marinade and add the herring fillets. Set aside in the refrigerator to marinate overnight.

2 Mix the sauce. Drain the herrings thoroughly and place them in the sauce. Set aside in the refrigerator for 24 hours.

Variations:
The garlic sauce can be replaced with mustard sauce. Mix 2 tbsp mustard, 1½ tbsp sugar, 1½ tbsp vinegar, 1 tsp salt and ¼ tsp freshly ground pepper. Mix thoroughly. Add 150 ml/5 fl oz vegetable oil, first drop by drop, then teaspoon by teaspoon, beating constantly. Stir in 6 tbsp chopped dill and 50 ml/2 fl oz sour cream.

TO DRINK
For the garlic variation, medium dry white wine
For the mustard variation, lager

LEVEL OF DIFFICULTY easy
PREPARATION TIME 48 hrs
PREPARE IN ADVANCE yes

OLD MAN'S MIXTURE

Serves 4

3 tbsp butter
2 medium onions
4 hard-boiled eggs
8 fresh anchovies, skinned and filleted or 1 x 125 g/4½ oz can anchovy fillets
freshly ground white pepper
4 slices white bread
finely chopped parsley

1 Peel and chop the onions. Melt 1 tbsp of the butter and sauté the onions until soft and transparent.

2 Shell and chop the eggs. Drain the canned anchovies, if using, and reserve the oil. Cut the anchovy fillets into small pieces. Add the chopped egg and the anchovies to the frying-pan with the onion. Stir over medium heat. Add a little anchovy oil if the mixture seems too dry or needs a stronger flavour. Sprinkle over a little white pepper.

3 Remove the crusts from the bread. Melt the remaining butter and fry the bread until golden brown and crispy.

4 Heat the 'old man's mixture' and divide equally between the fried bread slices. Sprinkle over a little parsley.

To drink
lager or schnapps

LEVEL OF DIFFICULTY
easy

PREPARATION TIME
30 mins

PREPARE IN ADVANCE
yes

PICKLED SHERRY HERRINGS
PICKLED SALT HERRINGS

Pickled Sherry Herrings:

Serves 4-6

4 Matjes herring fillets
2 onions, sliced
3 tbsp finely chopped dill

Marinade:
2 tbsp vinegar
2 tbsp oil
50 g/1¾ oz sugar
200 ml/7 fl oz tomato juice
10 crushed black peppercorns
3 tbsp sherry

1 Rinse the herring fillets and cut into chunks. Make alternate layers of herring, onion slices and dill in a glass jar or bowl.

2 Mix the ingredients for the marinade and pour over the herrings. Cover and place in the refrigerator for 24 hours before serving.

Pickled Salt Herrings:

Serves 6-8

4 large salt herring fillets, soaked overnight in water
2 onions, sliced
½ carrot, thinly sliced
½ small leek, sliced
1 tbsp peppercorns, crushed
2 bay leaves

Marinade:
6 tbsp vinegar
150 ml/5 fl oz water
85 g/3 oz sugar

Garnish:
1-2 red onions, sliced

1 Mix the marinade ingredients in a saucepan. Bring to the boil, remove from the heat and allow to cool.

2 Rinse the herring fillets. Leave them whole or cut into pieces, as preferred. Make alternate layers of herring, onion, carrot, leek and flavourings in a glass jar or bowl. Pour over the marinade. Cover, and place in the refrigerator for 1-2 days.

3 Serve garnished with sliced red onion.

TO DRINK
lager or schnapps

LEVEL OF DIFFICULTY
easy

PREPARATION TIME
30 mins + marinating time

PREPARE IN ADVANCE
yes

JANSSON'S TEMPTATION

Serves 4-6

6-8 large potatoes
2 large onions
8 fresh anchovies, skinned and filleted or 1 x 175 g/6 oz can anchovy fillets
2 tbsp butter
freshly ground black pepper
300 ml/10 fl oz double cream

1 Preheat the oven to 220° C/ 425° F, gas mark 7. Peel the potatoes and cut them in thin strips. Rinse under the cold running water and drain thoroughly.

2 Peel the onions and cut into thin slices. Drain the canned anchovies, if using, and reserve the oil. Cut the anchovy fillets into pieces.

3 Grease an ovenproof dish with 1 tbsp of the butter. Place a layer of potatoes on the bottom of the dish. Add the onions, anchovies and potatoes in layers, ending with potatoes. Sprinkle over a little black pepper.

4 Firm the mixture with the back of a spoon and pour over 200 ml/7 fl oz of the double cream and 2 tbsp of anchovy oil to strengthen the flavour, if liked. Dot the remaining butter on top and bake in the oven for approximately 45 minutes or until the potatoes are soft. Add more double cream during baking if required.

5 This dish can be prepared in advance and reheated in the oven just before serving.

JANSSON'S TEMPTATION

TO DRINK
lager

LEVEL OF DIFFICULTY
easy

PREPARATION TIME
1½ hrs

PREPARE IN ADVANCE
yes

CAVIAR MOULD

Serves 4

2 leaves gelatine
200 ml/7 fl oz bouillon or light stock
3 hard-boiled eggs, shelled
3-4 lettuce leaves
1 x 100 g/3½ oz can black caviar or lumpfish roe

Garnish:
lemon slices
pepper rings
dill
parsley
cooked, peeled prawns

1 Soak the gelatine leaves in cold water for approximately 10 minutes. Squeeze out the water and dissolve the gelatine in a little stock over low heat. Mix into the remaining stock.

2 Separate the yolks and whites of the hard-boiled eggs. Chop separately. Shred the lettuce.

3 Use four individual fluted moulds or dishes. Place a layer of caviar in the base of each mould. Pour over the stock so that it almost covers the caviar. Place the moulds in the refrigerator until the jelly has set.

4 Divide the chopped egg whites equally between the moulds on top of the caviar. Add stock so that it almost completely covers the egg whites and allow to set.

5 Add a layer of shredded lettuce to the moulds on top of the egg whites. Add the remaining stock. Place the moulds in the refrigerator until the jelly has completely set.

6 Dip the moulds quickly in hot water and turn out on to individual plates or on to one large serving dish. Garnish with the chopped egg yolks, shelled prawns, lemon slices, pepper rings, dill and parsley.

CAVIAR MOULD 139

TO DRINK
lager or dry white wine

LEVEL OF DIFFICULTY
medium difficult

PREPARATION TIME
1 hr + setting time

PREPARE IN ADVANCE
yes

CAVIAR SOUFFLÉ

Serves 4

3 hard-boiled eggs
salt
freshly ground black pepper
1 bunch chives, chopped
2 tbsp butter
2-3 tbsp caviar or lumpfish roe
1 tbsp mayonnaise
½ tsp cornflour
2 tsp grated Parmesan cheese
2 egg whites

1 Shell and chop the hard-boiled eggs, season with a little salt and pepper. Mix with half the chives. Grease 4 ramekins with the butter and place the chopped eggs in them.

2 Preheat the oven to 250° C/ 500° F, gas mark 10. Mix together the caviar or lumpfish roe, mayonnaise, cornflour, Parmesan cheese and the remaining chives.

3 Beat the egg whites until they form stiff peaks. Carefully fold into the caviar or lumpfish roe mixture. Put the mixture into the ramekins. Bake in the oven for 5-8 minutes until the soufflés have risen and are golden.

CAVIAR SOUFFLÉ 140

TO DRINK
beer

LEVEL OF DIFFICULTY
medium difficult
PREPARATION TIME
1 hr
PREPARE IN ADVANCE
yes

FISHERMAN'S BEST

Serves 6

6 large bloaters or other smoked fish
375 g/3/4 lb cooked, peeled prawns
3 hard-boiled eggs
1 large onion, finely chopped
3 tbsp finely chopped dill
3 tbsp finely chopped parsley
3 tbsp finely chopped chives
1 tbsp finely chopped lemon balm
black pepper
herb salt
75 g/2 3/4 oz butter
juice of 1 lemon
50 ml/2 fl oz brandy or gin

Garnish:
dill sprigs

Serve with:
sour cream
bread and butter

1 Fillet and skin the fish. Cut the flesh into small pieces. Roughly chop the prawns. Shell and chop the hard-boiled eggs.

2 Mix together the fish, egg, onion, dill, parsley, chives, lemon balm and pepper. Season with a little herb salt to taste.

3 Heat the butter and lemon juice in a saucepan. Fold in the egg and fish mixture. Cover and heat gently, without boiling. Stir in the brandy or gin. Remove the saucepan from the heat and add the chopped prawns. Add a little melted butter or lemon juice if the mixture seems too dry.

4 Divide the mixture between 6 crustades, bouchées or individual ovenproof dishes. Warm in a low oven for 5-10 minutes. Garnish with dill sprigs.

TO DRINK
lager or beer

LEVEL OF DIFFICULTY
easy

PREPARATION TIME
30 mins

PREPARE IN ADVANCE
yes

HERRING WITH MUSTARD SAUCE

Serves 4-6

1 kg/2¼ lb herring, cleaned and boned
3 leeks
2 tbsp butter
1½ tsp salt
freshly ground black pepper
1 bunch dill, finely chopped
2 tbsp breadcrumbs

Sauce:
2 egg yolks
2-3 tbsp mild mustard
50 ml/2 fl oz white wine vinegar
100 ml/3½ fl oz oil
40 g/1½ oz sugar
freshly ground pepper

Serve with:
boiled new potatoes

1 Rinse the herrings and cut away the fins. Set aside.

2 Rinse and slice the leek. Melt 1 tbsp of the butter and sauté the leek until soft. Grease an ovenproof dish with the remaining butter and put the leek in the base.

3 Place the herrings, skin side down, on a work surface. Season with salt and pepper and add a little dill. Roll the herring up, with the skin side outwards, and place them closely together in the dish on top of the leek. Preheat the oven to 200° C/400° F, gas mark 6.

4 Mix all the ingredients for the sauce together. Stir and season with salt, if necessary. Pour the sauce over the herrings and sprinkle over the breadcrumbs.

5 Place the dish in the oven and bake for approximately 25 minutes until the top has turned golden. Serve warm, lukewarm or cold.

HERRING WITH MUSTARD SAUCE 142

TO DRINK
lager

LEVEL OF DIFFICULTY easy
PREPARATION TIME 1 hr
PREPARE IN ADVANCE yes

SILLY DILLY
(Pickled Herrings in Dill)

Makes 10-12 small double sandwiches

3 salt pickled herrings (see recipe 137)
1 onion, chopped
2 tbsp capers
75 g/1¾ oz sweet pickled beetroot, chopped
1 tbsp sour cream or crème fraîche
1 tbsp melted butter
salt
freshly ground black pepper
sugar
vinegar (optional)
1 loaf day-old white bread
85 g/3 oz butter
finely chopped dill

1 Finely chop the herrings, onions, capers and beetroot in a mincer or food processor. Bind the mixture together with the soured cream or crème fraîche and the melted butter. Season with salt and pepper and, if liked, add a little sugar and vinegar to taste. Stir the mixture until smooth.

2 Slice the bread and cut out 20-24 small circles with a pastry cutter. Cover half of them with a layer, about 1 cm/½ inch thick, of the herring mixture. Place the remaining bread circles on top.

3 Melt the butter and fry the sandwiches on both sides. Place the finely chopped dill on a plate. As soon as the sandwiches come out of the frying-pan, roll the edges in the dill. Serve warm.

Variations:
Use pickled sherry herring (see recipe 137) instead of the salt pickled herrings and leave out the vinegar, salt and sugar.

TO DRINK
lager

LEVEL OF DIFFICULTY
easy

PREPARATION TIME
30 mins

PREPARE IN ADVANCE
partly

HERRING WITH HORSERADISH

Serves 4

600 g/1¼ lb herring fillets
1½ tsp salt
freshly ground black pepper
3 tbsp softened butter
2 tbsp grated horseradish
100 ml/3½ fl oz double cream
100 ml/3½ fl oz chili sauce
2 tbsp breadcrumbs

Serve with:
bread and butter

1 Rinse the herrings and pat dry. Preheat the oven to 220° C/425° F, gas mark 7. Grease an ovenproof dish with 1 tbsp of the butter.

2 Spread out the fillets, flesh side up. Sprinkle with salt and a little freshly ground pepper.

3 Mix together the remaining butter and the horseradish. Spread the horseradish butter evenly over the fillets and roll up. Arrange them tightly in the greased dish, seam sides down.

4 Mix the cream and chili sauce and pour the mixture over the herrings. Sprinkle over the breadcrumbs and bake in the oven for approximately 20 minutes.

HERRING WITH HORSERADISH 144

TO DRINK
lager

LEVEL OF DIFFICULTY easy
PREPARATION TIME 1 hr
PREPARE IN ADVANCE yes

PRINCE BERTIL'S PANCAKES

Serves 6

2 eggs
200 ml/7 fl oz single cream
2½ tbsp flour
1 tbsp melted butter
2-3 tbsp butter

Filling:
½ quantity Hollandaise sauce (see recipe 422)
500 g/1 lb cooked, peeled prawns
finely chopped dill

Garnish:
3 tbsp grated Parmesan cheese
2 tbsp butter, diced

1 Beat the eggs with a little of the cream. Beat in the flour, salt and the remaining cream. Set the mixture aside to rise for approximately 30 minutes. Mix in the melted butter just before frying.

2 Fry small thin pancakes in a greased crèpe pan or small frying-pan. Fry only one side and stack the pancakes on top of each other with the unfried sides facing upwards, interleaved with greaseproof paper, if they are not going to be filled immediately. Grease an ovenproof dish with the remaining butter.

3 Make the Hollandaise sauce and mix in the prawns. Divide the filling between the pancakes. Roll them up and arrange them, seam sides down, next to each other on the prepared dish. Sprinkle with cheese and dot with the diced butter.

4 Preheat the oven to 170° C/325° F, gas mark 3 and bake in the oven until the cheese has melted and the pancakes are thoroughly heated through.

TO DRINK
white wine

LEVEL OF DIFFICULTY easy
PREPARATION TIME 1 hr
PREPARE IN ADVANCE yes

FISH SAVARIN

Serves 4

Pastry:
125 g/4½ oz + 1 tbsp butter
175 g/6 oz + 1 tbsp flour
2-3 tbsp double cream

Filling:
150 g/5¼ oz smoked salmon
100 g/3½ Emmental cheese
4 lettuce leaves
250 g/8 oz cooked prawns
6 tbsp finely chopped dill
4 eggs
300 ml/10 fl oz single cream
salt
freshly ground black pepper

Serve with:
Hollandaise sauce (see recipe 422)

1 Grease a ring mould with 1 tbsp of the butter and coat with 1 tbsp flour. Make the dough. Rub the remaining butter into the remaining flour until it resembles fine breadcrumbs. Add the cream and work the dough together quickly. Set aside in the refrigerator to rest for at least 1 hour.

2 Roll out the dough and use to line the prepared mould. Chill in the refrigerator.

3 Preheat the oven to 250° C/500° F, gas mark 10. Cut the salmon into thin strips, dice the cheese, shred the lettuce and peel the prawns. Sprinkle the dill in the bottom of the mould and layer the prawns, salmon, cheese and lettuce on top.

4 Beat together the eggs and cream, and season with salt and pepper to taste. Pour the egg mixture into the mould; it should cover the filling.

5 Bake in the bottom of the oven for 15 minutes. Remove from the oven, cover with foil and bake for a further 15 minutes. Lower the temperature to 200° C/400° F, gas mark 6, and bake for a further 15-20 minutes. Invert on to a serving dish and allow to stand for a few minutes before removing the mould.

6 Serve the ring warm with Hollandaise sauce in a separate bowl.

FISH SAVARIN 146

To drink
dry white wine

LEVEL OF DIFFICULTY easy
PREPARATION TIME 1 hr + resting time
PREPARE IN ADVANCE yes

CRAYFISH GRATINÉE

Serves 4

16 boiled crayfish

Marinade:
3 tbsp olive oil
3 tbsp lemon juice
1 tsp paprika
1 drop tabasco
3 drops Worcestershire sauce
salt
freshly ground white pepper
100 ml/3½ fl oz dry white wine

Garnish:
120 g/4 oz white breadcrumbs
75 g/2¾ oz grated Parmesan cheese
2 cloves garlic, crushed
6 tbsp finely chopped dill
3 tbsp olive oil

1 Split the crayfish lengthwise with a sharp knife. Remove the stomach, which is situated behind the head, and the black intestine.

2 Line a rectangular ovenproof dish with foil. Arrange the crayfish next to each other, flesh side uppermost.

3 Mix all the ingredients for the marinade and spoon or brush over the crayfish. Leave in the refrigerator to marinate for 2 hours.

4 Preheat the oven to 250° C/500° F, gas mark 10. Mix the breadcrumbs, cheese, garlic and dill and spread the mixture evenly over the crayfish halves.

5 Drizzle a little olive oil over the breadcrumb and cheese topping and bake for 8-10 minutes. Serve immediately.

TO DRINK
dry white wine

LEVEL OF DIFFICULTY
easy

PREPARATION TIME
1 hr + marinating time

PREPARE IN ADVANCE
partly

GRAVAD LAX MOUSSE

Serves 4-6

2 gelatine leaves
300 g/10½ oz gravad lax, cut into pieces
1 ice cube
4 tbsp sour cream
1 tbsp gravad lax sauce (see recipe 423)
50 ml/2 fl oz light stock or bouillon

Garnish:
100 g/3½ oz gravad lax, cut into strips
mixed salad leaves
dill sprigs

1 Soak the gelatine leaves in cold water for approximately 10 minutes.

2 Make the mousse in a food processor. Place the fish pieces in the bowl together with the ice cube. Switch the machine on for a couple of seconds, add the sour cream and gravad lax sauce and switch the machine back on for a few more seconds.

3 Squeeze the gelatine, add to the bouillon and melt over low heat. Set aside to cool.

4 Stir the bouillon mixture into the mousse. Rinse a small ring mould or individual bowls with cold water. Pour in the mousse and set aside in the refrigerator for 2-3 hours.

5 Turn out the mousse and garnish with slices of gravad lax, salad leaves and dill sprigs.

Variations:
Leave out the gelatine and bouillon and serve the mousse as it is. Add small croûtons and hard-boiled egg halves. Alternatively, use as a filling for avocado halves. Decorate with gravad lax strips, small lettuce leaves and dill.

TO DRINK
dry white wine or sherry

LEVEL OF DIFFICULTY
medium difficult

PREPARATION TIME
30 mins + setting time

PREPARE IN ADVANCE
yes

HAZELNUT MUSSELS

Serves 4

24 mussels

Sauce:
2 shallots, finely chopped
2 cloves garlic, crushed
3 tbsp finely chopped hazelnuts
1 bunch parsley, chopped
4 tbsp olive oil or corn oil
1 tbsp water
salt
freshly ground black pepper
juice of 1 lemon

Serve with:
toast and butter or small bread rolls

1 Scrub the mussels under cold running water. Discard any that do not close when sharply tapped. Place the mussels in a large saucepan, just cover with water and set over high heat. Boil, covered, for 5-10 minutes or until the mussels have opened. Discard any mussels which have not opened.

2 Make the sauce. Mix together the shallots, garlic, nuts, parsley, oil and water. Season with salt, pepper and a little lemon juice to taste.

3 Strain the mussels, twist away one shell half and leave the mussels inside the base shell. Arrange them on a dish covered with rock salt so that they do not fall over. Spoon the hazelnut sauce over the mussels and leave in the refrigerator for 1-2 hours before serving.

Variations:
This dish can also be made with canned mussels in brine. Place them in thoroughly cleaned mussel shells which have been saved for this purpose. Choose the large farm produced mussels (1 x 225 g/8 oz can) and drain thoroughly before marinating in the sauce.

TO DRINK
dry white wine

LEVEL OF DIFFICULTY
easy

PREPARATION TIME
1 hr + chilling time

PREPARE IN ADVANCE
yes

LOBSTER THERMIDOR

Serves 4

2 boiled lobsters

Sauce:
2 tbsp vinegar
100 ml/3½ fl oz dry white wine
2 tsp French mustard
2 shallots, finely chopped
1 tsp dried tarragon
1 tbsp chopped parsley
2 tbsp butter
1½ tbsp flour
300 ml/10 fl oz single cream
1 egg yolk
50 ml/2 fl oz double cream
salt
freshly ground black pepper
2-3 tbsp grated Parmesan cheese
100 g/3½ oz small butter-fried button mushrooms

Serve with:
toast and butter

1 Split the lobsters in half lengthwise and remove the stomach and intestine.

2 Pick out the meat and reserve the liver. Break off the claws and the joints and remove the meat. Cut all the meat into small pieces.

3 Bring the vinegar, wine, mustard, shallots, tarragon and parsley to the boil. Boil until reduced by half.

4 Melt the butter and stir in the flour. Gradually stir in the cream and simmer until thick, stirring constantly. Strain over the wine and vinegar mixture. Remove the pan from the heat. Beat together the egg yolk and double cream and beat the mixture into the sauce. Season to taste and add half the cheese. Reserve the finest lobster pieces and mix the remaining lobster meat and the liver into the sauce.

5 Divide the sauce equally between the lobster shells. Top with the reserved lobster pieces and the mushrooms. Sprinkle over the remaining cheese. Keep the filled lobster halves in the refrigerator if they are not to be baked immediately.

6 Preheat the oven to 250° C/500° F, gas mark 10. Bake for 10-15 minutes until the lobster is thoroughly heated all the way through and serve immediately.

LOBSTER THERMIDOR 150

To DRINK
Champagne or sparkling dry white wine

LEVEL OF DIFFICULTY easy
PREPARATION TIME 1 hr
PREPARE IN ADVANCE yes

RHODE ISLAND LOBSTER SALAD

Serves 4

2 large firm tomatoes
100 g/3½ oz mushrooms, sliced
2 celery sticks
2 hard-boiled eggs, shelled and halved
2 boiled lobsters
4 green or mixed lettuce leaves, shredded
dill sprigs

Sauce:
200 ml/7 fl oz mayonnaise
3-4 tbsp chili sauce
small pinch cayenne pepper
1-2 tbsp brandy (optional)
½ red pepper, finely chopped

Dressing:
1 tbsp vinegar
1 tbsp water
2 tbsp oil
salt
pepper

1 Mix together all the ingredients for the sauce and pour into a bowl to be served separately.

2 Skin and seed the tomatoes. Cut them into strips. Thinly slice the celery.

3 Chop the egg whites and yolks separately. Slice the lobsters in half lengthwise and remove all the meat, keeping it as whole as possible. Slice the tail meat and return all the lobster meat to shells. Put the small pieces of meat from the claws and joints under the tail meat slices. Place the lobster claw, whole, in the front part of the lobster half.

4 Divide the shredded lettuce between four plates. Place one lobster half on each lettuce bed. Place the remaining ingredients, in a decorative fashion, around the lobster and garnish with sprigs of dill.

5 Beat together all the dressing ingredients or shake them together in a screw-top jar. Spoon over the lettuce.

TO DRINK
dry white wine or sparkling wine

LEVEL OF DIFFICULTY
easy

PREPARATION TIME
1 hr

PREPARE IN ADVANCE
partly

CRAB

Serves 4

2-4 crabs
water
3 tbsp rock salt crystals per 1 litre/1¾ pints water

Serve with:
gravad lax sauce (see recipes 423 and 424) or mayonnaise, toast and butter

1 Scrub the crabs under cold running water. Bring plenty of salted water to the boil, add the crabs and allow to come back to the boil. Boil vigorously for 20 minutes, turn off the heat and let the crabs cool in the cooking liquid.

CRAB GRATINÉE:

Serves 4

4 boiled crabs
100 ml/3½ fl oz vegetable oil
25 g/¾ oz butter
1 leek cut into strips
3 onions, finely chopped
2 cloves garlic, crushed
150 ml/5 fl oz fish or chicken stock
1 tbsp tomato purée
6 tbsp finely chopped parsley
1 tbsp French mustard
salt
freshly ground black pepper
pinch cayenne pepper
2 tbsp sherry
2 tbsp brandy

1 Divide the crabs so that the main shells remain whole. Break off the claws, remove the roe and all the crabmeat and cut into small pieces.

2 Heat the oil and butter and sauté the leek, onion and garlic without colouring. Add the stock, tomato purée and crabmeat and heat through. Stir in the parsley. Add mustard, salt, black pepper and cayenne pepper to taste. Stir in the sherry and brandy.

3 Preheat the oven to 250° C/ 500° F, gas mark 10. Scrub the crab shells thoroughly and divide the filling equally between them. Bake for 10-15 minutes.

TO DRINK
dry white wine, lager or beer (for boiled crab); medium dry white wine (for the crab gratinée).

LEVEL OF DIFFICULTY
easy
PREPARATION TIME
1 hr
PREPARE IN ADVANCE
yes

CRAYFISH MOULD

Serves 8

1.5 kg/3¼ lb boiled crayfish
10 gelatine leaves
250 ml/8¾ fl oz water
1 fish stock cube
2 bay leaves
½ tbsp dill seeds
juice of ½ lemon
200 ml/7 fl oz white wine
1 bunch dill, finely chopped

Sauce:
300 ml/10 fl oz mayonnaise
100 ml/3½ fl oz sour cream
6 tbsp finely chopped dill

Garnish:
crayfish heads
lemon slices
dill sprigs

1 Peel and gut the crayfish. Save a few of the nicest heads for the garnish. Keep the tails and the meat from the claws and scrape out everything edible from the bodies.

2 Soak the gelatine leaves in cold water for 10 minutes. Bring the water, stock cube, bay leaves and dill seeds to the boil. Squeeze the gelatine leaves and melt in the stock. Remove the pan from the heat and add the lemon juice and the wine. Discard the bay leaves. Measure the stock and make up to 500 ml/17 fl oz with water. Stir in half the chopped dill. Place in the refrigerator until slightly thickened.

3 Rinse a ring mould or other dish with cold water. Pour in a base of thickened gelatine and add the remaining dill. Layer with crayfish tails and gelatine, with the nicest crayfish pieces facing the edges and at the base of the mould. Put the claw meat and other small pieces of meat in the middle of the mould.

4 Place in the refrigerator for 3-5 hours or overnight. Do not leave longer than 24 hours.

5 Make the sauce. Mix the mayonnaise, sour cream and chopped dill. Season to taste.

6 Dip the mould quickly in hot water and loosen the edges with a knife. Invert on to a serving dish and garnish with crayfish heads, lemon slices and dill sprigs.

TO DRINK
white wine

LEVEL OF DIFFICULTY
medium difficult

PREPARATION TIME
1-2 hrs + setting time

PREPARE IN ADVANCE
yes

SALMON MOUSSE

Serves 4

160 g/5½ oz fresh salmon, poached, boned and skinned
200 g/7 oz smoked salmon, cut into thin slices
200 ml/7 fl oz double cream, lightly whipped
salt
freshly ground black pepper
½ tsp lemon juice
2 gelatine leaves
dill sprigs

Wine jelly:
2 gelatine leaves
200 ml/7 fl oz white wine
½ tsp salt

Serve with:
freshly toast and butter or fried bread croûtons

1 Carefully mix the poached salmon and 100 g/3½ oz of the smoked salmon in a mixer or food processor. Mix in the cream and season with salt, pepper and lemon juice to taste.

2 Soak the gelatine leaves in cold water for approximately 10 minutes. Wring out the excess water and melt in a bowl over a small saucepan of boiling water. Stir the dissolved gelatine leaves into the salmon mixture.

3 Line the base of four individual moulds or ramekins with one thin slice of smoked salmon. Fill the moulds with the salmon mixture and keep them in the refrigerator for 5-6 hours before serving.

4 Make the wine jelly. Soak the gelatine leaves in cold water for 10 minutes. Remove from the water and squeeze. Heat the wine with the salt, add the gelatine leaves and melt. Pour the gelatine into a shallow dish and allow to set in the refrigerator.

5 Turn the mousse out on to serving plates, garnish with sprigs of dill and chopped wine jelly. Serve with fresh toast or fried-bread croûtons.

SALMON MOUSSE 154

To drink
dry white wine

LEVEL OF DIFFICULTY
medium difficult

PREPARATION TIME
30 mins + setting time

PREPARE IN ADVANCE
yes

SALMON ROLL

Serves 8

300 g/10½ oz smoked salmon
3 tbsp butter
1 onion, chopped
freshly ground black pepper
1 egg yolk
50 ml/2 fl oz sour cream
1 large bunch dill, chopped
450 g/1 lb frozen leaf spinach, thawed
½ clove garlic, crushed
salt
4 sheets frozen puff pastry, thawed
1 egg, beaten

Serve with:
sour cream or smetana

1 Cut the salmon into small squares. Preheat the oven to 250° C/500° F, gas mark 10.

2 Melt half the butter and sauté the onion. Add the salmon and fry for 2-3 minutes. Season with black pepper. Remove the pan from the heat and add the egg yolk, sour cream and dill. Mix thoroughly and set aside to cool.

3 Roughly chop the spinach. Melt the remaining butter and fry the spinach. Add the garlic and season with salt, pepper.

4 Line a baking sheet with greaseproof paper. Roll out the dough into 4 lengths, 30 x 10 cm/12 x 4 inches. Place two dough strips on the prepared baking sheet. Brush the edges with beaten egg. Divide spinach equally between them. Top with the salmon. Do not cover the egg-brushed edges.

5 Cover with the other two sheets of dough and press the edges together with a fork to seal. Trim away any excess dough and cut 2-3 air holes or slits in the top. Brush with beaten egg. Bake for approximately 10 minutes. The rolls can be made well in advance, and then reheated in the oven before serving.

6 Place the rolls on a cutting board or serving dish and slice into portions. Serve with sour cream or smetana.

TO DRINK
lager, sherry or dry white wine

LEVEL OF DIFFICULTY
easy

PREPARATION TIME
1 hr

PREPARE IN ADVANCE
yes

SALMON TARTAR

Serves 4

250 g/8¾ oz salmon, skinned and boned
100 g/3½ oz trout roe
freshly ground white pepper
salt

Garnish:
½ red onion, finely chopped
lettuce leaves
lemon wedges

Serve with:
crème fraîche
butter-fried croûtons

1 Chop the salmon and mix with the trout roe. Season with pepper and salt to taste, if the roe is not salty enough.

2 Shape the salmon mixture into oval balls and place on chilled individual plates. Place in the refrigerator if they are not to be served immediately.

3 Place 1-2 tsp chopped red onion on top of each salmon tartar. Garnish with lettuce leaves and lemon wedges. Serve with ice cold crème fraîche in a separate bowl.

SALMON TARTAR 156

TO DRINK
vodka or dry white wine

LEVEL OF DIFFICULTY
easy

PREPARATION TIME
30 minutes

PREPARE IN ADVANCE
partly

MUSSELS WITH BACON

Serves 4

3 tbsp butter
1 clove garlic, crushed
4 slices white bread
1 x 225 g/8 oz can mussels in brine
4-8 rashers bacon
3 tbsp chopped parsley

1 Mix the butter with the garlic. Cut off the crusts from the bread. Drain the mussels.

2 Fry the bacon rashers. Remove them and fry the mussels quickly in the bacon fat. Stir in the parsley.

3 Melt the garlic butter and fry the bread slices on both sides. Transfer to individual plates. Add the mussels and top with the bacon.

TO DRINK
lager or white wine

LEVEL OF DIFFICULTY
easy

PREPARATION TIME
30 mins

PREPARE IN ADVANCE
partly

OYSTERS

6 oysters per person

Garnish:
crushed ice
lemon wedges

The oysters must be absolutely fresh and alive. If they are alive, the shells should be fully closed or they should shut when sharply tapped. They must be served freshly opened.

1 Scrub the oysters and rinse them under cold running water. Keep them horizontal all the time with the rounded shell halves downwards so that the juice does not escape.

2 Open the oysters. Use a double thickness of kitchen paper and a short, sharp knife, preferably an oyster knife. Place the kitchen paper in the hand in which you are going to hold the oyster, i.e. the left hand if you are right-handed and the right hand if you are left-handed. This is to protect your hand if the knife should slip. Place the oyster on top of the kitchen paper, belly side down. Insert the knife between both shell halves, at the top where the joint is located. Wriggle the knife to and fro a few times. Insert the knife as close as possible to the top shell and cut away the muscle which holds the halves together. Remove the top shell. Remove any shell splinters. Loosen the oyster from the lower shell but do not remove.

3 Place the oysters in their shells on oyster plates or a bed of crushed ice. Garnish with lemon wedges.

Variations:
Make a vinaigrette by marinating finely chopped shallots in white wine vinegar, seasoned with a little freshly ground black pepper. Strain the shallot vinaigrette and serve in a separate bowl.

TO DRINK
stout, beer or white wine

LEVEL OF DIFFICULTY
easy
PREPARATION TIME
30 mins
PREPARE IN ADVANCE
no

JOPPE'S PRAWN SALAD

Serves 6

800 g/1¾ lb cooked, unpeeled prawns
200 g/7 oz mushrooms
3 tomatoes
1 can asparagus spears
2 hard-boiled eggs
1 head lettuce
1 clove garlic
chopped dill
chopped chives

Sauce:
vinaigrette (see recipe 433) or chili mayonnaise with horseradish (see recipe 427)

Serve with:
toast and butter

1 Peel and devein the prawns. Clean and slice the mushrooms. Cut the tomatoes into wedges. Drain the asparagus. Shell the eggs and cut into wedges. Rinse the lettuce and separate the leaves. Make the sauce.

2 Rub the inside of a salad bowl with a cut garlic clove. Line the bowl with lettuce leaves and layer with the remaining ingredients. Sprinkle with dill and chives. Pour over the vinaigrette or serve the chili mayonnaise in a separate bowl.

TO DRINK
dry white wine, lager or mineral water

LEVEL OF DIFFICULTY
easy

PREPARATION TIME
1 hr

PREPARE IN ADVANCE
partly

PRAWN RING

Serves 6-8

1 kg/2¼ lb cooked prawns
freshly ground black pepper
salt
100 g/3½ oz dill, finely chopped
350 ml/12 fl oz double cream
4½ gelatine leaves
2-3 tbsp sherry or lemon juice

Garnish:
black caviar or lumpfish roe
cooked, peeled prawns
cucumber slices
dill sprigs

1 Peel the prawns and place them in a deep bowl. Sprinkle over a little pepper and add ½-1 tsp salt, depending on how salty the prawns are. Add the chopped dill and pour over the cream. Mix thoroughly. Cover with foil and set aside in the refrigerator for 10-12 hours or overnight.

2 Soak the gelatine leaves in cold water for approximately 10 minutes. Squeeze out the excess water, warm the sherry or lemon juice and melt the gelatine in it.

3 Strain the prawns and reserve the marinade. Beat the cream with the gelatine. Stir in the prawns and dill. Rinse a 1-litre/1¾-pint dish with cold water. Pour in the prawn mixture, cover with foil and place in the refrigerator for at least 3-4 hours, to set.

4 Dip the dish quickly in hot water and turn out on to a serving plate. Garnish with the caviar or lumpfish roe, prawns, cucumber and dill.

PRAWN RING 160

To drink
white wine, sherry or lager

LEVEL OF DIFFICULTY
easy
PREPARATION TIME
24 hours
PREPARE IN ADVANCE
yes

PRAWNS FLORENTINE

Serves 4

1 x 250 g/8¾ oz frozen leaf spinach
500 g/1 lb cooked prawns
2 tbsp butter
herb salt
grated nutmeg

Sauce:
2 tbsp butter
2 tbsp flour
100 ml/3½ fl oz milk and fish stock
100 ml/3½ fl oz dry white wine
150 ml/5 fl oz double cream
freshly ground white pepper
cayenne pepper
salt
1 egg yolk
120 g/4 oz cheese, grated

1 Preheat the oven to 250° C/500°F, gas mark 10. Thaw the spinach and drain off any excess water. Peel the prawns. Grease 4 scallop shells or individual ovenproof bowls with half the butter.

2 Roughly chop the spinach. Melt the butter and lightly fry the spinach. Season with herb salt and grated nutmeg to taste. Divide the spinach equally between the scallop shells or dishes.

3 To make the sauce, melt the butter and stir in the flour. Gradually stir in the milk and stock, wine, and cream. Simmer, stirring constantly, for 5-10 minutes until thickened. Season with white pepper, cayenne pepper and salt. Stir in the egg yolk and prawns. Do not allow the sauce to boil, otherwise the prawns will become chewy.

4 Pour equal amounts over the spinach and cover with grated cheese.

5 Bake in the oven for 8-10 minutes, until the sauce is heated through and the top is golden.

TO DRINK
dry white wine

LEVEL OF DIFFICULTY easy
PREPARATION TIME 45 mins
PREPARE IN ADVANCE yes

PRAWN CAKE

Serves 6

4 sheets frozen puff pastry, thawed
1 egg, beaten

Filling:
600-700 g/1¼-1½ lb cooked, prawns
200 ml/7 fl oz mayonnaise
50 ml/2 fl oz sour cream
salt or herb salt
freshly ground black pepper
cayenne pepper
2 tbsp finely chopped dill
1 small jar lumpfish roe

Garnish:
cucumber slices
lemon slices
dill sprigs

1 Line a baking sheet with greaseproof paper. Lay the dough sheets in pairs beside each other, overlapping by 1 cm/½ inch. Brush the edges with cold water before rolling out. Cut out two circles, using a plate as a template. Place the dough circles on the prepared baking sheet. Prick with a fork. Glaze with beaten egg. Set aside to rest for 20 minutes. Preheat the oven to 220° C/425° F, gas mark 7.

2 Bake the dough circles for approximately 10 minutes, until they feel light and brittle and are golden. Set aside to cool. They can be made in advance and then kept in an airtight container in a cool place, but not in the refrigerator.

3 Peel the prawns and reserve 20-25 for the garnish. Chop the remainder. Mix together 150 ml/5 fl oz of the mayonnaise and the sour cream and add the chopped prawns. Season with salt or herb salt, black pepper, cayenne pepper and dill.

4 Spread a thin layer of the remaining mayonnaise on one of the pastry circles. Sprinkle over a layer of lumpfish roe and arrange the reserved prawns on top.

5 Place the prawn filling on the other circle. Top with the circle that has already been decorated. Garnish with cucumber slices, lemon slices and dill sprigs.

PRAWN CAKE 162

TO DRINK
sparkling dry white wine

LEVEL OF DIFFICULTY
fairly easy

PREPARATION TIME
1 hr

PREPARE IN ADVANCE
yes

SALMON PLATE

Serves 4

frisée lettuce
4 large thin slices smoked salmon

Dressing:
1 tbsp lemon juice
3 tbsp olive oil
a little grated horseradish
salt
freshly ground black pepper

Serve with:
small, warm bread rolls or toast and butter

1 Rinse and prepare the lettuce. Arrange the lettuce leaves attractively on four dinner plates and place the salmon slices on top.

2 Mix the dressing and pour over.

3 Serve the salad with small warm bread rolls or toast, and butter.

TO DRINK
lager or dry white wine

LEVEL OF DIFFICULTY
easy

PREPARATION TIME
15 mins

PREPARE IN ADVANCE
yes

SHELLFISH PÂTÉ

approximately 16 slices

500 g/1 lb fillet of firm white fish
1 tbsp butter
1 tbsp breadcrumbs
salt
freshly ground black pepper
pinch cayenne pepper
3 egg whites
1 tbsp cornflour
400 ml/14 fl oz double cream
1 tbsp finely chopped dill
500 g/1 lb cooked, prawns
6 crayfish tails
meat from 1 crab

Green sauce:
400 ml/14 fl oz mayonnaise
200 ml/7 fl oz sour cream
2 cloves garlic, crushed
2 tbsp finely chopped chives
2 tbsp finely chopped parsley
2 tbsp finely chopped dill

1 Preheat the oven to 200° C/ 400° F, gas mark 6. Grease a 2-litre/3½-pint rectangular dish with the butter and coat with breadcrumbs. Cut the fish fillets into small pieces and finely chop in a food processor or food mill.

2 Stir in salt, black pepper, cayenne pepper and the egg white. Add the cornflour and the cream, a little at a time. Stir vigorously or work in the food processor until the mixture is smooth. Stir in the dill.

3 Peel the prawns. Reserve a few for the garnish and roughly chop the rest. Divide the crayfish tails and crabmeat.

4 Beat the remaining egg whites until they form stiff peaks. Fold them into the crab mixture. Make alternate layers of prawn mixture and crab mixture in the dish, ending with a layer of prawn mixture.

5 Cover with foil and place in a roasting tin half filled with hot water. Bake for 1 hour. Test with a skewer to see if it feels firm. Allow the pâté to cool slightly before turning out. Cover with foil and place in the refrigerator.

6 Mix all the ingredients for the sauce in a bowl and set aside for one hour for the flavours to infuse. Cut the pâté into slices and place on a serving dish. Garnish with peeled prawns and dill sprigs.

TO DRINK
dry white wine

LEVEL OF DIFFICULTY
medium difficult

PREPARATION TIME
2 hrs

PREPARE IN ADVANCE
yes

SEAFOOD ROLL

Serves 6-8

Pastry:
150 ml/5 fl oz water
100 ml/3½ fl oz single cream
50 g/1¾ oz butter
90 g/3¼ oz flour
3 eggs

Filling:
1 x 227 g/8 oz packet crab sticks
250 g/9 oz peeled prawns
1 x 200 g/7 oz can mussels in brine
300 ml/10 fl oz double cream
3 tbsp grated horseradish
salt
6 tbsp finely chopped dill

1 Preheat the oven to 200° C/ 400° F, gas mark 6. Line a rectangular baking tin, 30 x 40 cm/12 x 16 inches with greaseproof paper. Bring the water, cream and butter to the boil. Add the flour, stirring vigorously. Stir until the mixture comes away from the base of the pan. Set aside to cool. Add the eggs, one at a time, beating thoroughly between each addition.

2 Pour the mixture into the prepared baking tin and bake for approximately 20 minutes. Turn out on to a sheet of greaseproof paper and allow to cool.

3 Drain the mussels. Thaw the crab sticks and cut or snip them into smaller pieces.

4 Beat the cream. Stir in horseradish and dill. Season with salt to taste.

5 Spread the cream over the pastry base and add the mussels and prawns. Roll up, Swiss roll style, and chill in the refrigerator for 2-3 hours.

6 Place the roll on an attractive carving dish or arrange in slices on a large platter.

TO DRINK
dry white wine

LEVEL OF DIFFICULTY
fairly easy

PREPARATION TIME
1 hr + chilling time

PREPARE IN ADVANCE
yes

SNAILS IN GARLIC BUTTER

Serves 4

24 snail shells
1 can x 24 snails

Garlic butter:
150 g/5 oz butter
2 tbsp finely chopped parsley
1 tbsp very finely chopped shallots
1 tsp garlic juice from a crushed clove garlic
salt
freshly ground white pepper
3-4 cloves garlic, crushed

Serve with:
French bread

1 Wash and scrub the snail shells and allow to dry, face down, on kitchen paper. Drain the snails. Preheat the oven to 250° C/500° F, gas mark 10.

2 Mix all the ingredients for the garlic butter.

3 Place a little garlic butter into the base of each shell and add 1 snail. Fill the rest of the shell with garlic butter. Place the snails, with the opening facing upwards, on an ovenproof snail dish. If there is no snail dish available, put the shells into an ovenproof dish and surround them with crumpled foil to support them and prevent them from falling over.

4 Bake the snails in the oven for 8-10 minutes until the garlic butter has started to bubble but has not browned.

SNAILS IN GARLIC BUTTER 166

To drink
red wine

LEVEL OF DIFFICULTY
easy

PREPARATION TIME
30 mins

PREPARE IN ADVANCE
yes

TAGLIATELLE WITH SALMON SAUCE

Serves 4

200 g/7 oz mixed egg and spinach tagliatelle

Sauce:
1 large carrot
2 leeks
250 g/8 oz smoked salmon
2-3 tbsp butter
pinch saffron
100 ml/3½ fl oz dry white wine
300-400 ml/10-14 fl oz double cream
salt
freshly ground black pepper
cayenne pepper

Garnish:
50-100 g/1¾-3½ oz red lumpfish roe

Serve with:
grated Parmesan cheese

1 Cook the pasta in plenty of boiling salted water for 8-10 minutes, or until *al dente*. Drain.

2 Meanwhile, slice the carrot into thin strips. Rinse the leeks and cut away most of the green part. Cut the remaining part into thin strips. Cut the salmon into strips.

3 Melt the butter in a saucepan and add the carrot and leeks and cook slowly over low heat until soft. Sprinkle over the saffron and stir. Add the wine and cream and simmer for 3-5 minutes. Add the salmon strips and salt, black pepper and cayenne pepper to taste.

4 Place the pasta on a warm serving dish or divide between individual dinner plates. Pour over the sauce. Garnish with a spoonful of roe.

TAGLIATELLE WITH SALMON SAUCE 167

TO DRINK
dry white wine

LEVEL OF DIFFICULTY
easy

PREPARATION TIME
30 mins

PREPARE IN ADVANCE
no

TASTY TOAST

Serves 4

400 g/14 oz cooked prawns
100-150 ml/3½-5 fl oz mayonnaise
1 tbsp finely chopped dill
salt
freshly ground white pepper
4 slices white bread
60-85 g/2-3 oz butter
50-100 g/1¾-3½ oz lumpfish roe

Garnish:
1 tbsp finely chopped chives
lettuce leaves

1 Peel the prawns and roughly chop them. Mix the prawns with the mayonnaise and dill. Season with salt and pepper to taste.

2 Remove the crusts from the bread. Melt the butter and fry the bread until golden brown and crisp.

3 Place the prawn mayonnaise on top of the bread slices and top with a generous spoon of roe. Garnish with finely chopped chives and lettuce leaves.

TO DRINK
dry white wine or lager

LEVEL OF DIFFICULTY
easy

PREPARATION TIME
30 mins

PREPARE IN ADVANCE
partly

HOT PRAWN SANDWICH

Serves 4

1-2 leeks
2 tbsp butter
2 tbsp water
400 g/14 oz cooked prawns
4 slices white bread
1 egg
100 ml/3½ fl oz mayonnaise
1-2 tsp French mustard
1 x 100 g/3½ oz jar black caviar or lumpfish roe

1 Rinse the leeks and cut into thin slices. Melt 1 tbsp of the butter and sauté the leeks over very low heat until soft. If necessary, add the water. Set aside to cool.

2 Preheat the oven to 250° C/500° F, gas mark 10. Peel the prawns and remove the crusts from the bread. Spread the bread with the remaining butter.

3 Separate the egg. Beat the egg white until it forms stiff peaks. Beat the egg yolk with the mayonnaise and add mustard to taste. Carefully fold in the egg white.

4 Divide the leeks evenly between the bread slices. Add the prawns and top with a layer of black caviar or lumpfish roe. Cover with the mayonnaise mixture.

5 Bake in the top of the oven for 6-8 minutes, until the top has risen and is golden. Serve immediately.

TO DRINK
lager

LEVEL OF DIFFICULTY easy
PREPARATION TIME 30 mins
PREPARE IN ADVANCE partly

SWEDISH SALAD

Serves 4

1 medium-sized boiled lobster or
1 boiled crab
1 packet frozen green asparagus
125 g/4½ oz frozen petit pois
4 medium tomatoes
lettuce leaves
12-16 boiled crayfish tails, shelled
200 g/7 oz cooked prawns, peeled
16-20 boiled mussels
200 g/7 oz mushrooms, sliced

Dressing:
2 tbsp vinegar
6 tbsp olive oil
salt
freshly ground black pepper
pinch dried thyme

Serve with:
toast and butter

1 Thaw the shellfish pieces, asparagus and peas (if frozen). Break open the lobster or crab and remove the meat. Discard the inedible parts.

2 Cut the tomatoes in half, remove the cores and cut the flesh into fine strips. Mix together all the dressing ingredients and set aside.

3 Place the lettuce leaves on the base of a large serving plate. Place the remaining ingredients in separate groups on top. Alternatively, divide the ingredients between individual dinner plates as illustrated. Toss the mushrooms in some of the dressing and serve the remainder in a separate bowl.

Variations:
Other dressings that may be suitable are: chili mayonnaise with horseradish (see recipe 427), or Rhode Island Sauce (see recipe 428).

TO DRINK
sparkling dry white wine, Champagne or dry white wine

LEVEL OF DIFFICULTY
easy

PREPARATION TIME
30 mins

PREPARE IN ADVANCE
partly

DUCK BREAST SALAD

Serves 4

1 duck breast, broken into pieces
salt
freshly ground black pepper
50 ml/2 fl oz raspberry vinegar
500 g/1 lb raspberries
100 ml/3½ fl oz light stock
30 g/1 oz unsalted butter

Garnish:
several types salad leaves
sliced mushrooms

1 Heat a non-stick pan, add the duck breast, skin side down, and fry it in its own fat until almost cooked. Turn and fry the meat side lightly. Season with salt and pepper. Remove from the pan and keep warm.

2 Pour the fat from the pan and add vinegar and half the raspberries. Bring to just below boiling point and add the stock. Simmer until reduced to 4-5 tbsp. Strain the sauce and stir in the butter.

3 Divide the salad leaves between four plates. Cut the duck breast into thin slices lengthwise and arrange them in the middle of the plates. Garnish with the remaining raspberries and pour over the warm sauce.

To drink
light red wine

LEVEL OF DIFFICULTY medium difficult
PREPARATION TIME 30 mins
PREPARE IN ADVANCE no

CLUB SANDWICH ACAPULCO

Serves 4

1 grilled or roast chicken or
4 cooked chicken breasts
1 small head lettuce
2 tomatoes
1 avocado pear
150 ml/5 fl oz mayonnaise
1-2 tsp curry powder
8 slices white bread
3 tbsp butter
4 crisply fried bacon slices

Garnish:
tomato slices or red pepper rings
parsley

1 Remove the skin from the chicken. Cut the meat from the bones and finely slice.

2 Shred the lettuce. Slice the tomatoes. Peel the avocado pear, cut in half, remove the stone and cut each half into four wedges. Stir the mayonnaise until smooth and add curry powder to taste.

3 Toast the bread slices and spread with the butter. Divide the lettuce between four slices of toast, add the tomato slices and top with the chicken. Add the curry mayonnaise, avocado wedges and bacon slices. Cover with the remaining slices of toast and garnish with rings of red pepper or slices of tomato.

CLUB SANDWICH ACAPULCO 172

To drink
lager or mineral water

LEVEL OF DIFFICULTY easy
PREPARATION TIME 30 mins
PREPARE IN ADVANCE partly

DANISH LATE NIGHT SNACK

Serves 4

4 thin slices rye bread
butter
4 thick slices coarse liver pâté
8-12 slices salt meat, pastrami or similar cold meat
1 onion, sliced
Geléad Sky (see below)

Spread the bread with the butter. Spread the liver pâté on top. Cover with the slices of salt meat or other meat and garnish with thinly sliced onion rings and geléad sky (see below), which has been chopped, or cut into attractive shapes.

Geléad Sky:
3 gelatine leaves
200 ml/7 fl oz stock
1 tbsp sherry, port or Madeira

Soak the gelatine leaves in water for 10 minutes to soften. Squeeze out the excess water. Dissolve over low heat in a little stock. Add the remaining stock and wine to taste. Pour the gelatine into a long dish or mould and allow to set. Cut into 1 cm/½ inch wide strips.

TO DRINK
lager

LEVEL OF DIFFICULTY
easy
PREPARATION TIME
30 mins
PREPARE IN ADVANCE
yes

FRENCH FARMER'S SALAD

Serves 4

1 head of frisée lettuce or
40 young dandelion leaves
3 slices day-old white bread
1 clove garlic, crushed
3 tbsp butter or oil
300 g/10½ oz smoked, streaky bacon
freshly ground black pepper
2 tbsp olive oil (optional)
1 tbsp vinegar

1 Separate the leaves and wash and pat dry. Arrange them on individual plates.

2 Make the croûtons. Cut off the crusts from the bread and dice the slices. Melt the butter or heat the oil and fry them, together with the crushed garlic, until crunchy. Drain on kitchen paper.

3 Dice the bacon and fry it in its own fat. Arrange the bacon on the lettuce and pour over the frying fat. Alternatively, discard it and use a few drops of olive oil instead.

4 Sprinkle over the black pepper and dress lightly with vinegar. Place the croûtons on top.

FRENCH FARMER'S SALAD 174

To drink
robust white wine

LEVEL OF DIFFICULTY
easy
PREPARATION TIME
30 mins
PREPARE IN ADVANCE
partly

PICKLED FILLET OF BEEF

Serves 6-8 as a starter or 4 as main course

400 g/14 oz fillet of beef
50 g/1¾ oz salt
40 g/1½ oz white sugar
1 tbsp black peppercorns, roughly crushed
1 tbsp pink peppercorns, crushed
4 cloves garlic, crushed

Sauce:
200 ml/7 fl oz crème fraîche mixed with 1-2 tbsp French mustard and finely chopped chives or crème fraîche mixed with grated horseradish

1 Trim any fat from the meat. Mix the salt, sugar, pepper and garlic and rub into the meat. Place the meat in a plastic bag and tie a knot to seal it. Set aside in the refrigerator for 2-3 days. Turn the bag occasionally during this time.

2 Remove the meat from the bag and pat dry. Cut into thin slices and serve with one of the sauces.

Variation:
If the fillet is served as a main dish it tastes delicious with a potato gratin and salad.

Pickled Ham:
For 1 kg/2¼ lb ham (8-10 portions) make a mixture of 75 g/2½ oz white sugar, 50 g/1¾ oz salt, 1-2 tbsp crushed black peppercorns and 1-2 tbsp crushed juniper berries. Prepare in the same way as the fillet of beef but allow the ham 4 days in the refrigerator before serving.

TO DRINK
red or white wine

LEVEL OF DIFFICULTY
easy

PREPARATION TIME
several days

PREPARE IN ADVANCE
yes

CALVES' SWEETBREADS IN MUSHROOM SAUCE

Serves 4

4 bouchées, crustades or vol-au-vents, either ready-made or frozen uncooked

Filling:
100-150 g/3½-5 oz calves' sweetbreads
200 g/7 oz mushrooms
2 tbsp butter
1 shallot, finely chopped
2 tbsp flour
300-400 ml/10-14 fl oz cream or cream and light stock mixed
salt
freshly ground white pepper
1 tbsp Madeira, sherry or port

Garnish:
finely chopped parsley

1 Soak the sweetbreads in cold water for several hours. Discard the water. Cover with lightly salted cold water and bring to the boil. Drain and rinse the sweetbreads under cold running water and remove all the membranes. Cover the sweetbreads with boiling salted water and parboil for 10 minutes. Drain and set aside to cool. Reserve the cooking water to make the sauce later. Dice the sweetbreads.

2 Slice the mushrooms. Melt the butter and sauté the shallot and mushrooms, without covering, until all the liquid has been absorbed. Sprinkle over the flour and stir. Gradually, stir in the cream, cream and stock mixture or the cooking water from the sweetbreads. Simmer for 10 -15 minutes until thickened. Season with salt and pepper and add wine to taste. Stir in the sweetbreads.

3 Warm the mushroom sauce. Warm the bouchées, crustades or vol-au-vents in the oven if already cooked. If frozen uncooked, follow the instructions on the packet. Fill them with the warm sweetbread and mushroom sauce. Garnish with chopped parsley. Serve immediately.

CALVES' SWEETBREADS IN MUSHROOM SAUCE 176

To drink
dry white wine or light, fresh red wine

LEVEL OF DIFFICULTY
easy

PREPARATION TIME
1 hr + soaking time

PREPARE IN ADVANCE
yes

CHICKEN LIVERS IN ASPIC

Serves 8

8 chicken livers
1-2 tbsp butter
salt
freshly ground black pepper
8 thin slices boiled ham

Aspic:
6 gelatine leaves
400-500 ml/14-17 fl oz clear bouillon, stock or consommé
1-2 tbsp sherry
herb salt
freshly ground black pepper
juice of 1 lemon

Garnish:
1 head lettuce
8-12 mushrooms
8-12 radishes
2 tbsp finely chopped chives

1 Prepare the chicken livers and remove the sinews.

2 Melt the butter and fry the chicken livers over medium heat until they have browned on the outside but are still slightly pink inside. Season with salt and pepper and drain on kitchen paper.

3 Soak the gelatine leaves in cold water for 10 minutes to soften. Squeeze out and melt in a little stock over low heat. Mix with the remaining stock and stir in the sherry, herb salt, pepper and lemon. Set aside to cool.

4 Pour a little stock mixture into each of 8 individual moulds so that the bases are covered. Place the moulds in the refrigerator and allow to set.

5 Cut off any fat from the ham. Roll each chicken liver in a slice of ham.

6 Place the rolls, seam sides down, on to the set stock in the moulds. Pour the remaining stock over the rolls so that they are fully covered. Return to the refrigerator and allow to set.

7 Place 8 lettuce leaves on a serving dish or make a bed of shredded lettuce. Turn out the moulds, by quickly dipping them in warm water.

8 Garnish with sliced mushrooms, sliced radishes and finely chopped chives.

TO DRINK
light red wine

LEVEL OF DIFFICULTY
medium difficult

PREPARATION TIME
1 hr + setting time

PREPARE IN ADVANCE
partly

CHICKEN LIVER MOUSSE

Serves 6

400 g/14 oz chicken livers
1-2 tbsp butter
salt
freshly ground black pepper
2 shallots, finely chopped
1-2 tbsp brandy
200 ml/7 fl oz double cream

Garnish:
gherkins
sliced fresh mushrooms

Serve with:
toast or butter-fried white bread

1 Prepare the chicken livers. Melt the butter and brown the livers. Season with salt and pepper. Fry, covered, for 2-3 minutes. Remove from the pan and set aside to cool. Sauté the shallots, without colouring, and set aside to cool.

2 Place the chicken livers, shallots and butter in a food processor. Add the brandy and work, switching on and off. Pour in the cream while the machine is on full speed. Work for a few seconds until the mixture is fairly loose. Add more salt, pepper and brandy, as necessary. The chicken livers and shallots may also be put through a mincer and then mixed with the remaining ingredients.

3 Place the mousse in a small mould, smooth the top, and allow to set in the refrigerator for a few hours or overnight.

4 Spoon out the mousse just before serving. Garnish with fresh mushrooms and gherkins.

CHICKEN LIVER MOUSSE 178

TO DRINK
light red wine

LEVEL OF DIFFICULTY
easy

PREPARATION TIME
1 hr + setting time

PREPARE IN ADVANCE
yes

CHICKEN LIVER SALAD

Serves 4

1 kg/2¼ lb fresh leaf spinach
12 chicken livers
2 tbsp butter
salt
freshly ground white pepper
12 walnuts

Dressing:
2 tbsp lemon juice
5-6 tbsp olive oil
salt or herb salt
freshly ground white pepper

Garnish:
lemon wedges

Serve with:
white bread

1 Prepare the spinach by removing the toughest stalks, rinse and drain.

2 Make the dressing. Mix the oil and lemon juice together and season with salt or herb salt and freshly ground white pepper to taste.

3 Prepare the chicken livers and remove membrane and sinews.

4 Melt the butter in a frying-pan. Fry the chicken livers over medium heat until they are golden brown on the outside but are still pink in the middle. Season with salt and pepper.

5 Divide the spinach between 4 dinner plates. Add the warm chicken livers and pour the dressing over. Sprinkle with roughly chopped walnuts and garnish with lemon wedges. Serve with white bread.

TO DRINK
red wine

LEVEL OF DIFFICULTY
easy

PREPARATION TIME
30 mins

PREPARE IN ADVANCE
partly

CHICKEN LIVER TIMBALE

Serves 6

300 g/10½ oz chicken livers
3 eggs
2 egg yolks
300 ml/10 fl oz double cream
½ clove garlic, crushed
salt
freshly ground black pepper
pinch grated nutmeg
6-12 large green leaves, such as cos lettuce, swiss chard, iceberg lettuce or fresh leaf spinach
2 tbsp butter

Sauce:
2 tbsp butter
2 shallots, finely chopped
1 clove garlic, crushed
10-12 tomatoes, chopped
salt
freshly ground pepper
½ tsp dried basil

1 Prepare the chicken livers and purée them, together with the eggs and egg yolks, in a mixer or food processor. Bring the cream to the boil and add the to the chicken liver mixture in a fine stream while the machine is working. Add the garlic, salt, pepper and nutmeg. Preheat the oven to 170° C/325° F, gas mark 3.

2 Blanch the green leaves quickly in lightly salted boiling water. Drain on kitchen paper.

3 Butter 6 individual moulds or ramekins and line them with the blanched leaves. Divide the liver mixture equally between the moulds and place them in a roasting tin half filled with hot water. Bake for 30-35 minutes, or until the mixture has stopped rising. Test with a skewer.

4 Make the sauce. Melt 1 tbsp of the butter and sauté the shallots. Add the garlic, tomato, salt, pepper and basil. Simmer for 30-40 minutes until the tomatoes are soft. Sieve the sauce through a fine strainer so that the peel and seeds are removed. Bring the sauce to the boil again and continue boiling until thick. Beat in the remaining butter.

5 Carefully turn out the warm timbales on to a warm serving dish or individual plates and pour the sauce around them.

CHICKEN LIVER TIMBALE 180

TO DRINK
light red wine

LEVEL OF DIFFICULTY
fairly easy
PREPARATION TIME
1 hr
PREPARE IN ADVANCE
yes

FARMHOUSE PÂTÉ

Serves 12-15

600 g/1¼ lb lean shoulder of pork
100 g/3½ oz lard, thinly sliced
100 g/3½ oz smoked ham
300 g/10½ oz ox liver
1 large onion, finely chopped
2 eggs
2 tbsp cornflour
3-4 cloves garlic, crushed
salt
black pepper
3 tsp chopped chervil
1 tbsp paprika
1 tbsp soya sauce
1 tbsp butter

Serve with:
Cumberland sauce or mango sauce (see recipes 421 and 430)
gherkins
lettuce

1 Cut the pork into 5 mm/¼ inch cubes. Cut the lard and smoked ham into small dice. Preheat the oven to 200° C/400° F, gas mark 6.

2 Mince the liver using the finest blade in the mincer or food processor. Mix the liver, lard, meat and onion into a smooth mixture. Add the eggs, cornflour and all the remaining ingredients, except the butter, and mix thoroughly.

3 Grease a rectangular 1.5-litre/2½-pint mould with the butter. Place the mould in a roasting tin half filled with hot water. Cover the mould with foil and bake in the bottom of the oven for approximately 1½ hours. Test with a skewer.

4 Allow the pâté to cool in the mould and then set aside in the refrigerator for 4-5 hours or overnight before turning out.

Variations:
The pâté will look more elegant baked in a porcelain terrine. Allow the pâté to cool in the terrine with a weight on the top. Make a jelly with 100 ml/3½ fl oz meat stock, 50 ml/2 fl oz Madeira, 1 tsp soya sauce and 2 gelatine leaves. Pour over the pâté and allow to set. Serve the pâté directly from the terrine.

TO DRINK
red or white wine

LEVEL OF DIFFICULTY
medium difficult

PREPARATION TIME
2 hrs + setting time

PREPARE IN ADVANCE
yes

MELON WITH PARMA HAM

Serves 4

1 ripe melon (cantaloupe, honeydew, charentais or yellow fleshed watermelon)
8 thin slices Parma or Bayonne ham

1 Chill the melon. Cut in half lengthwise and scrape out the seeds. Cut the melon into wedges.

2 Place the melon wedges on a serving dish. Drape the slices of ham over the melon.

Variations:
Melon salad:
Cut a ripe melon in half and scrape out the seeds. Make balls with a melon baller or Parisian cutter. Alternatively, peel the melon halves and dice the fruit. Sprinkle with pepper and add a squeeze of lemon juice. Serve with boiled or smoked ham, cold chicken or turkey.

MELON WITH PARMA HAM 182

TO DRINK
white or red wine

LEVEL OF DIFFICULTY
easy

PREPARATION TIME
30 mins

PREPARE IN ADVANCE
no

SMOKED MEAT WITH CUCUMBER

Serves 4

1 large fresh cucumber
8 slices smoked meat

Sauce:
1 portion Hollandaise sauce (see recipe 422)
1 tbsp finely chopped chives

1 Make the Hollandaise sauce and keep in a covered dish over warm water.

2 Slice the cucumber into 5 mm/1/4 inch strips. Bring some lightly salted water to the boil in a saucepan and drop in the cucumber strips. Bring to the boil again and immediately turn off the heat. Drain the cucumber.

3 Arrange the boiled cucumber strips on a warm serving dish. Mix the Hollandaise sauce with the finely chopped chives and spoon over the cucumber. Arrange the smoked meat slices on top.

Variations:
Smoked fish may be substituted for the smoked meat.

TO DRINK
red or white wine

LEVEL OF DIFFICULTY easy
PREPARATION TIME 30 mins
PREPARE IN ADVANCE partly

HAM WITH MIMOSA SALAD

Serves 4

200-300 g/7-10½ oz cooked, sliced ham

Mimosa salad:
1 tart apple
1 pear
1 orange
2 canned pineapple rings, drained with 1-2 tbsp can juice reserved
1 tomato
50 g/1¾ oz grapes, halved and seeded
100 g/3½ oz frozen petit pois, cooked and cooled
2 hard-boiled eggs
100 ml/3½ fl oz double cream
100 ml/3½ fl oz mayonnaise

Garnish:
lettuce leaves

1 Peel the apple, pear and orange. Dice the fresh fruit and pineapple rings. Halve and seed the tomato, and dice the flesh. Mix the diced fruit, tomato, grapes and peas together in a bowl.

2 Shell the eggs, halve and divide into whites and yolks. Chop the egg whites and mix them with the salad.

3 Beat the cream and mix with the mayonnaise and a little pineapple juice. Season with salt and pepper to taste. Carefully fold the dressing into the salad.

4 Rub the hard-boiled egg yolks through a wire strainer and sprinkle over the salad so that they lie on the salad like fluffy mimosa flowers. Garnish with lettuce leaves.

Variation:
Mimosa salad is suited to all cold meats and poultry dishes. The double cream can be replaced with sour cream if a less fattening dressing is required.

HAM WITH MIMOSA SALAD 184

To drink
lager, light red or white wine

LEVEL OF DIFFICULTY
easy

PREPARATION TIME
30 mins

PREPARE IN ADVANCE
yes

OPEN ROAST BEEF SANDWICH

Serves 4

4 thin slices rough rye bread
1-2 tbsp butter
8-12 slices cold, roast beef

Scrambled egg:
4 eggs
2 tbsp water or double cream
salt
freshly ground black pepper
2-3 tbsp butter

Garnish:
lettuce leaves
2 tbsp finely chopped chives

1 Start with the scrambled egg. Break the eggs into a bowl. Beat them lightly and add water or cream. Season with salt and plenty of freshly ground pepper to taste.

2 Melt 2 tbsp of the butter in a heavy-based saucepan. Add the egg mixture and stir slowly over low heat until the eggs thicken. Take the saucepan off the heat before the egg mixture becomes too solid. Stir in the remaining butter.

3 Spread the bread with the butter. Arrange a lettuce leaf and 2-3 slices beef, depending upon the size, on each sandwich. Spoon the scrambled egg on top. Garnish with finely chopped chives.

OPEN ROAST BEEF SANDWICH 185

TO DRINK
lager

LEVEL OF DIFFICULTY
easy
PREPARATION TIME
30 mins
PREPARE IN ADVANCE
no

BOXER'S BEEF

Serves 4

200 g/7 oz fillet of beef
2 small red or yellow onions
4 slices white bread, crusts removed
2 tbsp butter
4 tbsp lumpfish or bleak (ablette) roe
4 egg yolks
salt
freshly ground black pepper

1 Cut the fillet into 4 slices and beat out very thin. It is important that the meat does not break. Finely chop the onions.

2 Melt the butter and fry the bread on both sides until crispy and golden. Place a raw beaten fillet slice on each. Top each slice with a circle of roe and a circle of chopped onion. Add a raw egg yolk to the middle of each roe circle, season with salt and pepper and serve.

BOXER'S BEEF 186

TO DRINK
lager

LEVEL OF DIFFICULTY easy
PREPARATION TIME 30 mins
PREPARE IN ADVANCE no

AVOCADO COCKTAIL

Serves 4

400 g/14 oz cooked prawns
3 avocado pears
4 tbsp lumpfish or bleak (ablette) roe

Dressing:
1 tbsp lemon juice
3 tbsp vegetable oil
salt
freshly ground white pepper

Garnish:
finely chopped red onion
dill sprigs

1 Peel the prawns and set aside in the refrigerator.

2 Make the dressing. Mix the oil and lemon juice and season with salt and pepper to taste.

3 Cut the avocado pears in half lengthwise. Remove the stones. Scoop out the flesh with a melon baller, Parisian cutter or a small spoon. Make layers of avocado balls and prawns in serving glasses or bowls. Top each with 1 tbsp of roe. Pour over the dressing and garnish with dill sprigs and chopped red onions.

TO DRINK
dry white wine, lager or mineral water

LEVEL OF DIFFICULTY
easy

PREPARATION TIME
30 mins

PREPARE IN ADVANCE
partly

AVOCADO SALAD

Serves 4

2 large or 4 small avocado pears
2-4 hard-boiled eggs (optional)
mixed salad leaves
15 walnuts, chopped

Dressing:
2 tsp vinegar
2 tbsp walnut or olive oil
1 tsp French mustard
salt
freshly ground pepper

Serve with:
bread and butter

1 Combine all the dressing ingredients in a screwtop jar and shake to mix.

2 Cut the avocado pears in half lengthwise; peel them and remove the stones. Cut into thin slices. Shell and cut the eggs into halves or wedges.

3 Arrange the avocado slices and the mixed lettuce leaves attractively on dinner plates. Garnish with egg wedges or halves. Sprinkle over the chopped walnuts. Spoon over the dressing.

AVOCADO SALAD 188

TO DRINK
dry white wine

LEVEL OF DIFFICULTY
easy

PREPARATION TIME
30 mins

PREPARE IN ADVANCE
no

BAKED POTATOES WITH VARIOUS FILLINGS

Serves 4

4 large potatoes

Smoked meat filling:
200 ml/7 fl oz sour cream
60 g/2 oz smoked meat
1 tbsp grated horseradish

Prawn filling:
150 ml/5 fl oz mayonnaise
200 g/7 oz peeled and chopped prawns
3 tbsp finely chopped dill
4 whole peeled prawns
dill sprigs

Crème fraîche with roe:
200 ml/7 fl oz crème fraîche
1-2 tbsp bleak (ablette) or lumpfish roe per potato
finely chopped onion

Pickled herring filling:
Spoon 1-2 tbsp sour cream on to each potato and arrange a few thinly cut Matje herrings pieces on top. Garnish with finely chopped chives.

Egg and anchovy butter filling:
2 hard-boiled eggs, chopped
8-10 anchovy fillets
½ onion, finely chopped
4 tbsp butter
2 tbsp finely chopped parsley

Mix the butter together with all the chopped ingredients and garnish with a few anchovy fillets on top.

1 Preheat the oven to 220° C/ 425° F, gas mark 7. Scrub the potatoes. Prick with a skewer or fork several times so that they do not explode in the oven. Cook the potatoes directly on the oven shelves or in an ovenproof dish in the lowest part of the oven. Bake for 45-60 minutes, depending upon size.

2 Remove the potatoes. Cut a deep cross into each and press inwards and upwards on both sides of the potato with thumb and forefinger so that the potato opens out.

3 Choose one of the fillings and spoon it into the potatoes.

TO DRINK
lager

LEVEL OF DIFFICULTY easy
PREPARATION TIME 1 hr
PREPARE IN ADVANCE yes

FILLED AVOCADO HALVES

Serves 4

2 ripe avocado pears

Filling:
see suggestions

Serve with:
toast and butter or butter-fried bread croûtons

1 Cut the avocado pears in half lengthwise and remove the stones.

2 Place a tasty filling in the hole left by the stone. Here are a few suggestions:

- Peeled prawns with mayonnaise or vinaigrette, garnished with dill sprigs.
- Black or red lumpfish roe, garnished with finely chopped red onion or chives and a lemon wedge.
- Drained canned mussels with vinaigrette sauce or mayonnaise flavoured with crushed garlic and finely chopped parsley.
- Finely chopped crabmeat mixed with celery cut in fine strips, diced red pepper, mayonnaise, lemon juice, and cayenne pepper.
- Approximately 20 raw sliced mushrooms marinated in 4 tbsp olive oil, 2 tbsp lemon juice, 1 finely chopped shallot, 1 tbsp finely chopped parsley and ½ tsp French mustard. Season with salt and pepper.
- Strips of gravad lax with gravad lax sauce (see recipe 423). Garnish with dill sprigs.
- Prawn, mayonnaise, dill and roe (see recipe 168).

FILLED AVOCADO HALVES 190

TO DRINK
dry white wine or lager

LEVEL OF DIFFICULTY
easy
PREPARATION TIME
varied
PREPARE IN ADVANCE
fillings only

AVOCADO GRATINÉE

Serves 4

2 tsp butter
2-4 avocado pears
herb salt

Sauce:
2 tbsp butter
2 tbsp flour
200 ml/7 fl oz milk
200 ml/7 fl oz double cream
salt
freshly ground black pepper
1/4-1/2 tsp grated nutmeg
170 g/6 oz Parmesan or
Emmental cheese, grated

1 Preheat the oven to 250° C/500° F, gas mark 10. Grease an ovenproof dish or 4 individual ovenproof dishes with the butter.

2 To make the sauce, melt the butter and stir in the flour. Gradually stir in the milk and cream and simmer for 5 minutes, stirring. Season with salt, pepper and grated nutmeg to taste. Stir in most of the grated cheese, reserving some for the topping.

3 Cut the avocado pears in half lengthwise. Peel and remove the stones. Place them, round side upwards, on the prepared dish or dishes. Sprinkle over a little herb salt.

4 Spoon the sauce evenly into the avocado halves. Sprinkle over the remaining grated cheese and bake in the oven for 10-12 minutes.

Variations:
Place a thin slice of dark bread topped with a slice of ham under each avocado half, then sprinkle over the sauce and bake. With a whole avocado per person, this dish becomes a filling lunch.

TO DRINK
mineral water or white wine

LEVEL OF DIFFICULTY
easy

PREPARATION TIME
30 mins

PREPARE IN ADVANCE
partly

VEGETABLE PÂTÉ WITH SPECKLED SAUCE

Serves 8

250 g/8¾ oz fresh or frozen broccoli
400 g/14 oz carrots
400 g/14 oz parsnips
salt
freshly ground black pepper
1½ tsp cornflour
3 eggs
150 ml/5 fl oz milk
2 tbsp butter

Sauce:
300 ml/10 fl oz crème fraîche
1 x 100 g/3½ oz jar bleak (ablette) or lumpfish roe

1 Preheat the oven to 170° C/325° F, gas mark 3. Thaw the broccoli if frozen. Prepare it if fresh. Peel and rinse the carrots and parsnips. Cut the vegetables in pieces. Boil them, separately, in lightly salted water for approximately 15 minutes.

2 Drain and finely chop or purée the vegetables.

3 Mix each vegetable with salt, pepper, ½ tsp cornflour, 1 egg and 50 ml/2 fl oz milk.

4 Grease a rectangular loaf tin with butter. Place half the broccoli mixture in the base, add the parsnip mixture, then the carrot mixture and finish with the remaining broccoli mixture. Bake in the oven for approximately 1 hour until the pâté is set. Set aside to cool.

5 Mix the crème fraîche and roe. Stir thoroughly.

6 Cut the cold pâté into slices and place on a serving dish. Serve the sauce in a separate bowl.

VEGETABLE PÂTÉ WITH SPECKLED SAUCE 192

TO DRINK
mineral water

LEVEL OF DIFFICULTY
easy

PREPARATION TIME
2 hrs

PREPARE IN ADVANCE
yes

GLOBE ARTICHOKES

Serves 4

4 globe artichokes
approximately 4 litres/7 pints water
2-3 tbsp salt
1 lemon

Lemon butter:
150 g/5¼ oz butter, softened
lemon juice to taste
salt

1 Rinse the artichokes. Break off the stalks as close to the base as possible so that any thin thread roots come away. Snip away the outer leaf tops if they are very spiky.

2 Bring the water to the boil, add salt and lemon cut into slices or wedges. Add the artichokes and boil them until done. The cooking time may vary between 30 and 60 minutes, depending upon freshness and size. They are ready when the leaves can be easily pulled away.

3 Beat the butter until light and fluffy and season with salt and lemon juice.

4 Remove the chokes from the centre of the artichokes. Serve the warm artichokes with the lemon butter.

Variations:
The artichokes may also be served with vinaigrette sauce (see recipe 433).

TO DRINK
mineral water

LEVEL OF DIFFICULTY
easy

PREPARATION TIME
1 hr

PREPARE IN ADVANCE
yes

GREEN BEAN PASTY WITH CHANTERELLES

Serves 6

500 g/1 lb green beans
500 g/1 lb chanterelles
3 sheets frozen puff pastry, thawed
1 egg yolk, beaten
150 ml/5 fl oz double cream
4 tbsp butter
2 tbsp finely chopped shallots
½ tsp dried thyme
salt
freshly ground black pepper
2 cloves garlic
1 bunch chives, finely chopped

1 Top and tail the beans and place them in cold water. Chop the chanterelles.

2 Preheat the oven to 250° C/ 500° F, gas mark 10. Line a baking sheet with greaseproof paper. Cut the puff pastry sheets in half. With a sharp knife, mark a line all around, 5 mm/¼ inch from the edge. Mark a pattern of diagonal lines inside the marked edge. Do not cut through. Place the sheets on the prepared baking sheet and brush with the egg yolk.

3 Bake for 8-10 minutes until well risen. Set aside to cool. Carefully cut around the 'lids' and remove. Scrape out the inside of the base sheets.

4 Put the chanterelles in a saucepan with 5 tsp of the butter. Add the shallots, thyme, salt, pepper and the whole unpeeled garlic cloves. Bring to the boil, covered. Simmer, uncovered, until all the liquid has been absorbed. Discard the garlic. Add the cream and simmer until the sauce has thickened. Keep warm.

5 Bring 2 litres/3½ pints of water with 4 tsp salt to the boil. Add the beans to the boiling water. Boil vigorously for 4 minutes. Rinse in cold water.

6 Warm the pastry cases in the oven. Melt the remaining butter in a frying-pan and shake the beans in it until well coated and warmed through. Season with black pepper. Fill the pastry cases with the beans, cover with the chanterelles in cream sauce. Sprinkle with the finely chopped chives and add the puff pastry lids.

GREEN BEAN PASTRY WITH CHANTERELLES 194

TO DRINK
the same wine as the main course

LEVEL OF DIFFICULTY
medium difficult

PREPARATION TIME
1 hr

PREPARE IN ADVANCE
yes

ASPARAGUS

Serves 4

1 kg/2¼ lb asparagus
2 litres/3½ pints water
5 tsp salt

Vinaigrette sauce:
50 ml/2 fl oz vinegar
50 ml/2 fl oz water
100 ml/3½ fl oz oil
2 tbsp finely chopped onion
2 tbsp chopped parsley
2 tbsp chervil
salt
freshly ground black pepper

Serve with:
Serve cold with vinaigrette sauce or olive oil. Serve warm with Hollandaise sauce (see recipe 422).

1 Peel the asparagus with a potato peeler. Carefully hold it at the tip and peel from the tip down the stalk only. Never peel upwards. Turn the stalk around carefully so that it is smooth all over. Cut away any woody pieces.

2 Lightly salt the water and bring to the boil. Divide the asparagus into 4 bundles and tie each bundle with cotton string.

3 Lower the bundles gently into the boiling water and boil for 15-20 minutes until the asparagus feels soft. Allow it to cool in the water if serving cold. Warm asparagus should be served freshly boiled.

4 Make the vinaigrette sauce by putting all the ingredients in a screw top jar and shaking vigorously. Alternatively, beat them in a bowl with a balloon whisk.

5 Remove the strings and place the warm asparagus on a warm serving dish lined with a linen napkin. Serve the sauce separately.

TO DRINK
mineral water

LEVEL OF DIFFICULTY easy
PREPARATION TIME 1 hr
PREPARE IN ADVANCE yes

ASPARAGUS WITH FISH ROE SAUCE

Serves 4

2 packets frozen green asparagus
200 ml/7 fl oz crème fraîche
100 g/3½ oz bleak (ablette) or lumpfish roe

Garnish:
lemon slices or wedges

Serve with:
4 slices butter-fried white bread

1 Cook the asparagus as instructed on the packet.

2 Stir the crème fraîche until smooth. Add most of the roe, reserving a little for the garnish. Stir the crème fraîche and roe mixture thoroughly.

3 Cut off the crusts from the bread. Melt the butter and fry the bread until golden brown and crisp. Cut in half diagonally to make triangles.

4 Divide the asparagus between 4 individual plates, spoon over the sauce and top with a little roe. Garnish with lemon slices or wedges.

ASPARAGUS WITH FISH ROE SAUCE 196

TO DRINK
mineral water, iced water or white wine

LEVEL OF DIFFICULTY
easy

PREPARATION TIME
30 mins

PREPARE IN ADVANCE
yes

SPINACH TIMBALES WITH MOREL SAUCE

Serves 4

Timbales:
250 g/8¾ oz frozen leaf spinach
4 eggs
1 tbsp flour
400 ml/14 fl oz double cream
120 g/4 oz cheese, grated
herb salt
grated nutmeg
1 tbsp butter

Sauce:
20 g/¾ oz dried morels
2-3 tbsp butter
1 shallot, finely chopped
1 tbsp flour
100 ml/3½ fl oz bouillon
100 ml/3½ fl oz milk
200 ml/7 fl oz double cream
1-2 tbsp sherry
salt

Garnish:
cress

1 Soak the morels in water for approximately 1 hour. Thaw the spinach. Squeeze out the water and chop roughly. Preheat the oven to 200° C/ 400° F, gas mark 6.

2 Beat together the eggs, flour, cream and cheese. Season with herb salt and grated nutmeg to taste. Stir in the spinach.

3 Grease 4 individual ovenproof moulds with the butter and fill with the spinach mixture. Place the moulds in a roasting tin half filled with hot water and bake in the oven for 20 minutes, or until they have risen. Set aside for a few minutes before turning out of the moulds.

4 Make the morel sauce while the timbales are baking. Drain and roughly chop the morels. Melt the butter and fry the shallots and morels. Sprinkle over the flour, stirring. Stir in the bouillon, milk and cream. Simmer over low heat for approximately 20 minutes until the sauce has thickened. Add sherry to taste. Season with salt if necessary.

5 Turn out the timbales on to a warm serving dish. Pour the warm sauce around them and garnish with chopped cress.

TO DRINK
mineral water or the same wine as the main course

LEVEL OF DIFFICULTY easy
PREPARATION TIME 1 hr + soaking time
PREPARE IN ADVANCE yes

TOMATO RING WITH MUSSELS

Serves 4-6

6 gelatine leaves
500 ml/18 fl oz tomato juice
50 ml/2 fl oz tomato purée
½ tsp Worcestershire sauce
½ tbsp vinegar
½ tsp dried basil
½ tsp herb salt

Garnish:
1 jar mussels in brine, drained

Sauce:
100 ml/3½ fl oz mayonnaise
150 ml/5 fl oz sour cream
2 tsp French mustard
1-2 cloves garlic, crushed

Serve with:
small bread rolls or croûtons

1 Mix together the tomato juice, tomato purée, Worcestershire sauce and vinegar. Add the basil and herb salt to taste.

2 Soak the gelatine leaves in cold water for 10 minutes to soften. Squeeze out and melt them in a little of the tomato juice mixture over low heat. Mix into the remaining liquid.

3 Rinse a ring mould with cold water and pour in the tomato mixture. Place the mould in the refrigerator for 3-4 hours until it has set.

4 Mix together the ingredients for the sauce. Stir thoroughly and taste.

5 Just before serving, dip the mould quickly in hot water and turn out. Decorate with lettuce leaves and the mussels. Pour the sauce into the middle of the ring or serve in a separate bowl. Serve with small bread rolls or freshly fried croûtons.

TOMATO RING WITH MUSSELS 198

TO DRINK
dry white wine or lager

LEVEL OF DIFFICULTY
medium difficult

PREPARATION TIME
30 mins + setting time

PREPARE IN ADVANCE
yes

TOMATO SALAD

Serves 4

8-10 tomatoes
1-2 red or yellow onions
1 tbsp finely chopped parsley

Dressing:
1 tbsp vinegar
1/2 tsp French mustard
salt
freshly ground black pepper
1/2 tsp Italian salad spice (optional)
1 clove garlic, crushed (optional)
3-4 tbsp olive oil

1 Wash and dry the tomatoes and slice them thinly. Thinly slice the onions and push out into rings or finely chop them. Place the tomatoes and onions in a bowl, or a large dish or on individual serving plates.

2 Combine the dressing ingredients in a screwtop jar and shake to mix. Taste and adjust the seasoning if necessary.

3 Pour the dressing over the tomatoes and onions. Chill in the refrigerator for 30 minutes before serving. Sprinkle over the chopped parsley and serve.

Variations:
For tomato salad with chives, replace the onions and parsley with a bunch of finely chopped chives. For tomato salad with mushrooms, replace a few of the tomatoes with thinly sliced fresh raw mushrooms.

TO DRINK
mineral water

LEVEL OF DIFFICULTY
easy
PREPARATION TIME
30 mins
PREPARE IN ADVANCE
yes

MY FAVOURITE MENUS

100 SOUP & STARTER RECIPES